TRAV

1138

BARBARIAN EYE

Lord Napier in China, 1834
The Prelude to Hong Kong

For
Nigel and Delia
and also for
Francis and Zara
Napier

BARBARIAN EYE

Lord Napier in China, 1834
The Prelude to Hong Kong

Priscilla Napier

BRASSEY'S
London • Washington

First English edition 1995

UK editorial offices: Brassey's, 33 John Street, London WC1N 2AT
UK orders: Marston Book Services, PO Box 87, Oxford OX2 0DT

North American Orders: Order Department, Brassey's Inc,
P O Box 960, Herndon, VA 22070, USA.

Library of Congress Cataloging in Publication Data
available

British Library Cataloguing in Publication Data
A catalogue record for this book is available from the British Library

Hardcover 1-85753-116-7

Typeset by M Rules
Printed in Great Britain by
Bookcraft (Bath) Limited

Contents

Part Four: Open Conflict

List of Illustrations
(Plates appear between pages 118 and 119)

Acknowledgements

In addition to my gratitude to Lord Napier and Ettrick for permission to quote from the letters and journals of William John, 9th Lord Napier, I have also to thank the Brickdale family for allowing me to quote from the letters of Midshipman Charles Brickdale, Royal Navy. My grateful thanks too to Mr Henry Johnstone for permission to quote from the letters of his great-great-grandfather Captain Henry Napier, Royal Navy and from the letters of Captain Thomas Bourchier, Royal Navy to Henry Napier which are also in his possession.

Bramley   PN
February 1995

Preface

'In the retrospect of Chinese patriots to-day it makes little difference that the opium traffic was a fully bilateral activity', writes John King Fairbank in *The United States and China*. 'In China the opium trade remains a classic symbol of Western commercial imperialism – foreign greed and violence demoralizing and exploiting an inoffensive people . . . A century later we can see it as part of an unavoidable conflict, Western expansion clashing head-on with China's traditional order. Conflict was bound to come. Opium provided the first occasion, though not the last.' 'Only in the light of the immediate occasion can the conflict be called an opium war' writes David Owen, in his meticulously researched *British Opium Policy in China and India* (published in the United States, 1936). Latter-day Chinese historians have shared this view. In his *Commissioner Lin and the Opium Wars*, Hsin-Pao Chang echoes Owen, and ICY Hsu, in *The Rise of Modern China* points out that opium was the immediate, but not the ultimate cause of the War.

In Central India, opium had been in daily use among all classes long before British rule was established. Coolies took it to get them through the long day's work, and in the North, Rajputs took it before battle to re-inforce their courage. The leaves of the plant whose seed-heads produced it – *papaver somniferum* – were still being eaten as salad (as it might be lettuce) in 19th century India. Bengal produced a stronger brew than could be grown in China, where this Indian opium soon found a market. The East India Company quickly muscled in on the lucrative trade, seizing its transport as their monopoly, out of the hands of the Portuguese, the Dutch and the Americans. The war was really fought over whether the Western nations should or should not be permitted to trade with China.

But it was the Opium War, and as such its waging, first by Britain alone and then by Britain and France combined, that has become more odious than ever now that drug-dependency increases in our world. The fact that opium was introduced into China by Arab traders in the 8th century, and went on trickling in from then on is little known or disregarded: and it is upon Britain that the entire odium is seen to lie. Some of that horror and disgust clings to all connected with it; and although, no more than his predecessors, Lord Macartney and Lord Amherst, was William John, 9th Lord Napier, connected with the importation of opium into China, the War broke out six years after his death in 1834, and he has had his share of the inevitable bad press.

Recently his own journals and letters have been rediscovered and restored to his family, and are now in the possession of his great-great-great-grandson, Nigel, 14th Lord Napier and Ettrick, who has kindly lent them to me.

Earlier incursions up the Pearl River by 17th and 18th century naval officers from Britain, or the abrupt 'open up or we fire' from the 19th century American captain in Japan, were more decided and arguably less harmful than the prolonged miseries of the two Opium Wars, in which attempted moderation, diplomatic pauses and slow pace were the watchwords. These efforts to proceed in a humane manner, as Captain Tom Bourchier pointed out, only resulted in greater misery all round. William John Napier must at least be credited with understanding (and advising the home government) that at the time of his mission to China, trade could have been opened and regularised, and opium smuggling halted, by the mere presence and threat of a convincing British force off the China coast; without the hateful need for destructive action. This took place six years later, after a lengthy shilly-shally that convinced the Chinese authorities that the British would really never act in earnest against them, and resulted in much bloodshed, rising hatred and the exaction of far more from the defeated Chinese Emperor than the original peaceful missions had asked. The chance was missed through no fault of Napier's; and great were the subsequent disasters. Those pretty ships under sail in the Pearl River, *Andromache* and *Imogene*, with their mild return of fire upon the Bogue forts were the unconscious heralds of China's near-destruction.

Some historians have condemned Lord Napier as a feather-brained naval reactionary with no ideas outside his own profession. Certainly, neither training nor Far East experience qualified him for the mission on which he was sent in 1834, with conflicting briefs from King William IV and Lord Grey's Foreign Secretary, telling him the truth; but his appointment in Canton was one that would have tested the most skilled diplomat to his limits. Even his Chinese opponents granted him 'a solid and expansive mind', and commented upon his calmness in speech and action. His newly returned letters and journals, and the recorded evidence of his contemporaries show him to have been a thoughtful and kindly man, with faith, patience, determination and a deep feeling for his fellow men, particularly the disadvantaged, amongst whom he came to include the Chinese people.

A loving husband and father, he in turn was respected and often loved by his subordinates – not for nothing was his second command known as 'the happy *Goshawk*'. His trust in the capacity and goodwill of the Royal Navy and its power to effect the rational solution (a trust shared with his monarch King William) led him into making decisions that seemed sound enough on the spot, but were far removed from the intention of his overlords, whose keynote was appeasement and who remained blandly unaware of the local conditions around the dangerous Bay of Canton. Napier's unflagging efforts to fulfil his virtually impossible mission, his sympathy with the Chinese poor who surrounded him and his dogged devotion to duty would effectively cost him his life and at a sadly early age.

No-one in the China–Britain conflict entirely escapes blame, but the time seems ripe for a reappraisal of the efforts made and the part played by William John in the early 19th century to open up normal trade with China to the European nations, and the disastrous results of Imperial China's refusal to play along with this plan.

Part One
Introduction

1

Sailor, Laird and Courtier

William John Napier, Master of Napier, going to sea in the fateful last years of the 18th century, had the luck to serve three years in HMS *Impérieuse* under the redoubtable Lord Cochrane. He therefore took part in most of the adventures and successes of this brilliant but incalculable red-headed commander. Cochrane was not an easy man to please, but his reports on young Napier were uniformly favourable. Other shipmates reported him as physically very strong, as brave, calm, and an excellent navigator. They also found him friendly, patient and good-humoured – just the man to send in maturity in charge of the third British mission to that difficult country on the other side of the world – the Chinese Empire.

William John, so called to distinguish him from his first cousin and contemporary William Napier, historian of the Peninsular War, was the eldest of the six sons of Francis, 8th Lord Napier, who was nine generations away from his illustrious forbear, John Napier of Merchiston Castle just outside Edinburgh, inventor of logarithms (and of the decimal point). William John was born at Kinsale in Southern Ireland, where his father's regiment was garrisoned. As a midshipman William John was in the *Defence* at Trafalgar, where he enjoyed the exhilarating experience of towing the shattered and captured Spanish three-decker, the *San Ildefonso*, into the safety of Gibraltar harbour on the night of the storm following the battle. The Captain of *Defence* was his kinsman, George Hope, 'and a precious taut hand was he', William John recorded later.

In *Foudroyant* he was known as a frequent pourer of oil upon the stormy waters of the cockpit, that dark reeking box of a place where junior officers, when not on deck, lived out their often all too brief lives. Navigation was his passion, and he would often take sights when he had no need to. In moments of leisure he would read Horace or play the flute, skylark in the rigging with the other midshipmen, mend his bagpipes, or entertain the gun room by singing the wilder Scots ballads. Contemporaries remarked upon his calm, he was not easily rattled. Patient, scientific, good-mannered, but at the same time able firmly to contain the excesses of shoregoing seamen, he seemed a man to come to reasonable trading terms with the proud and aloof ruler of the Celestial Empire, whose tea the British so much wanted. (None was grown in India until 1838.)

The officials of the Great Pure Realm were to feel differently. The Viceroy of Canton would decline to accept his letter of appointment from King William IV in 1834 on behalf of the Emperor Tao-Kwang (Glorious Rectitude), and agree to the translation of William John's name as Vile Labouring Beast – or Laboriously Vile for short – the rudest possible translation of the syllables Nay Peer. To them he was a Barbarian Eye, a dangerous spy.

All this lay far ahead. Joining *Impérieuse* not long after William John, was little Fred Marryat, later to win literary fame as Captain Marryat. He thought William John admirable – 'it was rare to find one like Napier, who with power to ensure despotism, was so magnanimous as to refrain, though he had a giant's strength . . . in the midst of tyranny he set the example of mercy, in the midst of ignorance he was learned and scientific'. His coolness and confidence in tricky moments, thought Marryat, made Cochrane hold in him 'the most implicit confidence'.

Blockading off Rochefort in *Impérieuse*, and in command of a boat surprising and chasing French vessels, attacking Arcasson's fortress, William John was learning his trade under a master. Though still only officially master's mate he constantly did the duty of lieutenant: 'I preferred his service to making application for other officers', Cochrane wrote. Soon they were off Corsica, taking a pirate ship manned by Albanian Turks, – 'the scimitar yielded to the cutlass' as Guthrie, the romantic doctor serving in *Impérieuse* described it – blockading Corfu, cutting out an enemy ship from Valona harbour, seizing every occasion to harass the French or their allies, or how otherwise end this interminable war?

In February 1808, *Impérieuse* was in the bay of Almeria, capturing enemy vessels despite heavy fire from Spanish batteries, when the war took a sudden twist for the better. Napoleon had turned against his Spanish allies, double-crossed their king, and imposed his brother Joseph Bonaparte on them as ruler. This the Spaniards were naturally resisting. For William John the event was particularly lucky as he was a prisoner at Port Mahon, having been taken when in charge of an unarmed merchant prize on the way to Gibraltar. He was freed, and able to join *Impérieuse* in harrying French troops from the sea as they poured into Spain along the coast road. *Impérieuse* helped to raise the siege of Gerona, and in the defence of Fort Rosas, during which both Cochrane and Napier developed a strong admiration for the gallantry and independence of the Catalan people.

Next they were sinking two French warships in the Bay of Cadaques and distributing the supplies of food their convoy was carrying among the local Catalans, and from there sweeping the south coast of France, harrying signal stations and making night landings to destroy coastal batteries. All stimulating stuff, but a more singular adventure awaited.

In Aix Roads south of Bordeaux, 12 French ships of the line with attendant vessels were watching their chance to escape the British blockade, sail westwards in their faster ships, and rescue their West Indian islands. William John was left in charge of *Impérieuse* on a stormy dark night of April 1909, while Cochrane himself took the explosion-laden small vessel he had devised, to break the mile-long angled boom by which the French anchorage was sheltered. He succeeded; and although not enough of his fire ships went through the gap he had shattered in the great anchored boom, those that did panicked the French. Morning found many of their great ships stranded. *Impérieuse* then defied orders to retreat and took on the remaining French fleet single-handed, knowing that however reluctantly, Gambier, the pacifically-minded C-in-C, would have to send reinforcements. The whole French fleet was only saved from destruction by what Napoleon called the 'mollesse' of Gambier in failing to follow up.

In all this, William John had distinguished himself, and when he perforce left *Impérieuse* to take his exam for lieutenant, Cochrane wrote him a fine report, ending 'if opportunity is afforded he may be highly useful to his country'. But would opportunity afford?

As a full-fledged lieutenant William John spent two years in the *Kent*, a 74-gun ship stationed in the Mediterranean and wearily employed in blockading Toulon, whence the French fleet declined to emerge. Much preferring small ships, he felt himself lucky, after a wounded swim following a boat-raid on Palamos, to be taken on by the *Sparrowhawk* sloop. 'I cannot convey the warm and sincere regard I had for him as a man and an officer', wrote Captain Pringle of *Sparrowhawk*. 'His superiors could with him have the pleasure of entering into and enjoying all the familiarities and intercourse of private life without its ever interfering in the least with the duties of an officer, a qualification which produces more good on board a man-o'-war than may be supposed'.

Made commander in the autumn of 1812, William John was given the sloop *Goshawk* – the delight of his life – she became the happiest of ships. They blockaded French-held Barcelona, storming batteries, spiking guns and 'constant skirmishing along the coast from the Bay to Rosas'. The tide was at last turning against Napoleon, who in a wave of mid-summer madness had invaded Russia; and on a starry night of December 1912 Ciudad Rodrigo, key into Spain, was successfully stormed by the British, George Napier leading and losing his right arm in the process. William John was now to suffer a loss that to him meant much more – his beloved ship.

He had, perhaps, grown over-confident in successful night raids along the French-held Spanish coast. At Tarragona he had anchored *Goshawk* 'in the very harbour, and engaged the battery for some hours', a shipmate recorded. 'In action Captain Napier always evinced the most perfect coolness'; but near Barcelona, 'in consequence of the wind battling and the heavy swell' the midshipman in charge 'missed stays when ordered to go about' and *Goshawk* grounded in the darkness, a bare mile or two from Barcelona. The hours of night were spent in an enormous effort to refloat her before daylight made her destruction certain: she was under the guns of Montjat Castle. To no avail: though all on board were saved, rowing away before dawn while *Goshawk* went sky high from their explosive charges. A court-martial exonerated them all from blame, the captain in charge of the court asking William John to dinner that same day, but the crew of *Goshawk* suffered a sad dispersal amongst the ships of the line still blockading Toulon.

William John became captain of the *Erne* in the West Indies, his arrival at Kingston in Jamaica saddened by the news that his younger brother, Francis, had died. Eight years of news, affection, family gossip, and naval talk could not now be uttered and heard, from Francis, – 'late 1st Lieutenant of HMS *Argo*, beloved of his messmates, and lamented even by the merchants and residents of Kingston'. Cast down by this loss, William John fell victim to the same 'vile yellow fever' and all but died also, his excellent sight was badly affected, he could no longer count all the Pleiades or make the minute starry observations that had been his delight. Maybe all this sadness turned William John's thoughts to poetry: He is next heard of reading aloud his ten verse lament to the ship's company the day after conducting the funeral of a young seaman in the intervals of a violent thunderstorm:

> '. . . vivid flashes in the sphere
> light for him the angry wave . . .'

In 1815, peace was made and the *Erne* was paid off, Europe being no longer 'plunged into the abyss of one arbitrary rule'. (Fichte.) There would be little doing at sea for some while, and William John after 12 years almost continuously at sea, after captivity, wounds, shipwreck, and ceaseless activity, during which he had only seen his family for a total of six weeks, went on half pay to look to them and his inheritance at Thirlestane in the Vale of Ettrick. In Scotland he met and married, in March 1816, Elizabeth Cochrane-Johnstone, great niece of his old commander in *Impérieuse*. They were second cousins, William John being the great grandson and Elizabeth, the granddaughter of Lord Hopetoun. Their wedding was a jolly gathering of Napiers, Cochranes, Johnstones and Hopes, with others either kin or 'conneckit'. They lived happily ever after, though William never lost his eye for a pretty girl nor his habit of light-hearted flirtation. Two boys and six girls followed in due order; and it was perhaps the desire to provide for all of what his friend Cochrane called his 'little productions' that in part propelled William John to the other side of the globe 20 years on. It could also have been the exploits of Cochrane, and the desire to emulate his cousin, 'Black Charlie' (Admiral Sir Charles Napier) who was currently the recipient of much réclame for his part in the naval side of Portugal's dynastic war. All these plus the urgent, exploring, enterprising spirit of his times.

Before marriage, William John had taken himself for six months to Edinburgh University to study agriculture, and for some years he lived a happy shore life on the Border – persuading his Ettrickdale tenants into more modern and effective methods of farming, and making roads along which they could, in all weathers, convey their cattle to market. He could be seen, Blackwoods magazine reported, 'carrying the end of the chain himself for many a weary day'. He bred a new line of sheep, afforested hills, and cherished the unfortunates of the district, particularly its lonely old women. He was made a member of the Royal Society of Edinburgh, Commissioner of the General Assembly of the Church of Scotland, and had a leading hand in the building of the Edinburgh Observatory and in the formation of the Selkirk Agricultural Society.

In 1823, he took his seat in the Lords as one of the representative peers of Scotland; but by voting both for Catholic Emancipation and the Reform Bill he alienated his fellow Scots lords and was not re-elected. Energetic and persevering, he became a well-known Border figure – tall, spare, and sandy-haired, striding or riding over hill and dale. 'His placidity of temper and benevolence were singularly engaging' one contemporary thought, and he was known locally as a father to the poor.

He was less placid in the Lords, arguing with passion for the passing of the Reform Bill and increase of the electorate, urging the excellence and responsibility of his countrymen – 'is it any longer possible to deny to such men a voice? . . . I am one of those Scotchmen who do love their country, better than any other country, and I have visited not a few . . . with all our imperfections which are neither small nor few, I do glory in the name and character of a Scotchman'; and it was 'for that perfect confidence which I repose in the integrity and good sense of my

countrymen' that he would vote, and urged his fellow peers to vote 'for
the Reform Bill'.

Maybe home life sometimes seemed a little quiet and dull to one who
had spent his youth under the aegis of such electric sparks as Nelson and
Cochrane. In 1824, William John was taken from his native hills to command HMS *Diamond* on the South America station. He left Elizabeth
with five small children and another one on the way, and Ettrick to the
charge of his trustworthy factor. His letters home breathed much enjoyment mingled with longing to be with them – 'the scenery is
mountainous and grand beyond expression', and Madeira made 'our
Wardlaw in comparison a mere mole-hill'. All the same, he went on
from Antigua, 'I never cease to think of our bonny green hills, and all
who reside among them . . . Take as much care of the old wives as you
can, and everyone else', he told his factor.

Like Darwin a few years later, he was amazed and delighted at the variety and richness of South America's natural growths, though less
enchanted by its inhabitants. He took the ambassador, Sir Charles Stuart,
to Bahia to meet the Emperor, 'who has gone there with his Court, his
Empress and his whore. Saving the Empress and one or two, there never
was a greater set of rogues, whores and thieves put together than Dom
Pedro and his Court'. Furthermore, slavery was still endemic and legal,
and ships of Brazil still raided the coasts of Africa for further supplies of
luckless Africans, though with these they mingled freely and without
racial bias.

William John was home by the summer of 1827 to rejoice in a new
daughter and a return to the family and the activities he loved. A seventh
child was soon on the way, and when King George IV died in 1830, his
successor King William IV, who had been shipmates with William John,
appointed him a lord-in-waiting, which involved spending some part of
the year in London, that forcing house of worldly ambition. From
Greece, Lord Cochrane wrote to urge William John to take service in the
Mediterranean. Political freedom was everywhere stirring – should not
William John with his liberal principles and naval abilities also take part?

Cochrane's function as gadfly to the authorities was ended by his
replacement on the Admiralty list in 1831. William John, who had urged
his cause throughout his disgrace, was the first to tell Cochrane the
good news, and received a correspondingly warm letter of thanks. Soon
Cochrane was back in beloved Scotland, happily testing the engines he
had invented in small boats along the Forth. Life seemed peaceful –
'happy may you both be!' Cochrane wrote to the Napiers on the arrival
of their fifth daughter. 'To rear your present and future little productions will prove the delight of after years'. By summer of 1833 life at

Thirlestane seemed set fair. An eighth and final child had been born, and since the Napiers already had two sons, the heir and the spare, no-one lamented the arrival of a sixth daughter.

Maybe London and the glories of its social life went a little even to William John's calm head. He loved the geniality of King William, and admired his generosity to his great brood of illegitimate children, the FitzClarences. He loved the grand dinners at Windsor Castle – the sumptuous wines and food, where the long table with its 420 candles in their gold candlesticks seemed to him 'like a blaze in a forest of golden trees'. He loved the pretty girls he sat next to at dinner, or the garrulous charming old princesses; he loved the bands and their jaunty music, the boat trips down the river to delicious cold lunches in great tents at Taplow; he loved the kindness of the royal family to his beloved Elizabeth. He enjoyed the junketing on the visits of the Empress of Brazil and her daughter, Donna Maria da Gloria. The throne of this very young Queen of Portugal had been largely secured to her by 'Black Charlie' against the forces of her usurping uncle, Dom Miguel, backed by all the reactionary parts of his country and indeed by the Pope, who had granted Miguel, a 57 year old debauchee, a dispensation to marry Maria da Gloria, his 13 year old niece. William John basked in 'Black Charlie's' fame and popularity, – popular since now that naval officers could no longer leap onto the enemy quarter-decks of Napoleon's ships, nothing took the fancy of the British public more than their doing the same thing in the interests of popular government on the continent.

In time William John's chance of interesting employment came up. He heard that a trade superintendent of experience and authority, but also of patience and calm, was needed to take charge at Canton, whence came vital supplies of tea (none was exported from India until 1838), and where local merchants, Chinese officials, and visiting seamen were often and dangerously at odds. He applied for the post to Lord Grey, Prime Minister, but there were delays over the appointment, even though it was warmly backed by King William.

Elizabeth had hastened north on the news that a dangerous epidemic of whooping cough was sweeping the Vale of Ettrick, and William John had to linger lonely in London, though celebrating the Trafalgar Day dinner, where in less than 30 years he was one of only three survivors, and welcoming Captain Ross back after four years in the Antarctic, for which he would be rewarded by having the *Ross Sea* called after him. Some of the Club members were for having Ross made to pay his four years' subscription: William John was able to put paid to that.

After four month's wait for an official decision Lord Grey told William John on 6 December 'that a ship was ready to take me out at Plymouth by the 12th. This is pretty sharp work'. Six days to get ready for five years at the other end of the world, during which he would have to drive north across the Border and back, settle all his affairs, say all his goodbyes, and be back in London to be briefed by Palmerston, Foreign Secretary, and by Charles Grant, President of the Board of Control of the East India Company, (though William John was stipulating that his task should be separated from the activities of the EIC).

Arrived at Thirlestane after travelling at full speed, the future Superintendent was told that *Andromache*, the frigate in which the family were to sail to China would not be ready by the 12th. There was time for mid-day dinner with his sister Lady Carmichael at Castle Craig on the way to Edinburgh for interviews with his lawyer. For the pleasure of their company he took his sister as well as his three eldest children with him, and found himself much moved by 'Sunday Service at the Iron Church where the Psalm 33 paraphrase was sung to the touching melody of "Martyrdom" '. At home, the Thirlestane burn was in spate and William John could not resist walking up the hill 'to bid farewell to the Black Spout, then roaring and foaming at prodigious rate from its rocky precipice'. An excellent dinner followed, 'surrounded with everything I loved at home', and a farewell to tenants and workers, with tears on both sides.

Plans for all the children had been made provisionally in advance. Maria and Georgiana were to come to China with their parents; Francis and Willie were to stay at Thirlestane with their tutor until Easter and then go to school at Saxe Meiningen in Germany, with parson brother Henry Napier, rector of Swyncombe in Oxfordshire, with overall responsibility. The four little girls were to go with their governess Miss Elmslie and the nursery maid to the Reids at Runnymede, after a jolly fortnight of junketing with kind Aunt Carmichael and Sir Tom at Castle Craig. How Elizabeth felt at being parted from them, and especially from her nine month old baby, Lucy, is not on record, but this was a way of life endured by many a parent and child in imperial times.

On the morning of 10 December, William John and his man Samuel Holton set off by starlight with four post horses to the phaeton. The continuous south-west gales and rain through which they drove almost non-stop to London at least gave the reassurance that in such contrary winds there would be no chance of *Andromache*'s putting to sea: she was probably still in dock and not even out in the Sound.

Two days later a message from Palmerston greeted William John in London – with the news that he had not been expected back for a fortnight – news he had not troubled to convey to Scotland. He himself had left London for Christmas in Hampshire. William John accordingly departed to say goodbye to the King at Brighton, finding time also to look in on an old sail-making friend. Saying goodbye, King William 'desired me to wear my uniform and appear always as a King's officer', and to write to him often. The King seemed not best pleased with the arrangements for the Resident at Canton, as well he might not.

The reasons for appointing William John seem obscure. He knew nothing of China, not much of trade, and had no training in diplomacy: his formative years having been spent under the King's Regulations and Admiralty Instructions, where nothing must be done 'to the derogation of God's honour', and at sea, where shilly-shally was the deadliest of sins. But trouble at Canton had too often been sparked off by sailors, who after a voyage from home sometimes lasting six months were frantic for the fleshpots of the shore, certain to get drunk, sure to create rows. William John was used to controlling sailors, and perhaps it was reckoned that if he could persuade Scots borderers to build roads they did not want to build, could cope amicably with Brazilian officials, with post boys and court ladies, he could probably keep the peace between Cantonese viceroys, foreign merchants and obstreperous sailors, and even persuade the first of these gradually to open up their country to a trade in ordinary goods which would benefit both sides and obviate the need for the present inflow of smuggled opium.

Over the New Year, Palmerston continued 'absent at his seat in Hampshire entertaining a company of ladies and their husbands', (in that order) but if Lord Napier would come to his house in Great Stanhope Street at noon on 7 January, the Foreign Secretary would meet him there for the necessary briefing. Arriving on the dot, William John was told that Palmerston had arrived at the Foreign Office at 3.00 that morning where he was still asleep. All day the patient William John waited in Whitehall. Appearing at 6.00, Palmerston said he must leave at once for a Cabinet dinner; since Lord Napier must depart for Plymouth early next morning, his instructions would be sent after him.

It says much for William John's good nature or for Palmerston's charm that after a little polite chat they parted 'on the best of terms'. The new Superintendent thus lost his one chance of discovering the Foreign Secretary's actual intentions as to policy in China. He was one of the rare ministers interested in foreign countries and knowledgeable about them, but China was a far country, he had many nearer home to consider, and his knowledge of this huge empire was sketchy. He may have felt that as the King's nominee and not his own, Napier could sink or swim without the government's specific advice. Lord Grey had simply advised caution and quiescence. To separate the British public from their cups of tea was to court political death.

Meanwhile, Shap Fell in mid winter had proved too much for the Napier's ancient carriage which had finally broken down at Manchester. Fearful of the delay for repairs, Elizabeth had sold the old coach for what it would fetch, and she and the girls and two maids plus all the luggage needed for a five year sojourn abroad went on by post chaise. They foregathered at Exeter, where William John told them that after all the breathless haste, *Andromache* was further delayed. This at least allowed the family to spend happy days with the Hopetouns, wintering in the south with a delicate daughter, and foregathering with other Scots exiles such as Lord William Kerr, rector of Totnes.

Andromache at last was ready, but at Plymouth the gales continued obstinately to blow up Channel. William John enjoyed himself buying an expensive chronometer at Cox's of Devonport and in calling on the port admiral, 'Sir William Hargood, a neat little old man, very quick in his movements, but who made dreadful havoc of the King's English in his conversation. He commanded the *Colossus* at the Battle of Trafalgar, where he got dreadfully cut up'. The girls meanwhile enjoyed their wind-buffeted walks along the Hoe.

On 4 February, 1834 *Andromache* anchored in the Sound, and two days later took the chance of the variable weather to set sail. Baffling winds slowed progress; after two days they were but 15 miles south west of the Dodman. Next day the wind obligingly veered to the east, carrying them down Channel, 'at 8.00 in the evening the Lizard lights showed NNW 3/4 W13, from which I took my departure for keeping the ship's reckoning'. Incalculable winds felt far more sympathetic than incalculable statesmen.

On the evening of 11 February, the barometer fell like a stone and the wind 'veered round to the westward and blew with considerable violence – a very heavy sea running from the SW and NNW crossing, which caused much uneasiness in the minds as well as the stomachs of the ladies'.

'I find the ship extremely easy in her motion', William John wrote unfeelingly; 'dips quick into the hollows of the sea but without violence, and rises again as quick without shipping a drop of water. The masts and rigging required securing this night, which was effected with some trouble.' The trouble was not his: he was a passenger, and for a time even the troubles of his beloved womenfolk were forgotten. The heedless official callousness was over. He was away once more in all the vigour and delight of a fine ship under sail at sea.

Part Two
Cathay and the Western World

2

The Land of Confucius

The country towards which *Andromache* was bearing William John through the spring gales of the Atlantic was a land almost as remote in thought and feeling as it was geographically far from the country he had left, armed only with contradictory instructions from Lord Palmerston and with his own faith, hope and charity, with which to understand and come to terms with the complicated Chinese.

From distant antiquity a vigorous black-haired people had dwelt in China around the great right-angled bend in the Hwang-Ho, the yellow river flowing through the yellow plain, where the dusty topsoil of a Northern Asia released from the Ice Age had blown consistently eastward to form a fertile earth 150 feet deep and 100,000 square miles wide. In due course, they spread south to the enormous valley of the Yangtse and from thence further south and west.

These, the self-styled Black-haired People, acquired from very early times a belief in Tien, the power of Heaven, a spirit rather than a person, whose righteous will men needed to follow rather than their own selfish desires. Life was a compound of Yang and Yin, light and shade, the brilliant and the dark. Yang was the bright sun, Yin the solid earth. Yang, needless to say, was male and active, Yin female and passive. Evil presented no problem: it was necessarily compounded with good. These concepts did not differ greatly from those inspiring other early societies: the Chinese hung on to them longer. Spirits both good and evil abounded, in mountain and river, in field and forest, and called for a perpetual calendar of propitiation and thanksgiving. Every season had its festival, and the four main points of the compass a particular significance.

Unlettered centuries succeeded one another: the legendary Fu- Hi taught the Chinese to live in families and groups, to tame and herd sheep, to build houses: the equally legendary Shen-Nung taught them to sow and plough and grow vegetables, to settle and live in villages. In the half-legendary years between 3,000–2,000 BC, as in most early communities struggling for survival and surrounded by jealous tribal enemies, a feudalism was established by the time of the Kings Yao and

15

Shun. These were central Kings with provinces administered and defended by lesser rulers appointed by them and responsible to them. These two, and their non-hereditary successor, Yu, consolidated a country whose enemies had been driven back, whose roads and markets had been established, who had in general been united by another even earlier figure of legend, Huang-Ti, the Yellow Emperor. All these, down the milleniums, acquired a golden aura – they had been rulers so virtuous, humble, strong and selfless that their legend set the tone for centuries. The Chinese looked backward to the best, rather than forward to the better. There *could* be no better than that Arcadian age. The only serpent in this Eden was the incalculable North China rainfall, varying as it does from zero to 45 inches, inducing either flood or famine.

* * *

The Chou dynasty in China roughly coincided with the great days of Greek civilization; but there was no contact, not even through the Scythian tribes, and little similarity. The seven hundred little city states of the Greek world carried on in continuous competition – a lively free-for-all around the Aegean; in China the so-called Hundred Families at least *aimed* for co-operation. Both peoples kept their women very firmly in what was thought to be their proper place. Women in Greece, before Euripides, were considered hardly worth talking to or being with; hence the free run for homosexuals. In both worlds women were feared for their Medea-like qualities, their alarming power; give them an inch and they would take an ell; therefore, do not give them an inch: they certainly displayed some very unpleasant qualities in their roles as Greek deities. The Chinese supreme being was impersonal, their many good or evil spirits sexless; the Greek gods were endlessly involved in sexual activity. The Chinese ideal was harmony; the Greek ideal individualism and triumph. Homer's Peleus tells his son Achilles always to excel all other men. ['Only be thou strong, and very courageous', Joshua was telling the troops of Israel in this Epoch.]

The Greeks were endlessly curious, but loved to sit about talking: the Chinese were endlessly industrious, and more ready to accept things as they are. Family life and respect for parents meant everything to the Chinese, and loomed only moderately largely to the Greeks. 'We pay a heavy rent for nine months' lodging!' Alexander the Great exclaimed in a moment of pardonable exasperation with his difficult mother – this sentiment could not have found utterance by any young Chinese. Both fought in bronze armour; Greece celebrating her warlike achievements in matchless verse; Chinese poets tending to sing about the timeless beauty of mountain, flower, and river; works rather more praiseworthy but distinctly less immortal.

The astonishing achievements of Greek civilization came and went like a brilliant rainbow, yet it forever marked the European sky. Advancing more slowly and lasting far longer in its original home, the Chinese achievement coloured the eastern sky with a dawn that left a permanent glow. 'The East is Red', sing young Chinese communists. Not so, but the East remains indubitably Chinese.

There was a sultrier side. Both peoples disposed of surplus girl babies, castrated surplus boys to make them useful house servants, and employed slaves without benefit of law, whose life and limb were at their absolute disposal. Yet a kind of yearning after righteousness was palpable in both. To both peoples religion was an all-pervading presence, a part of the air they breathed; their landscape as thick with deities and spirits as stars in the Milky Way.

The music of flute and bells, the rustle of silk – since the discovery of the silk-worm by the Yellow Emperor's wife – the story of Yu taming the untameable Yellow River, of Tang the Victorious who overthrew the wicked King Keih, of his son saying to an old builder in distant Fukien 'Enrich my mind with the treasures of your mind', induce in the western mind a certain cynicism. Not all can have been as beautiful, as well-ordered, as humble before the wisdom of age, as the tales have it. Tang was not a legend, with him was founded in 1766 BC the dynasty of Shang. Recorded fact emerges from the mist. By his time the Chinese believed in Tao, the Way, in which all things were made and in which they should lie. Man was endowed with the five virtues – kindness, good manners, knowledge, uprightness and honour – to be used or abused in free choice, but under threat of punishment from Heaven. Right relationships were of immense importance – the idea of Li, right behaviour towards everyone and everything. There were five special relationships – between father and son, ruler and subject, husband and wife, elder brother and younger brother, friend and friend. [Only in the last of these was there any question of equality.] Honour to parents was the magic check on wrongdoing, since this above all brings sorrow to a parent. When a father died, a three year period of mourning was decreed, providing a wonderful sabbatical to the tired business man, added to a blessed rest from wives and concubines and their demands.

No more than Christians were the Chinese faithful to their ethic, but in the same way it provided a framework, a settled notion of right and wrong, of an ideal of goodness bringing the reward of a mind at peace. Be all that as it may, the Indus Valley Empire passed away, the Egyptian,

(Tutankhamen was now Pharaoh,) the Assyrian, the Persian Empire, the Roman Empire: in 1834 the Chinese Empire was still very much there.

* * *

The Chinese were marvellously inventive; but not everything was devised by their acute minds. From further west came the use of bronze and of iron, painted pottery, tamed horses, the chariot, the growing of wheat, the domestication of animals. The dynasty of Chou succeeded that of Shang, conquering or invading dynasties became enervated in due course by an excess of good living in their sumptuous palaces, by wine, women and song; and, despite ancient doctrine, too often their manly Yang was overwhelmed by the Yin of a great tribe of maternal relations, concubines, and eunuchs. There were feudal wars as in Europe or India, kings driven back until they were rulers of but a small area known as the Royal Domain. Through it all civilization grew. Kingdoms waxed and waned, but people went on inventing, writing, composing. There is a curious tale from these years. Troubled by the increasing power of a Tartar tribe, the King of Tsin (or Chin) sent his musicians from the Middle Kingdom to play his own special music to the Tartar lord. In a few years the Tartar chief stopped fighting, stopped ruling, stopped bothering, simply lay all day listening to these sweet sounds; and the King of Tsin was able to invade and conquer without difficulty. Music, as well as religion, could prove the opiate of the ruler, if not of the people.

China was immensely formal, governed by strict rules in all aspects of civic and family life, ruled by an immense number of officials. To be one, it was necessary to pass a stiff civil service exam – there was no being the Duke of Norfolk without surviving a tough intellectual test as well as being proficient as archer and charioteer. The gentry, though sustained by family landholding, had to play an administrative or a political part, buffers between peasants and the higher officialdom. The gentry lived in the country in the big house, a family compound with stores of grain or rice against lean times, with fruit trees and a fish pond, and strong walls against banditry; but tended in due course to gravitate to the towns. In the peasant world family mattered more than community, community more than nation. There was almost no nationalism, China lived surrounded by lesser civilizations who wanted to absorb its way of life and were welcome to do so, since China was the Inner Land, the Flowery Land, the centre of the world. All outsiders were barbarians. About 220 BC the Chinese abolished primogeniture and the land was divided among sons, which made holdings smaller and smaller. Crowded together on their precious soil, since so much of China is mountain and desert that in time each acre had to support 1,500 people, the

Chinese were forced to cultivate personal relationships. Eventually it became almost impossible to be out of earshot of one another.

Officials kept the merchant class under by a process of squeeze. There was not much point in being W W Woolworth when officials could squeeze you for far more than half, rather as income tax does now, except that the officials kept the loot for personal use and not for the community. Nobody hoped to get rich by producing more, but by acquiring more of what had already been produced.

In the midst of all the ferocious feudal turmoil, – the Chou Dynasty, more often than not, was a 600 year long War of the Roses – wise men had survived, travelled from court to court, been allowed to live where they chose, and not infrequently had even been listened to. Even before Confucius, (Kung-fu-tse) two vital principles had emerged – a close relationship between humans and the natural world, and the idea that a king rules not by God-given right nor by hereditary succession but in virtue of his own righteousness. Lao-Tse, born around 600 BC, preached the Tao, the Way – 'all things depend on it for life, and it does not refuse them; it loves and feeds all things, but does not claim them for its own . . . Great virtue is like water, that nourishes every thing yet takes the lowest place of all . . . the wise man does not push himself forward nor make himself great . . . he has not a heart of his own, he makes the heart of the Hundred Families his heart . . . he meets the bad with goodness . . . The Great Way is very plain, but', Lao pointed out sadly, 'men prefer the winding paths'. During his time, to the far west, the Assyrian came down like a wolf on the fold on a small tribe of monotheists in Palestine.

* * *

Confucius was born in 551 BC when the Romans, another small but vigorous tribe, were still under Etruscan kings, when Croesus was piling up wealth in Asia Minor, Pythagoras was preaching his rum mixture of religion, mathematics, music, and natural science, when the ships of his fellow Greeks had penetrated as far south in the Atlantic as the Senegal River, and Darius the Great of Persia had conquered Thrace and Macedonia and crossed the Danube against the Scythians. By this time Chinese civilization, as well as the Egyptian and the Greek, was already old. Confucius was born in the promontory province of Shantung, jutting out into the Yellow Sea, where his state of Lu had been given to the great and good Duke of Chou, founder of the 1122–221 BC dynasty of that name. With this gift had gone the privilege of sacrificing to Heaven and Earth on the holy hill of Shantung province, Mount Tai.

Confucius, thus, grew up in a highly religious atmosphere and was much enamoured from his youth with ritual and ceremony, exactly performed. In such matters he was a perfectionist, and would never even sit down to a meal unless his seating mat were precisely aligned with the table. By the age of 17, he was holding office with meticulous efficiency; but when his mother died he revived the ancient practice of three years of mourning, during which he read, worked, and thought with unremitting persistence. The time accomplished, he set out on a journey in quest of further knowledge, studying and teaching on his way, with particular attention to the early kings and their rule of life, firmly replacing Yao and Shun on the religious/historical map of China as founding fathers.

Such kings, he taught, had made their realm happy by first purifying themselves. To effect purification, one must think rightly; to think rightly one must learn from experience, and so arrive at the truth. The pure in heart could control themselves, produce harmony in their families, and good order in state and kingdom. Self-discipline was the root of all things – 'the fault, dear Brutus, is not in our stars, but in ourselves . . .'.

Confucius preached reverence, uprightness, a revival of respect for all the fine old traditions of China. 'For a long time the Kingdom has been going the wrong way', a customs official said to the disciples of the sage, 'and now God is going to use your master as a bell to call the people back to truth and goodness.' It was a bell of infinite resonance. On one occasion his followers lost Confucius. Was he, someone asked them, 'a man as tall as Yu, with a brow like Yao's and the neck and shoulders of a hero, but looking as forlorn as a dog at a funeral'? Told the tale, Confucius laughed heartily, repudiated the first part of the description but said the part about the forlorn dog was excellent.

This forlorn dog left an imprint on his countrymen that endured down the centuries. He emphasized the need for learning, thought, and the continual purging of the heart as the route to happiness and harmony. He taught history, music, and poetry: pupils came from far and wide. Sometimes he held public office as a magistrate, sometimes he was himself imprisoned. He sought all over China for an honest prince who would take him on as minister, and, guided by him, lead the kingdom back into honesty and peace. He never found him; returning chastened and sad to his homeland where he opened his school again – 'I never get tired of learning, and I never get tired of teaching'. The times in which he lived were rarely peaceful and frequently disordered, but he persevered undiscouraged, preaching peace and order as the only way in which men should live; himself to die peacefully in his 70s.

Immense numbers of people listened to Confucius, and although the world in which he lived still contained its Caligulas and its Tiberius Caesars on the throne, men such as Kieh and Chow-Sin, who would torture their subjects to death and take pleasure in their pain, he believed in human perfectibility – 'Heaven desires our perfection: perfection is the beginning and the end of all creation'.

Aged 70, after many and often sad wanderings he had come back to his native land of Lu and completed his classic writings, mainly a collection of the great literature of China – the Books of History, of Poetry, of Ceremony, of Changes, and his own work, a short history of the State of Lu. From then onwards, for 2,000 years and more, every office-holder in China must read, mark, learn, and inwardly digest them all.

From these two wise men, and a third, Mencius (Meng-Tse) who died circa 300 BC and preached and taught very much as Confucius had done, came the lasting law and philosophy of life of this increasingly large empire on the eastern fringe of the Euro-Asian land mass.

* * *

Mencius taught that there was no enjoyment to be had from riches and the delights that riches buy, unless the ruler of the household or of the kingdom was wise and good. He should certainly be the patron saint of conservationists: he urged the King of Liang along the paths of conservation, in farming, forestry and fishing. The resulting surplus would mean more grain, more fish, more turtles, more wood for building and for fuel. Forests must be replanted, small fish thrown back, animals bred advisedly: he urged the King to see that mulberry trees were planted around the small farms, for shade and fruit and leaves to feed silkworms. 'When your people can feed the living and bury the dead contentedly, you have taken the first step towards gaining the whole kingdom.' He believed in ploughing back into the land, and the use of manure for its further enrichment. 'Set up good schools', he also advised, 'and you will never see grey-haired men on your roads bearing heavy burdens on their backs.' These too, in their 70s, 'should wear silk and eat flesh'. Plough deep, and weed well, he insisted, and with care 'the Black-haired people need never suffer hunger or cold'.

Mencius had preached peace, had declared that only a man who had no pleasure in killing men could unite the 11 kingdoms of China. But shortly before he died, its unity was set in train by the ruler of Tsin (or Chin, whence China) Chou-Tsiang, who by a course of consistent violence and treachery, dethroned the last Chou king, annexed the Royal Domain, and left completion of the task to his great grandson, who had enormous pleasure in killing men and who made himself master of all China, and once more, Son of Heaven, or First Great Emperor – Shi-Huang-Ti.

Though bloodthirsty, Shi was not impervious to wisdom; inheriting very young, he took advice from a wise and admirable adviser. But at 18, he suspected a palace conspiracy, had 400 officials executed, and banished his mother. Thereafter, he sat on the Dragon Throne with his sword on his knees, threatening death to any who dared to criticize him. But there were always those few just men, whose constancy made them the glory of China. After Shi-Huang-Ti had disposed of 27 of such, who had pleaded for respect of his mother, the young emperor was confronted by another, very old, and pleading the same cause. Taking off his long mandarin coat, and discounting the cauldron of boiling water kept handy for purposes of total immersion for the recalcitrant, this aged hero dared to tell the young man to obey the age-old precepts of parental reverence. To the astonishment of all, he was forgiven and rewarded, and the Queen Mother was reinstated.

Before bowing low, and stepping with dignity towards the boiling cauldron, this brave veteran had reproached the young emperor for his 'violent and presumptuous character . . . You do not control yourself, I am afraid for you and for your dynasty'. He had been right about the extreme brevity of the First Great Emperor's dynasty, but the Emperor himself prospered exceedingly, and his foundation of unity was solidly built, and lived on. As did the Great Wall, a defence against the incessant encroachments of Tartar tribes, roaming the wilds to the north and west of the Inner Kingdom, the Flowery Land. Shi-Huang-Ti did not forget the fierceness of his great grandfather, ruler of Chin, a western country of horsemen skilled in Tartar ways, who had swept the last of the Chou dynasty out of his way in 255 BC. The First Great Emperor did not delay in making himself master of all China, drenching it in blood in the process but laying the foundations of an immense resilient strength. He moved all over his huge domains, building roads, making canals, regularizing laws. His well-drilled, well-fed armies swept through the provinces like a cataract, at a cost of 500,000 lives, since all opposing armies as well as all opposing princes were butchered out of hand. He divided his Empire into 36 provinces (six being his lucky number) that were never again to be ruled by independent princes but by governors appointed by the Emperor and obedient to him – a system that endured.

As so often in China, a strain of poetry ran through the cruelties. Ordering all the weapons in China to be brought to him, Shi-Huang-Ti melted them down and had them re-cast into bells for his temples. He worshipped on the Holy Mountain in midwinter, he greeted each returning season at the gates of the great city he set up at Hien Yang, on the Wei river. He wanted this city to look like the Milky Way, its 100 glittering palaces massed as closely as those stars. From every corner of China he summoned skilled workmen to beautify them all. His greatest work was his Great Wall, built also at great cost in human life but ultimately to his people's advantage. He sent workmen, captured enemies, stone, and supplies from all over China, occasionally putting in a terrifying appearance himself, with his rapid movements, and his train of chariots following.

Safely established and glorified in his sumptuous palaces, he suddenly decided in 213 BC to make a complete break with the past. A strain of dangerous fanaticism ran through the Chinese soul, occasionally evidencing itself in deeds of arbitrary cruelty. Shi-Huang-Ti ordered all books, except technical ones, to be burned – all history, all poetry, all philosophy, all records of the past, all the writings of Confucius and other sages. A few copies, fortunately were hidden, and escaped the holocaust; and around 400 brave souls defied him and refused to burn their beloved books. The Emperor ordered them all to be buried alive, early martyrs to the noble cause of literature. In just the same spirit the Red Guards of 20th century China, more than 2,000 years later, once in power would organize the great smashing of beautiful statues and porcelain, because they had been made under the rule of the hated Emperors and must be blotted out. (They also ordained that a great many philosophers and wise men should be buried alive in the country, though only metaphorically.)

A great death-dealer himself, Shi-Huang-Ti contemplated his own demise with terror, searching far and wide for a potion of immortality and providing himself with a great terracotta army to march with him through eternity. But his tomb, in which the men who worked in it had been sealed into the outer passage, so that the secret of its locality could be kept, was soon rifled and robbed of its jewels, its jade, and its silk robes; for under a weak young ruler the imperial power had been seized. Liu Pang, son of a village headman, inaugurated the Han dynasty in 206 BC and led the original revolt. But while he was absent from the capital, pacifying the outer provinces, another rebel general marched upon beautiful Hien Yang, looted it as completely as could be, and then set it on fire. It took three months to burn – palaces, bridges, parks, temples – all the beauty and wealth gathered by the First Great Emperor. His son took less time to kill, the young man whom Liu Pang had spared and treated courteously. Returning, Liu Pang defeated the rebel leader, and by common consent the nobles and wise men begged him to be Emperor, of a dynasty lasting until 222 AD. Liu Pang was a peace-maker, a restorer. He rebuilt the villages and the bridges destroyed by the rebels, restored confiscated property to its owners, even reinstated some of the feudal nobles. Enemies were forgiven,

order restored. The harmony so dearly loved was seen to return. The
ways of Confucius were re-established. Liu Pang took the more imperial name of Kao-Tsu.

* * *

The peace and order did not extend to the Tartar tribes, among whom
were a small and insignificant tribe called Mongols, slowly swelling into
the power that 1,000 years later would conquer most of Asia and scare
Europe half out of its wits. A particularly cruel and cunning chief now
conquered and united all the tribes and with an alleged 300,000 horsemen swept round the western end of the Great Wall as if it had been but
a Maginot Line, and slaughtered and plundered as far south as the
Yellow River.

Kao-Tsu, enraged, set out with a great army, far west to the city of
Shansi. On the plain outside the city walls, the Tartar chief revealed that
he had tactics as well as numbers. His horsemen in great hordes had quietly surrounded the Emperor on all four sides, with men on black horses
to the north, bay horses for the red colour of the south, white horses for
the white of the west, greys for the blue of the east – an electrifying
spectacle combining art, intelligence, and menace in roughly equal
parts. An impartial judge would have awarded full marks for technical
merit and as many for artistic impression.

The Emperor was only saved by a beautiful young girl of his court,
who offered herself as a peace gift. She was well received by the Tartars:
none the less, they demanded more in the form of Danegeld. They
departed, for the while, with immense plunder, and Kao-Tsu had also to
give his daughter as wife to the Tartar chief. 'How shall I bear the winds
and frosts of that strange land?' her dramatic counterpart would be
made to lament on the Chinese stage a few hundred years on. This shat-
tering indignity for Kao-Tsu had fateful consequences; his daughter
taught her sons the ways and the lore of China; very slowly her infectious
way of life crept west into the wilds of Central Asia. Refusing medical aid,
Kao-Tsu died not long after from an old and unhealed wound.

The Han dynasty coincided with the Roman Empire; they knew dis-
tantly of one another, and their fates overlapped. The West knew a little
of China, her coveted silk had filtered through; and on Scythian gold
artefacts the twists of a Chinese dragon sometimes showed amongst the
formal Greek-influenced patterns. The Chinese knew almost nothing of
the civilization of the lands further west, and almost nothing of India:
they were now to learn. Tired of repelling endless Tartar raids, a descendant of Kao-Tsu decided to advance beyond the Great Wall and drive the
Tartars so far west that raiding would be impracticable. After many

battles they drove the Tartars beyond the Gobi Desert, a more effective barrier than any wall. The Emperor, Wu-Ti, heard that a tribe who hated the Tartars had moved off west in search of new lands, and sent a volunteer officer to persuade them to come back to lands he would secure to them, if they would become his allies. This adventurous young man was called Chang-Kien and became the Marco Polo of China, setting out west in 138 BC.

He did not lose heart when he was captured by Tartars and his 100 followers enslaved. After ten years, he had lulled his captors into the belief that he had become one of them, and escaped with one follower on their swiftest horses. Chang-Kien and his Tartar squire took the route north of the Tien Shan, the Heavenly Mountains; an endless journey of incredible danger and hardship, through a moon country of wind and dust and waterless leagues, ice-cold by night and burning hot by day. He came down into the lands between the Pamirs and the Caspian Sea, where he and his one follower found to their amazement broad and fertile plains, dotted with corn, cattle, houses and cities. Armstrong and Co, landing on the moon and finding there a flourishing human community, could hardly have been more surprised.

They discovered the lost tribe, happily settled by the Oxus river and declining to return to China's icy northern border. Here too, wandering for a year, Chang-Kien found Chinese silks. Whence these? From the Shin-Tu, he was told, a great rich country far to the south, with a steamy climate and warriors who rode to battle on elephants. China thus first became aware of India, hitherto cut off from her by Tibet and the Himalayas, and the steep and thickly wooded valleys of North Burma. Chang-Kien also saw, with great admiration, the magnificent horses of the Caspian plain, so different from the small tough shaggy rides of Central Asia.

Within sight of China, on his return through the southern route by way of Kashgar and Khotan, Chang-Kien was once more taken by the Tartars. This time he escaped after only a year, returning to the Emperor at Loyang, now the capital, to be fêted and honoured and listened to eagerly, with his tales of rice and wheat and beautiful horses, of gold and silver coins used as money, of men who made wine from bunches of purple fruit, (he had even brought back a root) of fabled Shin-Tu and its elephant-borne army, its ivory and carpets.

He was given the title of Great Traveller, and the Emperor Wu-Ti acted at once on his information, sending a series of well-provisioned and well-led armies into the west. All the little kingdoms of the region, and the pastoral tribes, were not unwilling to make peace and pay tribute in return for protection by this powerful man. Wu-Ti thus added the whole of Chinese Turkestan to his empire, a welcome region famous for its jade. At Khansu grew up the city from which the great caravans would start for the next thousand years – Yu-men, the Jade Gate.

* * *

Ever since the first man rode one, horses have always been objects of unscrupulous longing. The Emperor had *his* eye on Ferghana, where the eye of the Great Traveller had lit up at the sight of such fine steeds. From here his emissaries failed to buy horses, failed to be given them; and eventually stole some. The thieves were pursued and soundly thrashed; the delectable horses were led back. The wholesale defeat of the Emperor's first large army, sent to avenge this, did not permanently discourage him; China's already huge manpower soon provided another, this time victorious. (Her population at the time of Christ was reckoned at 60,000,000, stayed much the same until 1650, and doubled, or perhaps even quadrupled, by 1850, due to there being more food available. The west was now won.

In this way the love of fine horseflesh, so often operative in human affairs, opened up east and west to one another. Roman Empresses wore fine silk, and rich furs from the far north; the Chinese palaces enjoyed the glass of Syria, jewels, coral, the incense of Arabia. The Parthians, clever fellows, already celebrated for their departing flight of arrows, became the middlemen, operating from Tashkent; and taking some care that Romans and Chinamen never actually met. To Rome, China was Seres, the Silk Land: to China Rome was Ta-Tsin. In 97 AD, the famous Chinese general, Pau Chao, led his armies to the shores of the Caspian Sea, sending an envoy to Syria. Turning south, he was deflected from his journey by wide-eyed Parthians declaring with conviction that anyone who loved his wife and family and hoped to see them again would be mad to cross the Persian Gulf – this strip of sea inflicted people with strange sickness, and it took three years to cross and come back. Pau Chao was halted by this prospect. So that Roman and Chinaman never chaffered in the streets of Damascus, where St. Paul had recently lain blind from the shock of conversion.

A pre-Christian religion had already made its intrepid way across the mountains from India into China, in 67 AD. Under the Emperor Ming-Ti, Buddhism spread and flourished. Confucianism was a pragmatic way of life rather than a mystical faith – a long set of rules for the best method of living virtuously and happily on earth. Buddhism introduced a stronger spiritual element. Confucius believed in a future life, but he also believed in having a good time while here. The Buddhist aim of leaving passion and desire behind, of detachment from all things earthly, was very different; but the very nature of its other worldly quality may have supplied a deeply felt spiritual need which the old religion with its preoccupation with evil spirits did not. Islam was to arrive on a wide scale with the Mongols – this faith too was to seize and hold its corner of the vast Chinese world.

This immensely powerful empire now stretched from the Pacific to the Caspian, and from the Great Wall south to Tonkin; and its solid potency greatly affected the history of Europe. Pushed westward out of Asia by this irresistible force, the local tribes contributed to the fall of Rome, their displacement forcing, in due course, the Goths and the Vandals into over-running Europe, and in time contributing Attila the Hun. Later reinforced by the Mongols, this fear of the overwhelming masses from the East was to become forever operative upon the European consciousness. Even today, Russia still lives a life of deep-seated suspicion.

The Han dynasty came and went, succumbing in the traditional imperial manner to an over-production of powerful great-aunts, lovely but debilitating concubines, and ever-intriguing palace eunuchs; but ensuring, in the course of its 400 years, the stability which produced an immense flowering of invention – paper in the first century AD, painting on silk, fine pottery, beautiful carvings in that hardest and most difficult of substances, jade, in all its fascinating colours. Learning flourished, as did music and architecture. China was truly the centre of this eastern world; and the kings of all the subject tribes sent their sons to her capital of Loyang to be educated.

Strangely, the deeply entrenched hierarchy of China prevented her learned scientists in their long gowns from having anything to do with her highly skilled craftsmen. They were set apart from all manual work, never meeting the workmen who could have developed their ideas. There could be no Leonardos here, no Michelangelos, dirtying their hands with ceaseless experiment. In time China arrived at the admirable frame of mind when as a nation she did not covet *anything*, not even any longer the swift mares of Ferghana – she had it all.

* * *

Even the great Turkish invasion, sweeping round the north as far as Korea, or continuous Tartar infiltration from the same direction did not deflect this progress. The core of the Inner Land remained untouched, although the people of North China became and remained notably fiercer, from all this Tartar blood, and perhaps also from their savage winter climate. Even when the decline of central government brought the 360 years of strife known as the Six Dynasties, that led up to

the emergence of the Sui dynasty and reunification, China's essential
pattern of life prevailed – her ordered and regular festivities, worship on
the Mountain and at the temples, her Confucian mould. In the north,
however, men remained proud to call themselves the Sons of Han.

Shamanism continued from time to time to raise its sinister and superstitious head. Tao-ists continued to follow the way, and thus all forms of
religious feeling came to be catered for; practical goodness by
Confucius; a hermit life of thought and self-discipline by Lao-Tse; self-
abnegation, monasticism and other-worldliness by the Buddha, whose
benign countenance was soon to be carved everywhere in sandalwood
and jade. Tao-ists of the baser sort claimed magical powers; and the Han
Emperor Wu-Ti heard of their boasted elixir of life, summoning their
practitioners to Court, honouring them, and asking them to prepare
him a cup. But he had no better luck than Shi-Huang-Ti with his terracotta army of cavalry and infantry. A brave courtier seized the cup and
drank the elixir: if it truly gave eternal life the Emperor would be unable
to kill him; if not, he was glad to sacrifice his life to deliver his master
from the falsehoods of the charlatans who preyed upon him.

Somewhere around the year 700 another religion arrived, accompanied by an invasion more perilous than any. The setting-up was quiet.
Some Arab traders arrived at Canton; they were Moslems and a few of
them stayed and in due course were allowed to build a small mosque and
to raise a minaret, which accorded well with the pagodas to be brought
by the Buddhists from India. The Chinese tolerated all faiths, like the
Romans, who allowed all except those involving human sacrifice; (hence
their war with the Druids, so oddly resurrected of late in the form of
chartered accountants in long white robes and bi-focals). The Moslem
Arabs harmed no-one, did not invade, did not convert. But they brought
with them a tranquillizer made from *Papaver somniferum,* the white poppy
growing in Asia Minor – opium. It took on, flourished, slowly became an
addiction among the few who could grow or obtain it.

3

The Great Pure Realm

'The Princes of China are at each other's throats – let us get up from the mud in which we are lying', said the Tartar chief Liu Yuan to his son Liu Tsung. They were descendants of Tartar chieftains married to Chinese princesses, skilled in Chinese ways and possessing both paternal energy and maternal intelligence. They acted accordingly, and from 300 AD until nearly 600 China was ruled by Tartar princes. They rose from the mud to some effect, becoming Emperors of all north China. The remains of the later Chin dynasty moved south beyond the Yangtse, and China became two Empires.

Armies in China were looked upon as a form of public works, like wall-builders or canal diggers. Dynasties won power by the sword, but briskly dismissed their levies and ruled through their highly educated civilian officials. Their local gentry had many functions – public works such as canals, bridges and roads were under their supervision. They kept up Confucian values, ran schools and local temples. Even as late as the 1900s, over 400,000,000 people were run by less than 20,000 officials and about 250,000 holders of degrees. Family hierarchy left everyone knowing exactly where he stood, accepting the rules and the discipline in a way that led to the extraordinary stability of Chinese society, almost irrespective of who came or went on the Dragon throne. Feudalism had ended in 220 BC when primogeniture was abolished. Men were thus bound to the soil not by law but by the numbers who had to live off it. 'The back-breaking labour of many hands has become the accepted norm', Fairbank wrote of China in our century: it was true of others. Merchants were subservient to officials and of small account; but they could buy land and have their sons educated and thus move up the social scale. Education was not free, but it was cheap; families took good care that this immense advantage was lavished only on those boys who were clever and could be counted upon to work. Through thick and thin, under Tartar, Mongol or Manchu rule, China's society was based upon farming.

Liu-Tsung, the Tartar son, became in due course excessively tyranni-cal; but there were still brave men to stand up to him. 'Our coffins are at the door', two Mr Valiants-for-truth told the Emperor, 'here is a paper

on which we have written all the wrongs you have done.' (Few would
have stood up to Nero or Ivan the Terrible in this manner.) 'Am I like
Kieh, or Chow Sin?' Liu demanded furiously, as his two courtiers knelt
in tears before him: and there was a long pause of black silence before
he surprisingly said, 'I have been like a drunken man, and if you had
not had the courage to tell me, I might have gone on thus forever'.
Despite this admirable confession, Liu was not strong enough; other
tribes from Tartary swept in and devoured the north; cities fell, villages
burned, suffering rarely ceased. But all through this 'Period of
Darkness' the great Yangtse valley was further cultivated, and the south
yielded a steady harvest of precious metals and the products of its splendid forests.

The Chinese had developed the shadowy 'heavenly beings' of Indian
Buddhism into definite saints with names and characteristics, notably
Kwan-Yin, the goddess of Mercy – 'she who looks down and hears the
cries of the world', far more sympathetic than the sinister Kali and Co. of
Hindu mythology, and a being whom the Christian missionaries were to
have little difficulty in transmogrifying into the Virgin Mary. In AD 325,
permission for the building of Buddhist monasteries was given; but as so
often, this movement overreached itself; and in time these monasteries
became so rich, grand and powerful that there was trouble. Meanwhile,
securely perched on their remote mountainsides, they provided the happiest possible hunting ground for painters, poets and writers. In 400 AD
a Chinese monk called Fa-Hien penetrated to India in search of further
knowledge; it took him three years to get there over the mountains, and
the writings he brought back greatly strengthened the Buddhist movement in China.

Like Chang-Kien when he came upon Ferghana, Fa-Hien was astonished by what he saw in India – temples everywhere, and the Buddha's
actual footstep in the rock. He went down the Indus, where he found a
flourishing kingdom, then across to the Ganges basin and down that
great river, travelling for six years, copying the sacred books, drawing the
holy images, going as far south as Ceylon, from whence he took ship to
China. Fifteen years after leaving China he landed in Shantung, after an
exceedingly stormy passage, in which he prayed hard to Kwan-Yin, not
just to save his own life but to preserve his books and pictures; and
Kwan-Yin had not been slow to respond. His writings and his images
proved immensely influential.

Still more influential, but in a rather different way, was a missionary
from India, whose long name the Chinese could not be bothered with;
they called him Tamo. He arrived in 525 and widely reinforced Fa-Hien
in impressing Buddhism upon the Chinese. At Nanking, the southern

Emperor was already a Buddhist, and told Tamo proudly of the many holy books he had had translated, the many handsome temples he had had built.

This did not impress Tamo. 'You have done no good at all', he crisply told the Emperor. Goodness lay only in purity and truth, in depth and fulfilment of the spirit, in being wrapped in thought in the midst of stillness. The Emperor would find Buddha in his own heart, in meditation, in search after the soul's unspeakable treasures. Tamo then departed briskly for the Tartar Emperor's court at Loyang; where he was reported to have spent nine years sitting with his face to a wall in speechless meditation.

He was more actively productive in other ways. Furious with himself for dropping off to sleep during a meditative bout, Tamo was said to have cut off his eyelids and thrown them on the earth, where they proved more productive than the parts of our own dear Origen when similarly carried off balance by indignation at bodily tiresomeness. Although it was in fact probably some clever Chinaman who first thought of cutting up the fresh leaves of the camellia shrub, drying them, and then infusing them with boiling water, this brilliant notion was attributed to Tamo's eyelids, which had sprung into life and produced the first tea plant. This delightful beverage was above all to arouse the covetous desires of the West; and if Tamo had been rather more careful with his eyelids, a Chinese Emperor might still be sitting on the Dragon throne. Tamo had landed first at Canton, where Indian and Arab ships now came regularly, with rugs and scent and cotton cloth, incense and glass, and where they were introduced to this strongly refreshing drink. They took some with them: in addition to its other qualities, tea would keep during a long sea voyage. Here, for the moment, was another source of wealth for China, and the long slow camel-caravans that went winding to the west from the Jade Gate now carried chests of tea as well as bales of silk.

* * *

In 590, a Chinaman called Wen-Ti, Prime Minister to a failing Tartar Emperor, overthrew him and soon dealt likewise with the southern Emperor, uniting the whole once more. He and his son Yang-Ti, the brief Sui dynasty, achieved one famous deed. Ever since 486 BC, the Hwai and Yangtse rivers had been joined by a canal. Wen-Ti and his son began the Grand Canal, 200 feet wide, with stone embankments and an avenue of trees on either side. Both were cruel taskmasters; and for those who came up against the law in China, and for many who did not, it was a time of hard bondage. Hundreds of thousands were employed

on the canal, of whom a half were said to have died on the job; but the
Great Canal went on, a mighty work of man; through Nanking, on to
Suchow, and thence to Hangkow. The younger Sui, Yang-Ti, was so
enamoured of his canal that he had no leisure for governing his empire
and spent most of his time proceeding up and down the waterway with
a fleet of great pleasure ships followed by his wives in other equally lux-
urious pleasure ships, his generals and soldiers mounted on horseback
and trotting along in attendance, to the grave distress of the dwellers
nearby, who had to feed them.

Early in the 600s, China, as so often, produced the sufficient man,
who came to be called Tai-Tsung. Son of a northern general who was
prince of Tang, he looked with horror upon a country full of rebellion
and over-run by robber bands while the last of the Sui planned yet
another jaunt along his willow-fringed Grand Canal. Tai-Tsung gathered
his clan. Soon he and his father, and even his married sister, in the
active tradition before foot-binding, had put on their shining armour
and were riding south with 40,000 men to take the Siu capital of Chang-
an (City of Everlasting Peace) out of the hands of its aquatic monarch.
Here the young man from Tang was made Emperor and inaugurated the
Tang dynasty (best known in the West for its terracotta horses).

It took Tai-Tsung six years to set the Empire to rights and to begin (in
618 AD) 300 years of glory. He was a brave and clever general and merciful with it; disarming and sending home, but never slaughtering, his
conquered opponents. When China, from the Eastern Ocean to the
Jade Gate and from the Great Wall to Canton, had accepted his rule and
was ordered and quiet, he led his triumphant army into Chang-an to the
sound of music and drum and the noise of temple bells, wearing a
plumed helmet on his head and clad in silver armour. He was followed
by a bodyguard dressed in black tigerskins (panthers?), with a few captured chieftains behind him in the Roman manner, trailing their
discredited banners in the dust.

Tai-Tsung believed in the religion of Confucius and felt the need of
no other – 'Confucius is to the Chinese what water is to fishes'. He sent
out honest men to govern provinces and kept wise men to advise him.
His troubles were not over: news from Tartary was far from good. Over
the centuries the tribes had formed themselves into nations – powerful
Cathayans in the north-east, a small and insignificant bunch called
Mongols, living their wild and greasy lives near the source of the Amur
River, and, by far the most potent, the Turks to the far north, supreme
from Korea to the Caspian shores, a great crescent moon of restless
menace. With these last, on his way to power, Tai-Tsung had made an
alliance, but in his first year as Emperor these terrible fighters and

brilliant bowmen invaded China and swept to within a few miles of the gates of Chang-An, (whose peace seemed far from Everlasting).

Tai-Tsung drew out his army before his capital city, but himself rode out quite alone to confront the Turks. Such is the power of success and repute, that the two Turkish leaders dismounted and bowed low before him. Tai-Tsung let them have it. 'Is this worthy of men of honour, to forget all I have done for you, to break an alliance thus?' Shamed, the Turks agreed to renew the treaty and to take their armies back; and the alliance was sealed by the sacrifice of an unblemished white horse, to the horror of all Buddhists present, and had there been any there, all Christians likewise. Only once again did the Turks try a sally into China and once again were halted; mainly, once more, by the power of Tai-Tsung's personality. After which other Tartar tribes came to Chang-an to do homage, asking Tai-Tsung to be their emperor under the Turkish title of Heavenly Khan; and the Turks now sloped off westward – never again attacking the Middle Kingdom. Here they conquered Persia, Syria, Asia Minor, and eventually Egypt; and came at length to batter down the gates of Holy Byzantium on the distant Golden Horn – the strength of Imperial China yet again contributing to the downfall of a great western power. Meanwhile the Mongols, left more or less alone to the north-west, gathered themselves for their enormous leap.

Tai-Tsung had the prudence to maintain a standing army, but he continued to take the advice of wise men. In spite of their occasional remonstrance, he moved freely among his people – 'I compare their heart with my own; if I love them as a father, how should I suspect them of harm?' One wise councillor, Wei-Ching, spoke up once too often, and Tai Tsung stormed into his wife's rooms in the palace in a right royal rage, declaring à la Henry Plantagenet that he would never be master till he was rid of this wretched man.

'What wretched man?'

'Wei-Ching; he contradicts me in front of everybody.'

The Empress sensibly made no answer, but allowed her husband to cool his heels while she put on all her best clothes and richest jewels and reappeared, wearing flowers in her hair, gorgeous scent, and a demure expression. What is all this? Tai-Tsung demanded to know. 'I have heard', said the Empress, 'that a truly great Emperor has sincere and honest ministers. You have Wei-Ching; and I am come formally to congratulate you.' The soft answer had turned away wrath; and perhaps a lady with infinite leisure and wealth to make herself beautiful had no need of Women's Liberation.

Wei-Ching was reinstated, and his master's glories swelled. The King of Persia sent him a rat-catching terrier; the King of Samarkand sent two tame lions. Beautiful horses came from Turkestan, brocades and damask from Damascus. From Byzantium came embassies; Chinese garrisons kept peace in Bokhara and Tashkent. A Chinese princess went as wife to the ruler of Tibet, who built her a walled city as like to a Chinese town as could be contrived.

In the midst of all these splendours, of tribute from places 'so far away that no grass grows in them', Tai-Tsung continued to preach and exemplify the power of virtue. 'Without drawing a sword', righteousness kept the peace. The Emperor told his successors to follow the ancient kings, and not to copy himself. He had, he thought, loved magnificence too well, built too many palaces, sent far and wide horses and dogs and hawks. 'Because I have done much for my people they have forgiven me. Follow my rules and live in peace . . . Nothing is harder than to win an Empire: nothing is easier than to lose it.'

Living 100 years later than Justinian, more than 100 years before Charlemagne and 200 years or so before Alfred the Great, Tai-Tsung was all of these, conqueror, law-giver, learned man and patron of learning, operating on a vastly greater scale than any. But to all of these, if they had even heard of him, he was a being infinitely remote, as mysterious as the far side of the moon; and a heathen, separated from them by a huge gulf of faith and hidden from the Christian West by unimaginable misty distances of land and sea – to their great loss.

Literature meant a very great deal to the Chinese; even politicians, even Emperors were swayed by it. The *literati* in general had a great effect on public opinion. Once they decided, and conveyed to the generality, that a dynasty had lost moral claim to the throne, 'that dynasty became past saving'. (Fairbank.) Hence the frequent changes. In the early ninth century, when England was still battling with Danish invasion and in the literary line had not advanced much beyond *Beowulf*, the Chinese poet Po Chu-i was pointing out that 'the duty of literature is to serve the writer's generation; the duty of poetry is to influence public affairs'. Like other poets, Po was a civil servant. 'Where I believed I could bring alleviation to the sufferings of the people or remedy some defect of policy . . . I wrote a ballad, hoping it would be passed from one to another until it reached the Emperor's ear.'

He was not the first or last poet to sing the joys of the little garden, friendship, wine and music of an evening, as against the sweets of office. He was happy to live in a time and place where poetry could sway policy. A Buddhist, and one-time Governor of lordly Hangchow, eating lychees and growing magnolias, and only occasionally undergoing short banishments for saying the wrong thing, he grew mellower and more devout with age, happy to hear his ballads on the lips of Buddhist monks and singing girls alike, an intellectual enjoying the reclame now only allowable to pop-singers. He continued to read voraciously; perhaps, if culture ever spread so far, even the English might be induced to read, once they had settled with the Danes and recovered from the Normans. Perhaps.

* * *

The afterglow of Tai-Tsung's reign lived long. Not only Tibet and Korea, but now Japan as well sent princes to the great Emperor's school at Chang-an; and learned China's way of government and its family closeness, and copied China's elaborate and formal ceremonies. And although the Arab armies, inspired by the prophet Mohammed who had been Tai-Tsung's contemporary, over-ran Persia, Syria and Mesopotamia like a great river in flood, the Caliph Haroun-ar-Rashid sent embassies of friendship from Baghdad to his Tang contemporary counterpart, and many Arab dhows made their adventurous way from the Euphrates' mouth to Canton. A descendant of the Prophet came in person to Chang-an, and remarked upon Chinese order and justice and noted the remarkable skill of Chinese craftsmen; while Chinese junks sailed to trade in Ceylon and as far as Hormuz on the Persian Gulf.

China advanced steadily in all the arts of civilization while a disunited Europe battled still with heathen Norsemen and with the onrush of Islam. In enclosed gardens shaded by fine trees and watered by diverted streams, the Chinese grew honeysuckle and wisteria, roses, lilies, flowering trees, and above all, the peony. They played stringed instruments and sang a great repertoire of songs: everyone with any claim to education could write a poem, play a tune, paint a picture. They made carved stone bridges, and at times of festivity hung lanterns in their trees. Boats prowed in the shapes of dragons and tigers, and painted in bright colours moved over artificial lakes to the sound of music.

As usual, after a few hundred years all this proved too much for the Prince of Tang's descendants. Kao, the ancient founding father had sounded a note of warning 2,000 years earlier – 'lofty roofs and carved walls will bring the house to ruin'; but who that can grow peonies, eat lichees, and drift along in lighted dragon-boats to the sound of music over water will bother about founding fathers? Ming-Huang, the Emperor might endow a college of music and drama and employ a 500-piece orchestra, but he had also provided himself with a lovely concubine, who came to rule him with a rod of iron. Palaces had to be built, not only for her, because she demanded them, but so did her sisters and her cousins and her aunts; troops of dressmakers and embroiderers were kept busy on her clothes, and squadrons of cavalry posted south in relays to keep an all-the-year-round supply of ripe lichees flowing to that one alluring mouth.

This could have but one end, a Tartar revolt against an inattentive ruler, in which, as usual, thousands were killed and many a fair city burned. Surrounded by such forces, the Emperor Ming-Huang had to give up his lovely concubine. Like an English lord condemned by his peers, she was allowed the privilege of a silken rope, and hanged herself on a convenient pear tree, acting throughout with her habitual grace and elegance, which melted many a hard heart. This revolt was the beginning of the end for the Tang dynasty, which had produced a flowering of consummate art and some beautiful poetry. To the ancient wisdom that Confucius had collected together, his own sayings were added, as were the words of Mencius. 'Where there is teaching, there will be no class', Confucius had foreseen, and over the years many a poor herdsman boy and fisherman's lively son rose to learning and power through village schools that were cheap but not free, so that the frugal paying family took care to see that only the really clever and hard-working enjoyed this privilege. Great as were the skills in waterworks and architecture, the weakness of the system involved a kind of technical stalemate, owing to the gap between the long-robed scientist and the practical artisan, a complication which Confucius had not foreseen.

The Sung dynasty, one in the North, 907–1127, and one in the South, 907–1279, produced a like artistic richness, an epoch famous for its pictures. A Chinese artist did not paint from life. He studied his subject long, went away and thought, endeavouring to understand the true nature of what he had seen, to realize the willow tree, the bird, the flowering spray, to capture its spiritual essence before, in the privacy of his own room, he put brush to paper. 'You must envy a fish its life in the water', teachers insisted, 'and know its desires, otherwise it will look like a fish on a plate . . . A mountain must be like a prince, and other parts of your picture his vassals . . . share the movement of the spirit through everything . . . recognize true form and colour . . . the relation of things to each other . . . the strength and constancy of the pine tree . . . the grace and gentleness of the willow . . . the shoots of the bold bamboo pushing their way up through the hard ground.' These instructions, followed to the letter, established the enduring fame of Chinese art.

Wu-Tao-tze, a poor boy born near Loyang in the eighth century, became a devout Buddhist artist, and painted on the walls of one city such a devastating picture of the hell awaiting men who took animal life that all the town's luckless butchers and fishmongers were scared clean out of business. He also moved many to tears with his pictures of saints, dashing off the perfect round of their golden haloes without benefit of compass. In the Buddhist faith, trees and plants, rocks and stones were as much bound for Heaven, Nirvana, as were insects and reptiles; all were presented by the artist with the same loving attention as the face of the Buddha himself.

* * *

The last of the Tangs fell into the hands of intriguing eunuchs with the usual lust for power that sexual deprivation induces. Their corrupt rule inspired the inevitable rebellion: the last Tang Emperor was murdered in 907, and Chao-Kwang-Yin proved the necessary strong man to unite the country in 960, after 50 years of civil strife and its attendant destruction. The Sung dynasty, bringing 200 years of stunning artistic achievement, introduced also a practice of stunning cruelty, the foot-binding of women. An advanced civilization seems always to produce its dark side, and the process by which, for erotic reasons, the feet of little girls were bent double to give them a tiny appearance, could hardly have been darker. For four years, tightly bound while the bones were still growing, the feet of these children were clamped; millions of little girls enduring agonies of pain, days and nights of continuous anguished weeping, to hobble for the rest of their days, never able to go very far. This torment was endured by the women of China, the poor as well as the rich, for the next 1,000 years, adding immeasurably and quite needlessly to the sum of human misery.

Nor did boys, or such of them as were of no particular interest to any family, fare much better. Right up into the 20th century, unimportant boys continued to be castrated, since this rendered them innocuous and useful as domestic servants. Set against such a universal love of beauty, such a real reverence for every varied form of the natural world, this all seems strange and horrifying indeed; as if David Attenborough and the Curator of the National Gallery were to be convicted of open child-torture.

The astonishing creative activities went on, as if such suffering did not exist, or lived only by some inexorable law of nature. Under the Tang dynasty the Chinese had discovered an unusually fine white clay, had mixed it with powdered rock and sand, ground the whole into dust, and moistened it into the smooth white paste that makes porcelain. Perfected during the Sung dynasty, patterned and glazed and in time sold throughout the world, it was known as China-ware, and hence as china. Soon after this, the ingenious Chinese added printing to the sum of their discoveries. The first printed book in the world, in the form of a scroll, was a Buddhist holy work, the Diamond Sutra, printed in 868, 600 years before Gutenburg.

But peace, in this great inventive, artistic, casually cruel empire was never long lasting. By the beginning of the 12th century, the Turks had replaced the Arabs in western Asia – in Persia, Syria and Asia Minor their writ ran absolutely. This left a power vacuum, rapidly filled by the Cathayans or Khitans, a brooding presence in the north east, who during the years of Chinese weakness had occupied lands now known as Manchuria and Mongolia, and made both Korea and Tibet their vassal states. These, the Iron Tartars, had leapt the Great Wall and occupied much Chinese land to the north of the Yellow River. As once weak kings of Anglo-Saxon England had paid Danegeld to Scandinavian raiders to induce them to go away, so now the last of the Sungs paid Danegeld to the Iron Tartars, and with as little success. With still greater unwisdom, the Sung Emperor now called in another tribe, the Golden Tartars, to help him. Not surprisingly, they came, saw, conquered, and remained; exacting vast amounts of silver and gold from the Imperial store. China was fatally weakened, and when a more than sufficient man threatened her, she fell.

In the late 1100's, when Europe was still busy crusading in the Near East in an attempt to recover for Christendom its holy places, a remarkably tough and able little boy was deposited by his father, Yessugai, a Mongol Khan, into the care of one of his mother's kinsmen, to be brought up with this kinsman's ten year old daughter, Boitai, who was to be his bride. He took to her at once, and waved his father goodbye without a qualm. On his way home his father, Yessugai, was poisoned by a supposedly friendly host, and the perilous career of the little boy was launched. He was called Temujin, and was to become known as Genghis Khan, and to shake the whole of the known world.

Europe was little able to withstand him. Christendom had torn itself in two in the 11th century, (not long before William the Norman conquered England) by a passionate controversy that now seems not outstandingly relevant – as to whether the Holy Ghost proceeds from the Father alone or from the Father and the Son also. Before the Tartar hordes the separated Eastern Orthodox Church was powerless; the armies of Christendom divided went down like ninepins.

4

The Mongols

The dying Yessugai had sent for his son, but Timujin arrived too late to
see him. His danger was great, though his bold mother had seized the
Khan flag, hung with nine white yaks' tails, and now flew it from her yurt
on her son's behalf. Few among the Mongols concurred with this decision to exalt a mere boy, and for him a time of ceaseless danger and
hardship followed. Though Timujin was known as the rightful Khan, vir-
ulent enemies and rivals pursued him and his family and small faithful
band of adherents with ruthless intensity. At one time, he hid on a
wooded mountain till forced by hunger to attempt escape; caught by his
enemies he was placed in the dreaded *kang*, a square yoke of heavy wood
in which hands as well as neck were held. With superhuman strength he
broke from it, killed his guard, and escaped to his family. The torment
and ignominy of the *kang* had planted an implacable enmity in his heart;
but a loving side remained. As soon as he held enough followers for
safety he went back for Bortai, the little girl he remembered from his
childhood. They were married and although, in time, he collected other
wives and innumerable concubines, Bortai remained the bright and
constant element in his life, seated always in the place of honour, bearing him four sons as doughty as himself.

Kindness stopped here. In a few years, Timujin had strengthened
himself enough to attack an army of persistent enemies whose force was
twice as large as his own. Defeating them, he had 70 of their chiefs
boiled alive in large cauldrons. He was now unquestioned chief of the
Mongols, and proceeded to conquer all the Tartar tribes north of the
Gobi desert. Besides strength, cunning, and terrifying cruelty, Timujin
had undoubted charisma; hundreds of men who had no reason to do so,
left their homes to follow him even before his power and success were
assured. Sometimes defeated, often wounded, and twice left for dead on
the field, he never lost heart or failed of purpose. Men came to think of
him as someone more than human. More than 300 years ahead of Sir
Francis Drake he announced that 'the glory of a deed is in finishing it to
the very end'.

In 1206, when he was 44, Timujin called an assembly of tribes and was
proclaimed Grand Khan over them all. They added the forename

Genghis, meaning very mighty. He richly rewarded all those who had followed him when he was a hunted 12 year old, without power and
seemingly without a future, chased up hill and down dale by merciless
enemies. In China this while the last of the Sung dynasty presided over
a land making ever more exquisite porcelain and printing more and
more books. In India, the temple bells sounded and the Buddhists
prayed, bullocks ploughed the tawny fields and elephants swayed along
the dusty tracks. In Persia, the Turks had adopted the wisdom and the
ways of that ancient empire, and the skills of the Arabs; living in all the
magnificence of the old Caliphs and spreading their power in the eastern Mediterranean. In England, the long thrust against the absolute
power of monarchs had begun. No-one had the least idea of what was
about to hit them.

Genghis Khan was now faced with the problem of what to do with all
these fierce and restless horsemen now at his command. He was not
without religion, and he climbed a high mountain to pray. 'Boundless
Heaven', they heard him cry, 'send me help from on high, and men on
earth to fight for me; I go to avenge the blood of my kinsfolk, killed by
the Golden Khans.' His armies, superbly organized in bands of 100,
1,000 and 10,000, rode at speed over the enormous distances of central
Asia, over the deserts that even from an aeroplane appear interminable.
They drove their cattle with them and could live for weeks on a minimum diet of meat and milk, their horses grazing all the way, and in
winter scraping the snow and eating the meagre crop that lay beneath.
When in need, like the Masai in Africa, the Mongols opened the veins of
their beasts and drank their blood, closing the vein afterwards.

They went through Bokhara and Samarkand, Herat and Nishapur
like the wrath of God, which indeed Genghis Khan claimed himself to
be. The Mongols swept on over all western Asia and southern Russia, the
sons of Genghis conquering Persia, Iraq, Syria, North India. The destruction and killing that they wrought became a by-word for centuries. The
armies of Genghis enslaved the useful and killed off the useless (which
was perhaps more merciful than leaving them to die of starvation).
Finding that some of the vanquished would feign death, they beheaded
all; leaving great pyramids of heads along their way. They were quick to
learn from their enemies, adopting Greek fire, the use of siege engines,
knowledge of boat-building, and how to read and write. The death-toll
ran into millions; the wealth destroyed was uncountable. It was an experience that neither Asia nor Europe ever forgot. Yet Genghis, dying at
the age of 65, was long and deeply mourned by his own.

The Chinese Empire, still formidable, came last; and held out for 20
years against the Mongol hammer blows. Finally the last Sung Emperor,

a weakling, fled before Kubla Khan, grandson of Genghis, who proved a milder conqueror than his grandsire had been; he even left unspoiled the beautiful city of Hangkow. The Sung Emperor's young son, still a small boy, escaped to sea, where he was overwhelmed in a naval battle when the Mongols seized the Chinese junks and surrounded him. Seeing no hope, the Prime Minister took the little boy on his shoulders and jumped with him into the sea, where both were drowned. (All this suicide seems to argue that such a death was greatly preferable to the one meted out to those who fell alive into their enemies' hands.) Chinese resistance now ended and Kubla Khan reigned supreme.

* * *

Christendom was shocked to the marrow by the activities of Genghis and his family. The great pincer movement of the Arabs who took Spain in the 700's, (and remained there ruling for 700 years) only halted by Charles Martel of France at Tours in 714, while its other arm clanged steadily for centuries on the gates of Vienna, had been frightening enough, and its menace in the Mediterranean still held. But when the grandson of Genghis destroyed Moscow and devastated parts of Poland and Hungary, the peril seemed imminent indeed. The Bible's three wise men from the East who had worshipped Christ at birth seemed to be transformed into about 3,000,000 unwise men from the East apparently bent on strangling Christendom at birth. Something must be done; and only one course seemed likely to be effective in stopping this irresistible influx. The Mongols, and mighty China beyond them, must be changed into Christians.

Undaunted by the largeness of this enterprise, the Pope and the King of France each addressed letters to the Great Khan to this effect; and some enormously brave Franciscans set out to deliver them. Possibly there were thoughts aside from conversion in the minds of at least one of these potentates. Whilst fighting in Syria and Palestine in the Crusades, the English, French, and Austrian knights had been introduced to a number of delectable commodities – sugar and spice and all things nice – as well as rugs, silks, ginger, Damascene swords and brocade, velvet, cassia and the fine cottons of India. The taming of the desert tribes by the Mongols might lead the way to all this: even Popes and bishops were not above enjoying velvet and silks. Venice and Genoa had rapidly latched on to these possibilities and were to grow rich and powerful in becoming the latter-day Parthians, the buyers and sellers of the eastern Mediterranean. But the strongest motive was fear – the terror of seeing again those pyramids of severed heads, neatly separated into piles of men's, of women's, and of children's that Genghis had organized. The brave priests did not succeed, but they returned alive, and reported on the terrible dangers of the Asian route, and the tales they had heard of fabulous Cathay beyond them.

The West had long tried to establish contact with China, and via the Mongol invasion, they managed it. Genghis Khan had been at the gates of Peking in the same year as King John in England was signing the Magna Carta. The Khan was bought off, briefly; but the Sung dynasty was in no position to argue, exhausted with wars between the Chin north and the Sung south, and a particularly bad Yellow River flood in 1194. This huge stream fairly regularly burst its banks, changed course, and made havoc of all the well-tilled fields. Soon Genghis Khan was back again, and took Peking with great slaughter: he was not really a suitable subject for Christian conversion. 'A man's greatest pleasure', he announced, 'is to defeat his enemies, to drive them before him, to take from them all they possess, to see those whom they cherished in tears, to ride their horses, to hold their wives and daughters in his arms.' The stoutest missionary heart might quail before such a soul; everyone in the greater part of Asia and much of Europe had had to join him, submit to him, or succumb to him. His descendant, the Emperor Mong-Ke was a much better bet; his mother had been a Nestorian princess, and via Father William of Rubruck, he informed King Louis IX of France that 'There is only one eternal God in heaven', a fact with which King Louis was already familiar; adding the less familiar thought that there was only one sovereign on earth and he himself was it. But Father William of Rubruck spoke to King Louis in admiration of the Khan's endless supplies of silk, of the skill of Chinese doctors and craftsmen, their paper money, their brush writing, their strange but fascinating script. Here were the Seres, the 'silk people' known to antiquity, Cathay beyond the ravaging tribes of Central Asia.

Relations between east and west took a smart step forward in the reign of Kubla Khan, grandson of Genghis, and greatest of the Yuan dynasty. It was he who finally conquered rich Cathay and became Emperor as well as Great Khan, an honour he inherited when he was at the Summer Palace he had built at Shang-Tu – 'at Xanadu did Kubla Khan . . .' Combining the duties of Great Khan and Son of Heaven, he kept his capital in Peking, and in order to keep its food supplies flowing, he completed the 1,100 mile long canal by bringing it thither from Hangkow, with a paved highway all along its side. Terrible as it had been, the Mongol invasion had once again opened up the road to the east, and enterprising Venetian feet were soon padding along it, notably those of Marco Polo's father and uncle. When they went back to Venice, Kubla Khan told them to bring back with them at least 100 Christian priests and a flask of holy oil from Jerusalem; they succeeded in collecting only two Franciscans, both of whom fell by the wayside when the Polo family were on their way to Peking again with Marco, who stayed for 17 years. The holy oil at least arrived safely.

* * *

Kubla Khan employed the observant Marco Polo as a sort of travelling agent, and he was lucky enough to be sent through Shensi, Szechuan, and Yunnan, and even into Tibet and Burma. He also went down the coast from Peking, where Kubla Khan had established the capital of China, to Hangkow, which Marco Polo thought the most beautiful city in the world. Like his native Venice, Hangkow had canals as streets, lagoons, and sea-going ships tied up at its quays. There were arched stone bridges, paved ways, courtyards, and painted boats, the sound of music drifted over calm water. Marco Polo admired the Chinese immensely for their polite manners and their smiling faces, for their honest dealings, reverence for parents, and absence of noisy feuds. 'They behave like gentlemen and eat very properly . . . there is so much good-will and neighbourly feeling that one would imagine the people of one street to be all of one family . . . They treat foreigners who visit them for trade most cordially, entertain them kindly, give them helpful advice . . .'

Chinese skill in hydraulic engineering astonished all who saw it. When Marco Polo came to Hangkow and saw the beauty and order of this great town, exceeding anything existing in Europe, he could hardly believe his eyes – the lakes, the bridges, the trees, the paved streets, the well-behaved people. The difficulty of Chinese writing – at least 4,000 characters had to be mastered – meant that literacy was not widely disseminated, but it created a large scholarly class to handle the administrative problems of a vast empire, and the learned man became the most important, the intellectual dominated. Galileo would have ruled, rather than Christopher Columbus, or King Henry V of England. Commerce as well as the army and the navy depended on the literate mandarinate; however many people conquered China – the Mongols, the Manchu – the mandarinate stayed as the essential factor without which China could not be run. To this, and to the sacred bonds of family, the remarkable changeless stability of China was due; here Confucianism, Taoism and Buddhism could happily co-exist – most of the time – until the wealth and power of the ever-increasing Buddhist monasteries turned feeling against them. Rival religions did not 'disturb tranquillity': in the 16th century China would accommodate Jews, Christians and Moslems.

Failing the arrival of the 100 Christian priests for whom he had asked

the two Polo brothers, Kubla Khan and his Mongols had all become
Buddhists; and as Marco Polo went about China it may have crossed the
mind of this extremely observant and perceptive young man that these
highly civilized people were the 90 and nine just men that needed no
repentance; and that Europe, with its incessant clang of steel sword on
steel armour, its forever besieged castles, its feuding Montagues and
Capulets, might be the sinner who did.

He thought it all staggeringly wonderful; and returning in a Chinese
junk as far as Ormuz, was able to observe the feasibility of the ocean
route. Far from being hailed as the Great Traveller when he arrived
back in Venice, or honoured in any way, he was simply disbelieved. This
was a great age of faith in Europe, and all over the west huge and beautiful cathedrals were being built to the glory of God, at Burgos, at
Salisbury, Coutances, Bourges, Wells, Beauvais, Lincoln, the heady tow-
ers of Rheims – built in the main by men who themselves lived in daub
and wattle huts. To medieval Europe the idea of a great empire at the far
end of the world run on roughly Christian principles without benefit of
Christ, would be deeply disconcerting. Marco Polo was soon in prison for
a minor civic offence.

Fortunately for posterity, in prison Marco Polo found himself alongside a born journalist, who listened to him, and recognized a good
story when he heard one. Exaggerating little, except the grandeur of
Marco's reception when he arrived at the court of the Great Khan, the
journalist prisoner committed the whole amazing story to paper; and
despite there being as yet no printed books in Europe, it was widely and
enthusiastically read over the next centuries, and particularly by a
Genoese seaman called Christopher Columbus, who, when he set sail
from Palos in 1492, would carry a letter of greeting from the King of
Spain to the Great Khan of Cathay. Although he never reached this fabulous continent to deliver his letter in Peking, but happened upon a yet
more fabulous pair of continents on the way, the idea of this immense
and ancient empire as a goal for discovery remained in the European
mind.

Another reader of the adventures of Marco Polo was Prince Henry of
Portugal, son of an English princess, and to be known to posterity as the
Navigator. For a long while he brooded on the problem of getting ships
to far Cathay. Africa, the great dark continent of *terra incognita*, lay in the
way; and now the old silk road was barred. Although many of the
Mongols had become Buddhists, and were now settled in Tibet, and
deeply devout monks, many more further west had embraced Islam,
still involved with its long struggle with Christendom for the soul of
Europe and the Middle East, and since the Crusades, more deeply

opposed to the western Christians than ever. Between these and their goal of China now stretched an implacable phalanx of scowling ayatollahs; and when the Turks took Egypt, the line of defence was complete.

To Prince Henry, the idea of the enormous oceans as the future highway of the world belongs: he was the pioneer, although his ships never got to China in his lifetime. His captain, Bartholomew Diaz, rounded the Cape of Good Hope in 1488, calling it Cabo Tormentoso for its fierce storms, but subsequently changing his mind to something more cheerful. Vasco da Gama followed this up in 1497, and went further; by 1555, the Portuguese vessels were up the Indus, where they very regrettably sacked and burnt Tatta, before making off further east. In so far as anything so vast as the Indian Ocean could be called a lake, this stretch of water had become an Arab lake; they had sailed to and settled in Mombasa, Calicut, Malaya, the East Indies – those coveted spice Islands – converting all these to Islam as they went. After a considerable struggle and one successful pitched sea-battle, the Portuguese turned the Indian Ocean into a Portuguese lake, with their strong-points at Hormuz, Goa, Calicut, and in Sumatra. Once arrived in the Spice Islands, it was but sharp left, or hard-a-port, and then straight on for China.

* * *

The Christian West had not abandoned its hope for the soul of China, and Father John of Monte Corvino was soon on the track of the Polo family, though he arrived in Peking only in 1294, after the death of Kubla Khan. He was allowed to proceed, baptized several thousand converts, trained a choir to sing Gregorian chants, and in 1307, was made 'Archbishop of Cambaluc', the Mongol name for Peking briefly taken up by Europeans. After this burst, the Christian efforts in China were swallowed up, for the time, by the tide of Buddhism.

The Mongols had soon given up any attempt to impose their way of life on the Chinese; although the poorer among them continued defiantly to wear furs, drink fermented mare's milk, and allow their women's feet to grow naturally. Kubla Khan on the other hand was determined that his son *should* become Chinese; he made him practise brush writing every day and listen to long lectures on Chinese history from former Sung officials, most of whom he kept on in his admirable administration. But Kubla's lame young kinsman, Timur-i-Leng, whom the West called Tamerlane, would have none of this and went south to conquer India. Wading through blood, he took Delhi; but luckily for the Indians he disliked their climate so much that he soon left. Turning his attention westward, he did little to cement East–West relations by killing great numbers of people in the Near East, Russia, and around the Black Sea,

leaving a tribe of Crimean Tartars to trouble the Czars of all the Russias
for many years. They were forcibly removed by Stalin in 1944.

Chinese *amour propre*, a little dashed by the Mongol conquest, was
consoled by the fact that their dynasty, the Yuan, lasted less than a hundred years. A strong sense of Chinese superiority, felt to be due to their
own purer virtue, had sustained them through the Han dynasty, and
the Tang, and was now to be reinforced by the Ming (Bright) Dynasty,
1368–1644. This was founded by a capable rebel who began his career as
a Buddhist monk, and then served under a military official whose
daughter he married. Styling himself Duke of Wu, he slowly won
province after province and eventually became Emperor and Son of
Heaven under the name of Hung-Wu (Boundless Valour). What with
this prolonged effort of conquest, and having 26 sons and 16 daughters
(Boundless Fertility) Hung-Wu was unlikely to have much attention for
ties with the West, although Friar Oderic of Pordenone spent three years
at Peking in the 1320s. In Europe, things looked unpromising for the
Christians. In 1361, seven years before the founding of the Ming Dynasty,
the Osman Turks, grown strong in Asia Minor, invaded and took Greece
and set about the conquest of south-eastern Europe with great éclat and
considerable success. It was all that Christendom could do to keep its
end up, without attempting to convert Asia.

* * *

As yet undisturbed by Western ideas, and with no idea of how great had
been the results of Chinese strength and resistance against the milling
tribes of central Asia upon the fate of Europe, China under the Ming
Emperors reverted to full Chineseness, almost as if the Mongol invasion
had never been. Skilled craftsmen began lacquer-work and enamelling,
bronze and jade continued to be beautifully wrought. The spirits of former Emperors were worshipped in magnificent tombs; and luck-bearing
new pagodas – an import from Buddhist India – sprang up all over, like
sacred trees, always with an odd number of storeys, 5 to 13, since odd
numbers were Yang and even numbers merely Yin. Painters flourished,
with their exquisite scenes from nature, and there were new and beautiful colours and designs in porcelain. The famous blue of willow-pattern
had come from Persia and was known by the Chinese as Mohammedan
blue. Hung-Wu set up a great porcelain factory in Kiangi province.

The Ming Emperors sent their junks sailing so far that they reached
the coasts of East Africa and made incursions into the Indian Ocean
that preceded the Portuguese voyages from the opposite direction.
Uniquely, and unlike either Arab or European, the Chinese went home
again. Pushed by no compulsively convert-making faith, and without that

valuable but dangerous gift of intense curiosity that ancient Greece had bequeathed to Europe, they felt no need either to go forward or to stay in Africa. The Chinese knew that they had it all made, they no longer needed to know more. They believed that nature, the elements of wind and water, existed in a close relationship with human behaviour. Right conduct was harmony with nature, and without it disaster would ensue. The Emperor, the Son of Heaven, kept up the harmony between man and nature not only by worship of its forces but by doing right, by acting wisely. Advised by his learned men, he governed by virtue, his goodness sustaining his people. Who could want anything better? The practice, humanly speaking, could not always accord with the theory; but the system wore extremely well. By the time Lord Napier stepped ashore in 1834, 'the Chinese officials were no less self-confident and self-righteous than the late 18th and early 19th century English, and they were also stubborn'. (Professor Jerome Ch'en, *China and the West.*)

For 3,000 years or more, through countless generations the peasants of China had laboured under harsh winter skies and the scorching noons of summer, planting rice in the south, reaping corn in the middle lands, herding buffaloes and geese, building houses, cutting wood, drawing water in changeless continuity. They lived sometimes in caves, sometimes in boats, sometimes in courtyard one-floor houses of complex design. They worshipped, died young, survived into a respected old age, but more commonly fell earlier before flood or famine, fire, disease or invasion, and held (more or less) to the maxims of Confucius. Their state structure and national way of life miraculously survived – the idea of virtue, the practice of matters less virtuous – the whole at once unyielding, subtle, tenuous, but immensely strong and tenacious. The Chinese people lived apart, in a conscious apartheid of their own desiring, under the noble ideal of a ruler qualified by his goodness.

In 1615, a Portuguese ship cast anchor at Canton. The Chinese thought her crew amazing – the strange shape of their ship, their tightly-fitting clothes, their oddly round eyes – 'wide open like a cat's!' The Portuguese behaved with exemplary good manners; quietly traded their pepper and spices for tea and silk and went away again. But next year, there were eight ships instead of the original one. Hard on their heels came the Jesuits – dedicated, fearless, intelligent, and prepared to exercise an infinite patience.

5
Hopeful Contact with Europe

With the first galleon from Portugal had come a letter from her king politely asking permission to trade with the Emperor of China's subjects. Unluckily the letter's arrival at Peking coincided with a visit from an Arab trader, who warned the Emperor not to trust the Franks, men of bad behaviour who came to trade and then stayed to conquer. ('You see the licentiousness of these foul unbelievers' as Saladin's secretary wrote when the Queen of Jerusalem married again rather too rapidly after her husband's assassination.) Meanwhile, the next Portuguese captain took the words out of the trader's mouth by building a fort near Canton. This confirmed imperial suspicions. But the Arabs, having lost the battle for naval supremacy in the Indian ocean were now somewhat at a discount; the Emperor paid less heed to these words of warning than he might have done.

Soon the Portuguese, acting helpfully in the matter of some pirates, were allowed by the Emperor a settlement on the handy peninsula of Macao, ideally situated for trading with Canton, which lay only across the Bay of Canton and up the Pearl River. The Americas had been awarded by the Pope to Spain; but the share he allowed to Portugal included India, the East Indies – the longed-for spice islands – and by implication, China. Not surprisingly, the Protestants, Dutch and British, did not long concur with this arrangement. Somewhere, at the other end of the world, was fabled Cathay, an immense and ancient empire ruled autocratically by an Emperor; and although by the 18th century Dr Johnson was to point out that this same Emperor was advised by a council of wise men, (his highly educated mandarins, who always had access to him) the impression of an arbitrary and sometimes cruel despotism remained, and all Europeans approached his shores with apprehension. All traders alike had their eyes fixed mainly upon the spice trade, still immensely lucrative. But if one went on to China, silk and tea and porcelain were also to be had. The difficulty was to find anything that China would buy; but Arab, Portuguese, and Dutch alike had solved this problem by importing small but increasing amounts of opium. Trade flourished, with Chinese merchants as anxious to buy as Europeans were to sell; but diplomatic relations, or indeed any kind of relations between Western kings and Chinese Emperor were as far as ever from becoming established. In Chinese eyes there was still only one Empire, ruled over by the world's one Emperor. All other countries were subject and tributary.

Fear still lived on both sides of the East–West divide. In China it was a fear of the new, of brash and pushy ideas that would upset the well-established order, the rule by virtue, ideas that would 'disturb tranquillity'. In the West the fear was still compounded with horror. In the racial memories of Europe the terror inspired by the old unstoppable hordes from the East still dwelt – fear of Darius the Persian, fear of Attila the Hun, of Tarik the Moor, of the *ordos* of Genghis Khan and his son, Ogotai, of the sons of Juchi and their Golden Horde, of Tamerlane the Merciless, of wave after wave of Mongols sweeping over the flat lands of south-eastern Europe, of the scimitar-wielding Turk at the gates of Vienna. The need to tame China while there was yet a breathing space, by Christianizing her, was a thought living on in the European mind. But by the time Lord Napier hove over the horizon this was fortified by a number of non-Christian aspirations as to trade.

These hopes did not muddle the Jesuit aim. They approached China with respectful caution, first learning the mandarin tongue in Macao, then awaiting permission to proceed. It took Father Matteo Ricci 20 years to cover the distance between Macao and Peking. He had learnt the form, and brought with him watches, clocks and scientific instruments as presents for the Emperor. Ruthlessly intolerant of other Europeans and especially of other Christians, in far countries the Jesuit missionaries displayed all the sense and sensitivity that at home they so dramatically lacked – making music up remote South American rivers to lure shy primitives out of their forest – in China they more or less turned Chinese in dress, language and customs, growing pigtails when the Manchu rulers made these compulsory, eating with chopsticks, and sitting cross-legged on a mat to discuss philosophy, science, mathematics and astronomy.

They made thousands of Chinese converts; with great common sense allowing these to go on worshipping their ancestors, which is not so very far from worshipping saints, nor from the Apocryphal 'Let us now praise famous men, and our fathers that begat us'. In one matter the Chinese declined to be converted, setting their faces like a stone against learning geography. Among his other presents to the Ming Emperor, Father Ricci brought with him a map of the world, showing five continents. The Chinese knew quite well that there was only one continent, one Empire, one ruler of all the world. The existence of five continents was a piece of awkward arithmetic that the Emperors managed quite quickly to put from them and obliterate, just as the French have managed to dismiss from their collective mind another awkward sum – of the 52 judges who

tried and condemned Joan of Arc, 51 were Frenchmen. By 1747, the
Ming official encyclopaedia stated that Father Ricci's ideas were mere
fantasy, 'nothing more than a wild, fabulous story'.

* * *

Imperial wisdom did not always include a refusal to cut down the moun-
tainside trees for firewood, so that the plains of China were often
flooded; and despite the Great Wall they were sometimes flooded by
invasion. A respectfully treated standing army was no part of Chinese
philosophy in the 17th century, although under Emperors of a conquering bent, their armies had swept over more than half Asia in their
'ordos', from which word we derive 'hordes'. (Even Alexander the Great
in 332 BC had halted respectfully when he saw the innumerable camp-
fires of their armies twinkling beyond the Oxus.) China now relied on
peasant levies swept from the land and sent untrained against intruders.
Chinese forces had never been negligible; but before the Manchu influx
in 1644 they ultimately gave way. Even the Mongols had by now learnt
the pleasant ways of the Chinese gentry; they settled on their farms and
sent their sons in for the civil service examination, forgetting former
fierceness. The Manchu had forgotten none of theirs.

The ending of the Ming dynasty in the face of invasion had a fey and
fated quality about it. The last Ming Emperor but one had an innocent
passion for carpentry; living in a haze of happy creation amongst the
wood-shavings, this 15 year old boy allowed his mighty heritage to fall
entirely into the hands of the eunuchs, one Wei in particular, who had
poisoned his capable young father and who exacted huge sums for
favours, which he used to build temples and have them dedicated to
himself. Most dangerously of all, Wei had sacked all the generals from
whom he received no bribes, and replaced them by nonentities who
paid up handsomely but neglected the armies.

Only the Empress, Precious Pearl, (an orphan who had been adopted
by a famous scholar and later chosen as wife out of a large selection of
beauty and charm presented to the Emperor) stood firm, trying hard to
persuade the Emperor into a better idea of his responsibilities. The
Eunuch Wei longed to poison her also, but she was too dearly loved by
the Emperor. When this young man lay dying, sped on his way perhaps
by the ever-busy eunuchs, she was able to persuade him, in the teeth of
Wei's opposition, to appoint his able younger brother to the succession.
'If I obey you now', Precious Pearl told Wei, 'you will kill me sooner or
later; and if I refuse to obey, you will only kill me a little sooner. But if I
die resisting you to my utmost, I can face without shame the spirits of the
Emperors in another world.' The dying Emperor told his brother to

care for this beloved Empress, but to trust Wei. His wiser sibling cared for Precious Pearl, but briskly disposed of Wei.

It was too late. Chaos had already come again. There was revolt in Shensi, revolt in Szechuan, Manchu Tartars were advancing on Peking. Li, captain of the Shensi rebels, reached the capital first, slaughtering and burning all the way. Peking was carelessly defended, its one remaining good general was facing the Manchus with his army. The mighty walls of Peking still stood, and the city might have resisted siege almost indefinitely. But there was the usual obliging eunuch who was prepared for a consideration to open the gate by night. Soon Li and his men were in the Outer City and the smoke of burning buildings rose to high Heaven.

From his palace on a nearby hill that night the Emperor saw all around him the blaze of the fires and could distinguish the distant shouts of triumph or terror, the anguished screams of women. Early in the morning he went to the audience hall to await the ministers whom he had summoned to council, But no-one came. There was silence and stillness amongst all those scarlet pillars under their yellow-tiled roofs. No footfall echoed on the floors of marble; the Emperor stood in a total paralysing solitude. After a while, the last of the Ming dynasty, heartbroken by this desertion, took off his dragon robe, put on a ragged coat, returned to his garden outside the City, and hanged himself on a tree.

* * *

General Wu, still fighting in the north, and hearing that Li had occupied the Forbidden City and named himself Emperor, did what seemed to him the only possible thing: he stopped fighting the Manchu and asked them into China to help against the rebel Li. Hearing of their approach, Li and his men looted everything in Peking that they could carry and departed for Shensi, burning the City and palaces as they left. Arrived in a smoking Peking, the Manchu politely but firmly declined to depart, and with the minimum of local fuss took over; thus inaugurating the last of the dynasties – the Manchu Ching.

When the Manchu armies thundered at the gates and swarmed over the Great Wall, under Jesuit persuasion the Portuguese were enlisted to help the last Ming Emperor. But the influence of Cantonese officials, jealous in their fears that the trade might be moved further north up the coast, prevented the Portuguese army from actually being used. After marching halfway across China they had another very long march back to Macao, an effort comparable to Chairman Mao's in the 20th century. Firing away with superior artillery learned from the Jesuits, the last Ming army held out in the south west, before defeat and flight into Burma. The last Ming Empress was a Christian, and her son, born in 1648, was hopefully christened Constantine, after that mighty convert, the first Christian Emperor of the West; but he fell into Manchu hands as a small boy and, not surprisingly, was never seen or heard of again.

General Wu, far from possible Ming claimants in the south, and sensibly accepting the *fait accompli*, was made a prince by the Manchu; but not all fell into place so simply. As always, appalling bloodshed and enormous devastation came from conquest and resistance, followed by hunger, starvation and disease. This was 1644: about now, on the European scene the horrors of the Thirty Years' War were about to draw to an exhausted close. In France, the Sun-King was reigning, and two years earlier his uncle, Charles I of England, had lost his head. The enterprising Peter the Great was Czar of all the Russias, Prussia was moving towards prominence among the petty princedoms of Germany, two successive Ferdinands ruled in the Austrian Empire, exercising an implacable and brutally persecuting Catholicism that would narrow the domains, perhaps terminally, of the Hapsburg Empire. Italy was still only a geographical expression, Spain in a state of post-imperial stupour, and Greece still vassal to an Ottoman Sultan whose empire dominated the surround of the eastern Mediterranean. India basked in Mogul power and order, a warmth by no means illuminating her Hindu population. America was still a British colony in constant danger from Red Indians, where for another 100 years Britons would be fighting for her life against the equally constant threat of her being overwhelmed by the French. No-one in the entire wide world was in a position to menace or to succour China in her hour of weakness and division.

From boyhood, the new Emperor had been determined to rule China, because of the way in which a well-remembered forebear had been treated by the Chinese, causing him to swear a great oath that he would one day conquer them and avenge these treacherous deaths – 'I hate you with an intense hatred and hereby make war upon you'; and he had set light to the paper whereon this was written and sent it smoking up to Heaven. Once satisfied, the new Emperor adapted easily to Chinese ways, since for years past the Manchu in their hard-wintered but fertile valleys had also had an Emperor, the same Six Boards of government, the same echelons of examination-passing civil servants and mandarins. The first Ching Emperor died young; and China was now to rejoice in a Sun-King of her own. Kang-Hi (Lasting Peace), after the routine years of bloodshed and devastation, settled down into a model ruler.

* * *

Like Louis XIV, Kang-Hi too inherited as a small boy. At 14 he took power into his own hands, and ruled wisely from then on. His domain stretched from the cold north, where in winter the Amur river froze and Siberian tigers padded along its ice, to the mountainous and sub-tropical forests of Yunnan, full of the heat-loving birds and beasts of India. Kang-Hi rose every day at dawn to councils with his ministers. Between bouts of archery and hunting at Jehol he set himself to mind-improvement, never ceasing to learn. Familiar since boyhood with the Chinese classics, he learned mathematics and physics from the Dutch Jesuit, Father Verbiest. He watched his officials carefully, holding familiar discussions with learned men and peasants alike; tireless, active, and all-seeing, worshipping upon the Tai Shan mountain as King Shun had done 2,000 years earlier, and kowtowing before the tomb of Confucius in Shantung. The sage had taught that the spirits of the dead lived on but needed comfort and love in the form of gifts just as they had in life on earth. In everything Kang-Hi sought to carry on the good traditions of his forerunners.

Lasting peace did indeed ensue after he had received homage from all the Mongol tribes, and then led a great army across the Gobi desert to trounce the Tartar chief who continued to harass them. 'O sovereign Heaven . . . I have vowed to give the blessing of peace throughout the land I hold from You . . . but the Tartar Chief tramples Your laws underfoot. I hold from You the right to make war upon the wicked', prayed Kang-Hi; and made it to some effect, suppressed a rebellion in the south, and took Taiwan, of late the haunt of pirates, Japanese and others. More Chinese than the Chinese themselves, he instituted a dictionary of 80,000 characters, and an encyclopaedia of several hundred volumes. He wrote poetry, and promulgated his own Sixteen Rules of Living. He encouraged foreigners, and reinstated a Jesuit, as President of the Board of Astronomy, in place of an Arab who had got the calendar wrong.

Kang-Hi established contact with Louis XIV of France, and the Jesuits translated Chinese classics into French and wrote a history of China which aroused great interest in Europe. (Later on Voltaire, Rousseau and other leaders of the Enlightenment were to talk of the Chinese rule of life with avidity – here was a righteous empire without benefit of clergy.) Jesuits also translated for a Russian boundary commission sent by Peter the Great, settling it without difficulty in Chinese interests. Kang-Hi loved discussing Europe with the Jesuits, and the theorems of geometry were his kind of crossword-puzzle recreation. He felt no fear of foreigners or their influence, and in 1692 the Chinese Board of Ceremonies decreed that Christianity could be taught and churches built anywhere in China.

Upon this harmonious scene Christian internal faction raised its ugly head; the distant frown of Rome scorched up the hopeful harvest field.

The early Jesuits, and in particular Father Ricci, had not sought to disrupt Chinese religion. They had told their listeners that Confucius and Mencius had indeed spoken with the spirit of Tien, of God; but that now an even brighter light had been revealed, in the coming of Christ. There were difficulties – Confucius had believed in original virtue, in man's essentially good nature corrupted by his failures; and would-be converts put up a stout resistance against St. Paul's Original Sin, with its need for forgiveness and for redemption through Christ. For good reasons the Jesuits had accepted ancestor-worship; it was such an essential and immemorial feature of Chinese life and appeared to do no harm to anyone. But now the Roman Catholic Archbishop of Manila laid objections to the practice, and there were rows and rages that 'disturbed tranquillity' and disgusted the Emperor Kang-Hi. Finally the Pope came down on the wrong side, forbidding ancestor worship.

Kang-Hi reacted with a Henry VIII-like indignation – what the hell had the ceremonies used by the subjects of the Son of Heaven to do with him? 'How can the Pope know about the ceremonies of China?' he demanded of the Jesuits; asking, reasonably enough, 'Would I dare to judge the customs of Europe, when I know nothing about them?' Already the Jesuits had been banished from Japan and their flock had been exterminated; Kang-Hi was not so extreme; he kept a few Jesuits at his court who were astronomers or other scientific experts, sent away the rest, and ordered all the Christian churches to be converted into schools or town halls. Papal intransigence had wiped out 100 years of Jesuit work and worship, and the priests left China with their hearts half-broken. In 1724, all conversion was forbidden; and this hopeful contact between Europe and China ground to a bitter halt.

In 1722, Kang-Hi departed this life in a truly Roi Soleil blaze of hospitality. To celebrate his 60 years on the Dragon Throne, he invited every man over 60 in his entire realm to dinner. Immense numbers came, there was a superb banquet, and the skies above Peking glittered with fireworks. With his usual savoir faire the Emperor died a few months later, leaving his great Empire prosperous and united. On the other side of the world Queen Anne and her great general, the Duke of Marlborough, had consolidated a strength that in the coming century was to send the British to the shores of the Great Khan.

6

Friction

Since Marco Polo the Venetian had first made his way overland to the court of the Chinese Emperor in Peking in the 13th century, relations between Western Europe and the Celestial Empire had been spasmodic and unhappy. By sea, the Portuguese as ever had been first in the field, acquiring Macao as a trading port in 1586, as a reward from the Chinese Emperor for driving off piratical raids on his realm. The Dutch had first rounded the Cape and sighted the coast of China in 1595. Four years later John Mildenhall from England had headed a mission from Queen Elizabeth I to the Emperor of China, who had been persuaded by the Jesuit missionaries at his court not to receive it. By 1603, the year of Queen Elizabeth's death, the Dutch had driven the Portuguese from Amboyna and Tidor, thus greatly increasing the value of the peninsula of Macao to the still potent Portuguese. In another four years the enterprising Dutch had acquired a settlement in Taiwan and a share of China trade.

The English had appeared again in 1615, in a spirit of compromise (with Holland at least). After a preliminary brush with the Dutch, it was decided that the two nations should unite 'to open a free trade to China'. In Chinese eyes all these foreigners were barbarians, but by 1637 trade at Canton was established with both nations.

Less compromising had been Captain Weddell, forebear of the discoverer of the Antarctic Weddell Sea. A treaty had been made with the Portuguese at Goa, whereby the British were allowed to trade through Macao, and in 1634, Captain Weddell had cast anchor in the Bay of Canton. He was refused entry to the Pearl River, and after prolonged and unsuccessful negotiations with the Chinese authorities he despaired of being allowed to water his ships or victual them, and so attacked and silenced the forts, forced the Bogue, (or Bocca Tigris, Tiger's Mouth) the narrow entrance to the river, destroyed the war junks and thus compelled the Chinese Viceroy at Canton to allow British trade.

An unpromising beginning; but 800 years before this a more lethal enemy had made a quiet entrance. Sometime earlier than 700 AD the Middle East had arrived, in the form of Arab traders. They settled, built a mosque at Canton, and set up a small unobtrusive Islam, firing no guns, seeking no converts, making no trouble. But they introduced, to the ruin of millions of Chinese, the commodity of opium, grown in the fields of Turkey.

The year 1635 produced a more desperate invader of Canton than any British sea-captain. From across the Great Wall the Manchus from the Siberian plains had assaulted the Celestial Empire and all China had been convulsed. The Manchu Khan took the imperial throne from the Ming Emperors, and in 1644 besieged Canton. Knowing their probable fate, the Cantonese put up a stout resistance, but in vain. Barbaric Manchu soldiers took the city, sacked it, and massacred most of its inhabitants. A million bodies at least, it was reckoned, had floated down the Pearl River and away into the cleansing sea. Thereafter, though the framework was preserved, ferocious Manchu soldiers manned the ancient gates and walls of Canton, and a Manchu Viceroy ruled there under the Manchu Emperor in Peking. It was hardly surprising that another British trade mission, arriving in 1664, met with failure; though Oliver Cromwell had paved its way by a treaty with Portugal in 1659 opening the ports of both countries to each other.

In the midst of all this, the clever Dutch had quietly introduced Europe to the practice of drinking tea; and the desire for this delightful and expensive drink dominated the situation from then on.

In 1666, a superbly equipped embassy from Holland arrived to approach the Emperor in Peking. Its leaders 'kowtowed' in the approved fashion and did all that was most conciliatory; and for these acts of obeisance some slight trade concessions were made – and cancelled a few months later. The Russians fared no better. After their defeat on the Amoy river in 1689, they were considered as 'a subject nation' and made to perform the kowtow (a Tartar practice) to the Manchu Emperor, the Tartars having conquered Amoy in 1681. In the same year, a seaman of HMS *Defence* killed a Chinaman in a shore brawl, and his commander, Captain Heath, refused the huge indemnity demanded by the local mandarin and simply sailed away. The Tartars had greatly increased the Customs duties at Amoy and Canton, and the Russians, for all kowtows, were soon dismissed from Peking. At Chusan, on the other hand, a Factory or warehouse was allowed by the Emperor Kang-Liu to 'the red-haired people'.

Possibly the Dutch and the British, coming from so far away, were looked on as less of a menace by the Chinese than were the Russians so closely bordering the Celestial Empire. By 1702 the redheads were trading unmolested at Chusan, Amoy, Condow, Mocha and Canton, and by 1715 a regular system of trade had been established at Canton. Under this, the supracargoes, though obliged all to live in one house and not set up family establishments, could at least inhabit Canton and trade there during the season in which the monsoon allowed their ships to arrive in Chinese waters. Merchant ships could come up the Bay of Canton as far as the Bocca Tigris, where the supracargoes came to meet them in smaller vessels, agreed duties with the Hoppo, or chief customs officer, and then proceeded upstream with the goods to sell at Canton.

In 1719, Peter the Great of Russia made another effort to trade with the Chinese, sending an envoy to Peking, who brought rich presents, performed the kowtow to the Emperor and was allowed to remain as envoy. But he was so ill-treated that he was soon obliged to return to Russia.

As the century progressed the system by which Portuguese, English, Dutch and presently Americans could trade seemed more or less established, however limited. The journey across the oceans was still perilous, the treatment by Chinese officials still captious, but the tough and enterprising could at least live with it, and the rewards were great.

* * *

The 18th century as a whole showed no marked improvement in the alternation of frustration and aggression. In the 1720s a series of rows developed between the Chinese merchants of Canton, who in 1720 had formed themselves into a 'Co-Hong', to agree prices for cargoes, and the supracargoes, who objected to the system, preferring, no doubt, to bargain individually. Next year, the accidental death of the Hoppo officer at Whampoa, the basin up-river where merchant ships unloaded into smaller craft, caused the local mandarin to imprison eleven of the East India Company's officers in Canton. These lodged so strong a protest, pointing out that it was just such an arbitrary action that caused the Company to leave Chusan and Amoy, that the mandarin who had ordered the arrest was degraded and punished. For by now a great many powerful Chinese, including the Emperor, had realized that large private fortunes were to be made through foreign trade. But this freeing of John Company's officials did not really clarify the situation, any more than did the stopping of a ship in the river whose gunner had accidentally shot a Chinese boy, and the subsequent dropping of all proceedings because the Emperor had died.

He was succeeded as Emperor by a vigorous fourth son who had murdered his rivals, and the authorities at Canton were ordered to increase the impositions upon traders in 1727. This caused the supracargoes to threaten to leave Canton and trade only at Amoy, whereupon some reliefs were granted, only for the original impositions to be renewed soon after. At this, the supracargoes forced their way into the Viceroy's presence to protest, which did nothing to resolve the dispute. Chien-Lung, succeeding to the Celestial throne in 1736, did at least abolish the extra ten per cent duties, but at the same time insisted that all the foreign barbarians were to deposit their arms with the local mandarin.

Five years later, yet another brisk naval officer appeared in the Bay of Canton. Commodore Anson, on his way round the world, anchored at Macao, was refused a permit to go to Canton by the Hoppo, threatened to arm his boats and shoot his way up river, and was at once granted a permit.

Throughout the 1750s, ineffectual attempts were made by the merchants to curtail the taxes on their goods, particularly the illogical Chinese method of imposing duties on her goods in accordance with the measurement of each ship. The British now made an attempt to reopen the trade at Limpo, but did at least send out three Englishmen to learn Cantonese. Warehouses known as Factories were set up, but in spite of this considerable concession by the Chinese, in 1755 trade became legally confined to the Co-Hong, and there was a further insistence that the foreigners should not wander about the countryside shooting duck with their fowling pieces. This seemed fair enough; given an inch, they would take an ell.

Two years later Chien-Lung confined all foreign trade to Canton, and forbade any foreigner to resort to Chusan, Limpo and Amoy. At Canton, violent altercations continued, as did personal attacks of some ferocity by the Chinese on the supracargoes – the traders meanwhile continuing to find it all worthwhile (a little surprisingly). Mr Flint, one of the luckless Englishmen who knew Cantonese, was imprisoned for four years, and Captain Shattowe, sent out by the East India Company Court of Directors to redress this injury, was totally unsuccessful.

In the 1760s, the Dutch appointed a resident commissioner at Canton, and in 1767, three years later, the French monarchy, in a final burst of expansiveness, sent thither ten resident supracargoes, while a royal decree from Louis XV opened the China trade to all French subjects. John Company, perhaps feeling threatened by these rivals, ordered its supracargoes to remain permanently in China, and not go chasing off home to England on leave. A year later, in 1771, the Company paid a large sum of money to dissolve the Co-Hong, who now held all trade in their hands. (Obligingly dissolved, they quite rapidly reassembled themselves.) By the end of this decade the Company were sternly resolved to make their supracargoes take their jobs seriously. They were forbidden to marry, or to keep separate establishments of a more dubious kind. They were *all* to dine and sup *in* the Factory and *at* the same table. (For this, extremely good food and wine, and splendid tableware were provided.)

* * *

Whenever a state of calm and mutual forbearance was arrived at, some untoward event would sooner or later upset the precarious balance. In 1780, a French sailor who had killed a Portuguese was handed over to the Chinese authorities and at once strangled. Four years later came an incident whose appalling impression haunted the westerners for years. A gun of salute fired from the British merchantman *Lady Hughes* accidentally killed two Chinese boatmen. The captain of the ship was inveigled to Canton on a promise of investigation into the matter, and there seized and imprisoned, not to be released until he handed over the man who had in all innocence fired the gun. Eventually he did so, and the seaman, imprisoned for some while without trial and subjected to inhuman treatment, was eventually strangled on direct orders from the Chinese Emperor. The firing of complimentary salutes was thenceforth prohibited to all British ships, by the home authorities; but from that day no Briton, however much to blame, was ever again handed over to Chinese justice. (Indignation in Britain would probably have been much less intense had it been known that the seaman in question, far from the blue-eyed Anglo-Saxon stripling of their imagination, had in fact been an elderly Portuguese. Not that the principle differed; he had been a British subject.)

The end of this momentous century arrived with but little improvement in the awkward relationship between far west and far east. In 1785, a Chinaman was strangled for killing an Englishman; and from afar the Court of Directors reprimanded their supracargoes for their threatening behaviour after the execution of the *Lady Hughes'* gunner. Ships' captains were ordered from on high to deliver any offender who had caused a Chinese death to be dealt with by local authorities. This sounded well enough in London; but in Canton, where the probability of torture and the certainty of strangling without trial were better known, it rang hollow and was widely disregarded. In 1801, the Select Committee of the Company applied to the Viceroy of Canton for a copy of Chinese law, of which they were sent printed extracts. Perhaps the newly dawned 19th century would produce more equitable dealings between East and West.

* * *

Before this, in 1792, and in spite of being on the brink of a 20 year life-and-death struggle with Napoleonic France, the British government had launched Lord Macartney on an embassy to the Chinese Emperor at Peking. In preparation for this, some assistance was demanded from the East India Company, who could so greatly benefit if the Embassy succeeded. The 'Chairs' or leaders of the Canton Factories told Dundas and Pitt that they did not think the Macartney embassy would do any good; all the same they voted £30,000 to help it on its way.

Lord Macartney was handsome, urbane, and intelligent, an envoy (it was hoped) to appeal to the equally urbane and intelligent Chien-Lung. His mission was designed to impress the elegant and civilized court of the Chinese Emperor with the elegance and civilization of Britain, and reinforced by a wealth of extremely handsome presents. As John Company had predicted, it was a dead flop.

7
Chien-Lung

In 1736, Chien-Lung had ascended the Dragon throne. Like his grandfather Kang-Hi, he was to reign 60 years, keeping mainly to the lines that this famous monarch had laid down. The Chinese people continued in their ancient ways while the Manchu among them tried hard not to follow the Mongol path and lose their rugged vitality. Inter-marriage was forbidden, Manchu women were not to bind their feet, no Manchu was to engage in trade, still less in manual labour. Garrisons of Manchu 'bannermen' continued to be kept in large towns. Two officials were appointed to important jobs – a Chinaman with the needful learning and administrative ability, and a Manchu to check on him; a plan occasionally disturbing to tranquillity. The Chinese still disliked their Manchu rulers, and their Tartar troops even more; but the notion entertained in British India and at home in England (and picked up by Lord Napier) that the Chinese as a people were ripe for revolt against their Manchu rulers was far wide of the mark.

Everyone had a place in this hierarchy, though it seems unlikely that everyone was happy with it. But at least they knew where they stood, and promotion for the highly intelligent was always possible. Such a huge empire could not be all joy, and never was. Children still suffered, and many still starved or went on extremely short commons; but order, that blessing of the poor, still prevailed. Once a year, in midwinter, the Son of Heaven worshipped on the Holy Mountain, he and all his court dressed in blue, the colour of winter, the Emperor bowing low before spiritual powers even greater than his own. But all alike kowtowed before him (a considerable exercise involving three prostrations with the nose pressed to the ground, with three bows between each prostration). His rule was still arbitrary and absolute; but he still took counsel. On Confucian principles he still needed to be righteous, a difficult quality to combine with absolutism.

Chien-Lung was a great ruler by any standards. He saw his councillors every day at dawn, he travelled widely throughout his vast domains, keeping provincial officials up to the mark, he read the classics, and exercised a strong personal rule. He set up a huge state library, and encouraged the arts: that he did not consider George III his equal is understandable. But although the Manchu had lived near the Chinese border so long that they had adopted the Chinese way of life and their Confucian principles, a tough warrior still lurked within Chien-Lung's dignified frame, clothed in the most beautiful of Chinese silks, and he ruthlessly destroyed all the books of whose ideas he disapproved, even entering private houses to get at them.

Like his grandfather Kang-Hi the Emperor Chien-Lung led his armies westward to victory. Once again there was a Tartar rebellion, once again a Manchu Emperor led a Chinese army across the desolate wastes of the Gobi desert to defeat a Tartar horde. Chien-Lung swept on, meaning to finish it for good and all. He took Turkestan, which from then on owed allegiance and paid tribute, adding them to Manchuria and Mongolia. Taking no chances, he added Tartar-occupied Tibet to his domains. The Tartars here were now all Buddhists, but who knew what they might become or be up to, in that icy mountainous region made inaccessible by nature? Manchu soldiers now guarded that high cold plateau around Lhasa, where Chinese mandarins also kept an eye on things, (and on the Dalai Lama) on behalf of the Son of Heaven. Though not part of his empire, the rulers of Burma, Siam and Tonking also paid tribute to Chien-Lung.

In spite of all this massive power, Chien-Lung was far less relaxed than his grandfather had been. He was suspicious in particular of Europeans, who had been trading up and down his coasts, at Chusan, Amoy, and even Tientsin: he confined them all to the port of Canton, where they were allowed only to trade through the Hong Merchants, and were subject to the changeable and arbitrary rules of the local authorities. How not be suspicious of all these differing Europeans – Russia on the move to the northward, Britain and France active in India, Spanish, Dutch and Portuguese in the East Indies? Coming in with tireless persistence on the south-west winds of autumn and departing on the north-east winds of spring and early summer, European traders had become a regular feature; Chien-Lung, acting on advice, made sure that the traders should not settle at Canton. They were allowed to build water-front warehouses and to live in them during the limited trading season, but they were to bring no wives or women, to depart on the monsoon, and never to enter the walls of Canton city itself. Strict customs officers superintended the landing of every cargo, and disobedience or trouble from any trader was followed by the closing of the trade. At the same time it was all very paying for both sides. In Chien-Lung's time 20,000,000 lbs of tea per annum were exported. At first hugely expensive in the West, selling from £5 to £10 a pound in the 16th century, it had become steadily cheaper and more readily available, creating a huge demand. The Chinese insisted on being paid in silver and showed only a limited appetite for western goods, with one exception – opium.

The Europeans reacted with almost an equal suspicion of the Chinese. Why were they so prickly? Why did they refuse to allow any foreigner to learn Chinese, threatening the death penalty for anyone who taught them? Why did they torture suspects and imprison wrongdoers without trial? The traders who came yearly to Canton had not, in spite of the honesty and good manners of the Hong merchants, acquired either admiration or respect for the riverfront dwellers who were their main contact. The banished Jesuits had brought reports of China and her remarkable civilization which encouraged great European curiosity and a strong desire to know this wonderful but seemingly forbidden land. Her goods also excited great cupidity; but the men who braved the dangers to come in search of them were not such as to disarm Chinese suspicions or promote East–West harmony or mutual comprehension. Themselves suspicious, and often arrogant, they approached China with mingled apprehension and swagger, although of course this was not true of everybody who sailed up the river to anchor at Whampoa, port of Canton. Amongst the educated of Europe there existed a kind of respectful awe, a reverence for this ancient and long civilized Empire. Even their sketchy knowledge had taught them that the Chinese people had been staggeringly inventive, and certainly their artifacts were of a beauty and skill to command universal admiration.

* * *

The traders felt differently, artistic impression cutting less ice. The Chinese were heathen, and therefore bad; this discounted all else. The Chinese were reputed to be cruel, their tortures outclassing in ingenuity and prolongation anything thought up by the Spanish Inquisitors; but the Western adventurers who brushed their shores most certainly afforded them few examples of humanity. In 1661, Dutch ships arrived at the famous and undefended Buddhist island sanctuary of Pu-To-Shan on Chusan, where they pillaged the temples, burnt and sacked the shrines, and treated the monks in barbarous fashion. In the 18th century the Dutch massacred most of the Chinese in Java, while the Spanish exterminated a much larger colony of Chinese who had settled in the Philippines but declined to accept Catholicism. The Portuguese too had not been blameless; and in the Indian Ocean British and French merchantmen pillaged and sank Chinese junks trading en route for Ceylon.

The Europeans had been far from emanating sweetness and light, and the Chinese hated them all indiscriminately and had many excuses for referring to them as barbarians, for barbarously had these men, far from home and beset by dangers and hardships, treated them. The Chinese also found Europeans physically unappealing; they smelled of mutton fat; great noses stuck out of all their faces. The Russians were devils with green eyes like lanterns and heads far too big; the Portuguese were Sea-Devils; the Dutch had sunken eyes, red beards, and feet 14 inches long; they and the English were Red-haired Devils. The European tendency to grow hair on their faces made them seem like beasts. Greedy and omnivorous, these foreigners had 'the nature of dogs and goats', forever devouring and forever unsatisfied. All were seen as 'physically hideous and socially repulsive' (Professor Jerome Ch'en). All were suspected of cannibalism; and when Europeans attempted to employ young Chinamen as men-servants, the officials to whom they applied feared that these would end up as pot-roasts. The official Ming history declared firmly in 1517 that Portugal was south of Java, and that she had sent an envoy 'for the purpose of buying small children to cook and eat '.

The Red-Haired Barbarians evoked a particular horror not connected with their actual crimes. Since everyone in China has black hair, the devils of Chinese mythology have always been depicted with red hair: in the same way, since everyone in Europe has a fair skin the Devil of Europe is always depicted as black, less from reference to Africans or Indians than because he was alleged to be smudged with the fires and smoke of Hell. In China, the Dutch and the British aroused exactly the same atavistic fear and horror as did Jamaicans and Bengalese arriving in large numbers in Britain in the 20th century – ("Black as Old Nick and buying up the whole street!") These were handicaps of which the British in the 19th century and blacks in the 20th were alike unaware: William John had hair of an alarming tawny hue, as well as those strangely alien blue eyes. At this point, Australian aborigines were being gunned down, largely because their smoky looks had hellish connotation. *Heathens do not count* was the unconvincing but generally held conviction; and why in forty thousand years had aborigines failed to stop killing their small children or invented so much as a wheelbarrow? It was an age when the temptations of racial dislike were resisted by scarcely anybody, bar the poet William Blake, a few missionaries and churchmen, or sailors desperate for a woman in any size, shape or colour.

* * *

British trade with China was inextricably bound up with the problems of India. More by accident than design, the opium monopoly from the poppies of Bihar and Bengal had become – by the time Hastings retired as Governor General in 1785 – too valuable to the East India Company to risk losing. Without its revenues, how maintain the Indian administration?

The determination of the British Government (Pitt's India Act of 1784) and of the East India Company's directors in London *not* to sell opium to China had proved unequal to the determination of the men on the spot to make fortunes by so doing. Dutch merchant seamen, Americans, Parsee entrepreneurs and British get-rich-quick adventurers all combined to make sure that the trade would continue to flow: not in East India Company ships, because that would endanger the permission to trade that the Chinese Emperor had given the Company, but in the holds of *any* avid captain prepared to sail opium round the Malay Peninsula and up the coast to Canton between the monsoon winds.

For all the efforts of Cornwallis to set British rule in India upon a just and equitable basis, the state of Bengal was still wretched when he returned home in 1793, and the opium monopoly revenue was still a necessity. And when the Napoleonic wars broke out in 1793, the revenue from opium landed in China (with which to pay for tea) was more than ever vital. How tide the British population through 20 years of loss, hardship and economic stress if deprived of their cups of tea? At the other side of the world, thousands of South Chinese seemed unwilling to endure the continuous toil, poverty and hardship of their lives without opium's instant but fatal alleviation.

Lord Napier had been preceded in China by two other emissaries, operating on a different and more imposing scale. Both had been equally unsuccessful. In 1792, when Lord Macartney landed, Chien-Lung was 83 and wrapped in imperial mystique – very grand, very gracious, very hospitable and blandly indifferent to the aspirations of lesser folk, amongst whom King George III of Great Britain was, in the Emperor's mind, emphatically numbered.

Macartney and his suite of the noble and the expert, his Marine band, his troop of cavalry, his artists and scientists had come a long way, in all the dangers and discomforts of the age of sail. King George's envoy had an intelligent face, marred by bulging cheeks, like a small boy comfortably pouching quantities of food he could not yet swallow. (Chinese comments upon this peculiarity are happily hidden from us.) Velvet-coated, with powdered hair and faultlessly white knee-breeches, Macartney had drawn the line at the kowtow, but was prepared to accord the Emperor the honour he gave his own King, that of a low sweeping bow. Only to God would the earl go down on two knees. To this exception from the rule the Emperor Chien-Lung had graciously agreed, although amazed that anyone should object to the ordinary courtesy of pressing his face to the ground three times to the beat of a drum.

At the mouth of the Pei-Ho the junks sent to convey Macartney to Peking arrived, and his lordship stepped hopefully on board. He did not

know that the sails of the junks bearing him up-river to the imperial reception were emblazoned with the words 'Tribute Bearer'. The blazon was in
Chinese, and what the eye does not see the heart has no reason to grieve
over. Nor did Macartney know that he was about to receive the politest of
receptions followed by one of the most resounding set-downs in history.

* * *

The attempt of Lord Amherst's mission to regularize trade and establish
diplomatic relations in the year 1816 had been equally unsuccessful,
although by this time Chien-Lung had been gathered to his fathers and
become an unusually worthy object of ancestor worship; and now a
lesser man sat on the Dragon throne in the traditional yellow silk, and
worshipped on cold Mount Tai every midwinter night. Opium was now
flowing in freely; the West, and particularly Britain, impoverished by 20
years of desperate war against Napoleon's attempt to dominate Europe,
no longer had enough silver to pay for its tea.

This trade situation was inherited by Henry John Temple, Lord
Palmerston, on becoming Foreign Secretary in the Ministry of Lord Grey
in the 1830s. Although the word opium is never mentioned in his briefing
of William John, nor even the word drug, Palmerston knew very well how
dependent the China tea trade was upon the revenues brought in by the
growing and export from India of those chests of the stuff, and of the part
played by such revenue in bearing the costs to John Company of the
Indian administration. But of Chinese law, of their customs and way of life
he had, in common with most Europeans of his day, but the haziest
notion. The little that he knew, or that the Foreign Office knew, had been
imparted to William John to read as he sailed slowly half round the world.

'Napier's appointment was significant', writes Professor Ch'en, 'not
because of any clearly defined instructions from Palmerston . . . but
because he came as his king's representative, empowered to negotiate as
an equal with the Chinese Viceroy at Canton. Thus, he came armed with
the assumptions of modern diplomacy to China, only to find that that
ancient Empire was not a nation state and did not share those assumptions. Trade was not regulated by any treaty until 1842.' By this time,
sadly, blood had flowed, and in the Chinese heart enmity had settled.

In the spring of 1834, when Napier set sail from Plymouth for Macao
and hence Canton, a lasting friendship between Britain and China still
seemed to many besides himself a hopeful possibility. In his small creak-
ing cabin on board *Andromache* he set himself to study the limited
available facts on this relationship. Reading them, his native goodwill
underwent some diminution, and his heart a certain hardening. Would
it be *possible* to come peacefully to terms?

Part Three

Voyage to the Celestial Empire
and Confrontation in Canton

8

Macartney's Mission

The monotony of a very long voyage by sea under sail had fortunately to be broken by the need of frequent stays in port, to replenish with fresh food and water supplies. Rough weather in the Chops of the Channel had failed to delay *Andromache*, 'it blew always with a leading wind so as to make a good day's run, and on Sunday 16th about noon observed the Island of Porto Santo in the SW', William John reported. He kept a critical eye on the ship's handling, but wisely kept his views to himself. Madeira would now give them all a chance to stretch their legs and go places.

If they ever got there. 'It is my private opinion that the ship was steered too much to the Eastward, so that we made the wrong island in the present instance, and to leward of it. The proper course is to run down the longitude of Madeira and pass to the Westward of Porto Santo. In the afternoon passed under the lee of the Town of Porto Santo and at 7 o'clock – fair wind and beautiful weather – we shortened sail and humbugged all night at a distance from the island of Madeira instead of carrying on to the Brazen Head and coming to anchor if possible.' This kind of dawdle was no way to get to China. 'This Channel-groping manoeuvre discomposed my tranquillity for the night', William John reported crossly.

'The Master, Mr James, has been long in the Packet service and ought to be a good Navigator. He pays great attention to the Chronometers and *looks the Sailor* every inch of him. I fear the Captain is a timid man in the government of his own ship, he does not carry as much sail as he might do, and never works the ship himself, but leaves it to his first Lieutenant, Mr Hill, who is a noisy would-be-smart sort of man and a bad officer.' Such disparagement is unusual for William John: perhaps the luckless Mr Hill had made eyes at one of his daughters, still only 16 and 15. It all seemed rum to him; his idea of bliss being to work his own ship himself whenever possible. Or why go to sea? (Captain Chads afterwards became a distinguished admiral.)

At Madeira it seemed that the Portuguese civil war was far from being over. The only one of Dom Miguel's ships that had escaped capture by 'Black Charlie's' squadron was sheltering here, and the Governor,

Da Souza, on whom William John paid a courtesy call, was 'busy making batteries and preparations for defence, a determined partisan of Dom Miguel's'. So, he found, were most of the British merchants – 'Naturally all attached to the despotic side, they are in enjoyment of privileges which will depart from them under another system of government'. On the other hand, 'all Murgados, or land owners of any respectability, have been seized or banished for their liberal opinions. Out of 80 principal people banished for their politics are to be found above 30 Vicars, the most respectable of the Clergy'.They wanted reform, and to be allowed to marry, 'desirous of moral change, and the comforts of domestic life'.

Peasants were squatting on the lands of the displaced, but appeared hardly to be working them and were making a sorry mess of things, and were 'in a great state of misery and degradation. Any man with a hat on his head or a shoe to his foot is said to be a Pedro-ite or Reformer', and thus under a cloud. Great complaints about the quality of the Madeira wine had lately come from England, and William John heard that this was because a habit had grown up of planting potatoes and vegetables between the vines; these needed manure, which produced wire-worm and led to the destruction of the vines.

The Napiers were at once swept ashore by William's friends from old days, hospitable as ever. While Mamma rested, WJ and his daughters were soon riding away with the Consul, Mr Veitch and his daughters, high up in the hills to his home, Jardin da Sierra, 3,000 feet up. Arriving at dusk, they were glad of the blazing fire, for in Madeira it was scarcely the end of winter; vines and chestnut trees were bare, and 'Madeira Mahogany and orange trees only showing their leaves of green'. Next day he had the joy of riding with his two girls past glorious scenes remembered from his youth – The Abyss of the Corral, the magnificent views, the ride down to Funchal, 'a display of nature not to be seen in the tamer regions of Ettrick', and he rejoiced in the open-eyed wonder and admiration of his children.

Scientific as usual, he paused fascinated by a newly-constructed water mill, and described it in his journal at length. The high ranges of Madeira's mountains were still covered with snow, and he could not help regretting a little the joys of former visits, the lush green vines and ripening grapes, the smell of innumerable flowers, when 'the whole air in the cool of evening exhaled the sweets of nature'. No-one, thought William John, who did not come upon it after 50 or 60 consecutive days at sea could comprehend the stunning and extravagant beauties of the island.

There were, however, always the two Miss Veitches to admire. 'At present the prettiest flowers were the two young ladies.' They further won William's heart by telling him what a treat it was to make friends with his two daughters. Back in the town, William John took his wife to the Mount Convent, which she had expressed a wish to see. Eliza was carried in a palanquin up the steep hill, while the two girls rode, their father happily striding alongside. His old Convent friends greeted him delightedly. It was good to see them all again after eight years and to remember all their kindness. The Napiers dined nearby on the Mount with the ever hospitable merchant Webster Gordon, also a Scot, from Selkirk; Veitch, the consul, was from Galloway, William noted appreciatively.

Tied up alongside *Andromache* was another ship bound for the Cape, and William John was pleased to find his cousin Major John Napier on board of her, on his way with his wife and daughter as a settler to South Africa. Perhaps the Major was a bit of a self-dramatiser, but William could only applaud his resolution in emigrating, instead of staying in Somerset to mourn his lost inheritance of Tintinhull and envy his younger brother Andrew's lot, who had married an heiress, Miss Laetitia Berkeley, and had several sons, who would inherit Pennard. *Nil desperandum*!

It was sad to leave Madeira, with its beauties and its friends, but the Napiers spent the last evening with the Gordons, who had asked several local young friends in, with whom Maria and Georgiana happily danced quadrilles. They were reft away from the fun smartly at ten o'clock, *Andromache* weighing anchor soon after, making sail for Teneriffe. Here the Spanish officials came on board as soon as the ship hove to, off Santa Cruz, and forbade all communication with the shore, 'for fear of our giving them cholera'. This luckily did not prevent the Spaniards from selling *Andromache* 'a supply of Bullocks and vegetables and wine for the Ship's Company,' while William's personal purchase was '2 quarter casks of best Vidonia and 4 of Common or Cargo. I think Vidonia infinitely superior to the Madeira drunk in England.' It was a pity not to be able to show the girls the Island and take them up the Peak, to go down into its crater, and observe its other wonders of height and precipice and the immense vistas of shining sea.

They sailed south the next day, and firmly shutting himself into his hot little cabin, William John set himself to further study of China and its relationship with the west, carefully transcribing the dates and details into his notebooks. He had been unable to resist a last glimpse of Teneriffe's Peak, rising at sunrise next day to see it 70 miles astern at a great elevation above the horizon. 'It had been obscured all the day before.' There in the sunrise it showed, agleam and lofty. He turned to the perusal of the affairs of China, no less obscure and much less lofty.

At the same time he felt unable to resist recording in his diary *Andromache*'s method of sailing – what navigation! 'We made a circuit of 300 miles at least to keep clear of the Islands instead of taking the straight course from Teneriffe to St Iago, as we ought to have done. This adds considerably to the length of the passage.' However, he concluded, it was useless to fret, and he settled down to a close study of all the available facts.

* * *

Some slight advantages had accrued to Britain, he read, from the embassy under Lord Macartney that had arrived on board HMS *Lion* at the mouth of the Pei-Ho river in August of 1792. They had at least been received with friendliness and dismissed with dignity. Chien-Lung had thanked George III for the 'respectful spirit of submission' which that monarch was far from exhibiting. He had also, and this was a major concession, accepted the British refusal to kowtow. The stumbling block had been Chinese insistence that the junks that bore Macartney and his suite of 100 persons and rich presents up river should wear flags announcing that they were 'Tribute Bearers' from Britain: this obstacle had been surmounted, it will be remembered, by the announcements being in Chinese characters, so that no Briton could read or be offended by them. A further concession was made in that the Viceroy at Canton had waived the old objection to foreigners being allowed to learn Cantonese. But this was all.

The Emperor Chien-Lung was at this time 83 years old, the essence of civilized dignity in his long silken robes embroidered with the Imperial Dragon. Since the Chinese reverenced the wisdom with which long experience endows the intelligent aged, he was now generally considered to be at the height of his powers. He was lodged at his summer palace at Jehol, in the cooler hills to the North of Peking. He received the British mission courteously, and Lord Macartney, resplendent in his velvet coat embroidered with gold, had bowed low and politely. In six weeks, spent between Peking and journeys to Jehol, Macartney had four audiences with Chien-Lung; and achieved virtually nothing. The Emperor had remained throughout an embodiment of dignified good manners, but the very gleam of his embroidered dragon – symbol of power and fruitfulness – exuded an immense and unassailable superiority.

Macartney was impressed by the 'grandeur and elegance' of the Emperor's surroundings; he found them all in such good taste that 'they diffused over the mind a pleasing serenity and repose', he wrote. Regarded as divine, the Chinese Emperor was surrounded by an all-but religious ritual and ceremony. Chien-Lung too was pleased – so splendid an embassy sending 'tribute' underlined his position as supreme master of the world. He entertained the British mission royally for six weeks, listened politely while King George's words of goodwill were translated for him, and received graciously that monarch's letter handed to him by Macartney in a gold box inset with diamonds. The envoy had brought with him no fewer than 600 cases of presents, containing the best that Georgian craftsmanship could produce; and Chien-Lung, intimating politely that the moment for departure had come, had sent Macartney and his suite home loaded with presents, and even sent gifts to the officers and men in the naval ships waiting off the mouth of the Pei-Ho to transport the visitors home – 'so that they too may share in my all-embracing kindness'.

* * *

Two long letters were sent in reply to King George. Macartney had stayed steadfastly calm, polite and urbane throughout; but his urbanity may have faltered a little when he learned their content. 'It behoves you, O King' Chien-Lung proceeded, in the cause of putting George III in his place, 'to respect my sentiments and to display even greater loyalty and devotion in the future'.

The Emperor proceeded in polite but firm tones, to refuse all, but every one, of Macartney's far from outrageous requests. The sending of an envoy to Peking as a permanent arrangement 'is contrary to all usage of my dynasty and cannot possibly be entertained'. Anyone who came would be forbidden ever again to leave China, would not be allowed to move outside Peking, nor to correspond with his home country. And if the Emperor sent an Ambassador to London 'how could you possibly make the necessary arrangements for him? . . . The thing is utterly impracticable.' As for controlling the merchants at Canton – 'Peking is nearly two thousand miles from Canton and at such a distance what possible control could any British representative exercise?' the Emperor asked, not unreasonably.

> If you assert that your reverence for Our Celestial dynasty fills you with a desire to acquire our civilization, our ceremonies and code of laws differ so completely from your own that, even if your Envoy were able to acquire the rudiments of our civilization, you could not possibly transplant our manners and customs to your alien soil . . .
>
> Swaying the wide world, I have but one aim in view, namely to maintain a perfect governance and to fulfil the duties of the state: strange and costly objects do not interest me.

He had only accepted the presents because he appreciated the humble spirit in which they had been sent.

> We possess all things. I set no value on objects strange or ingenious, and have no use for your country's manufactures . . .
>
> As the tea, silk and porcelain which the Celestial Empire produces, are absolute necessities to European nations and to yourselves, we have permitted, as a signal mark of favour, that foreign hongs should be established at Canton, so that your wants might be supplied and your country thus participate in our benevolence . . . Our dynasty, swaying the myriad races of the globe, extends the same benevolence towards all . . . If other nations, following your bad example, wrongfully importune my ear with further impossible requests, how will it be possible to me to treat them with easy indulgence? Nevertheless, I do not forget the lonely remoteness of your island, cut off from the world by intervening wastes of sea, nor do I overlook your excusable ignorance of the usages of our Celestial Empire. I have consequently commanded my Ministers to enlighten your Ambassador on the subject . . .

As to the barbarian wish to disseminate their religion –

> Ever since the beginning of history, sage Emperors and wise rulers have bestowed on China a moral system, and inculcated a code, which from time immemorial has been religiously observed by the myriads of my subjects. There has been no hankering after hetorodox doctrines . . . The distinction between Chinese and barbarian is most strict, and your Ambassador's request that barbarians should be given full liberty to disseminate their religion is utterly unreasonable.

Kindly, Chien-Lung allowed King George the benefit of the doubt.

> It may be, O King, that the above proposals have been wantonly made by your Ambassador on his own responsibility . . . Upon you, who live in a remote and inaccessible region, far across the spaces of ocean, but who have shown your submissive loyalty by sending this tribute mission, I have heaped benefits far in excess of those accorded to other nations.

In addition, the Emperor warned King George not to be led astray by subordinates into allowing his traders to land and attempt to trade at Chekiang and Tientsin, from whence they could be immediately expelled by loyal officials of the Empire, who 'tremblingly obey and show no negligence' he added, in conclusion.

The Macartney mission had its comical side; but also its deeply tragic one. The British envoy had been told to assure the Emperor that if he would accept British goods in exchange for Chinese, the British Government would undertake to stop the import of opium into China. This request was refused, with endless bitter consequences. Perhaps the Son of Heaven felt that the making of bargains was beneath him. Britain, for all its power and glory, was to be placed firmly once again in its Chinese pigeon-hole, on a par with China's tributary nations of Vietnam, Cambodia or Burma. These Britons were but subject nationals who had made the long sea journey from England 'impelled by your humble desire to partake of the benefits of our civilization.'

* * *

Two countries – in the politest of terms – could hardly have been more at cross purposes. Over the years the opium trade was thence to increase to huge proportions, until the economy of India under the East India Company became largely dependent on it. A terrible chariot had started rolling and would carry China, and eventually the Chinese imperial house, rolling downhill with it. The immemorial silks and splendours, the elegance and the ceremony would be no more. Neither any more, come to that, would be the red-coated cavalry of Britain, prancing behind Macartney, her gold-laced officers, her footmen in 'rich green and gold livery', bearing lavish gifts.

William John, studying the Foreign Office briefs and the books on China that he had been able to collect before his pierhead jump on board *Andromache*, must have sighed with the complexity of it all. The cabin was hot, *Andromache* was nearing the tropics. He sought the tranquillity of the upper deck, in that brief moment between dusk and nightfall when the possibility of taking exercise began. Pacing the starlit desk awhile, to the soft rushing sound of the sea, lit by phosphorescent gleams, he laid aside his task for a moment. The situation seemed baffling, and if his increasing knowledge deepened his concern, it did not daunt his determination or his courage. As he looked ahead into the beautiful night, he was more than thankful that he had brought his wife and daughters with him – something at all events of the comfort of home.

Long ago, in ancient Greece, Sophocles had written of seafaring as man's first and greatest achievement. William John was too well used to life at sea to think of it on such terms; but he truly loved seafaring. Pacing the quarterdeck, with his wife's arm tucked under his own, in the mildness of the tropic night, he was able – and well enough content – for the moment to let the future take care of itself.

For all Macartney's reports of the elegance, cleanliness, and civilized prosperity of Northern China under its Ching emperors, and of the stunning artistic achievements he beheld, all was barely realized in the West, in part because no-one from the West was allowed in. China was a world of tradition and of social immobility, an 'urbane, sophisticated, sensitive culture;' but its nature was inconceivable to the tough, beady-eyed, aggressive traders, who were allowed only to Canton, and who noted only the eternally poor and suppressed people, the half-starved coolie, the women tottering on their bound feet. A stony misapprehension coloured the views of both East and West.

In the main, things stayed as they had been before. China was impervious. As for this strange foreign wish for trade – 'There is nothing we lack', the hopeful British had been told. Not even British woollens, the traders wondered, for the icy winters of North China? Nor clocks, nor other ingenious devices from Europe? 'We have never set much store by strange objects', the Emperor had responded aloofly. Next year war with revolutionary France had broken out at home, and no treaty with China had come of it all. No foothold for an envoy had been found at Peking.

What did come of it was a great increase of interest in England in all things Chinese. The supplies of silk and porcelain had increased already, and rich men were sending paintings of their coats of arms to be reproduced on special armorial china. Decorated china gave an idea of the Chinese scene, and soon little hump-backed bridges could be found in the gardens of the grand and fashionable, painted Chinese red, and with lattice work balustrades. Mandarin ducks with exotic plumage floated on the steely waters of ducal lakes. Chinese Chippendale chairs were made. By the end of the 18th century, many people owned Chinese porcelain and an immense number drank tea.

William Alexander, the water-colourist who went with Macartney to Peking, and produced a picture of his meeting with the Emperor, as well as of other Chinese scenes, gave an emphasis to an already existing image of a beautiful and exotic civilization at the other end of the world, an image that had hovered hazily in Europe ever since the opening of the old Silk Road. In 1814, the despatch of Napoleon to Elba was celebrated in London by the building, at the Prince Regent's suggestion, of a Chinese bridge across the lake in St James's Park to the design of John Nash. It had a seven-storied pagoda on the crest of the bridge, and elegant small pavilions at each end. During the celebrations, fireworks which were set off from the pagoda unluckily set fire to it, and the top four tiers fell into the lake, and the most of it was destroyed.

No matter; the Chinese scene had seized and now held the British imagination. Coleridge's great dream of Kubla Khan had been inspired by the spell of this far land. And although, even from the restricted view from Macao or Canton, the British traders and seamen and the missionaries they had brought with them, could see that this immense and ancient empire was beginning to crumble, England still felt its powerful pull. Not only for Chinese tea and silks, but for the beauty and learning of it all, they wanted very much to get in there, to wonder, to admire, to learn, and of course to trade, since the Chinese insistence on silver rather than goods in exchange for their tea made its purchase increasingly difficult.

This desire was implacably opposed by the Chinese authorities. They dreaded new ideas, and preferred to dwell as far as possible on a separate planet, to dismiss the rest of the world into its customary state of insignificant apartheid.

At the same time they badly needed the revenue to be had from selling tea.

William John, (who was thin enough in all conscience) saw himself hopefully as the thin end of a wedge whose insertion would be beneficial to both countries, and to the rest of the Western world as well.

At Peking, Lord Macartney had seen, but too clearly, the seeds of Imperial China's decay. 'China is an old crazy first-rate man of war', he had pronounced after two audiences with the Celestial Emperor, 'which a fortunate succession of able and vigilant officers has contrived to keep afloat for these one hundred and fifty years past, and to overawe the neighbours merely by her bulk and appearance. But whenever an insufficient man happens to have the command upon deck, adieu to the discipline and safety of the ship. She may perhaps not sink outright; she may drift sometime as a wreck, and will then be dashed to pieces on the shore; but she can never be re-built on the same bottom.'

The insufficient man was not yet due.

9

Homework on Passage

Sighing at intervals, William John proceeded with his brief. Despite Lord Macartney's attempts at peaceful accommodation, matters in the early 19th century, he read, grew worse rather than better. Nothing could stop British sailors, after the hard tack and deprivations of the long passage from England, from becoming drunk ashore and involving themselves in rows with the Chinese and, since the affair of the *Lady Hughes* gunner, nothing could make British captains hand their men over to Chinese justice. In 1799, while trying to steal from HM Schooner *Providence* by first cutting her cable, a Chinese sampan-owner was wounded by a shot from the ship; losing balance, he fell from his sampan and was drowned. Demands were made for the culprit, but Captain Dilkes of HMS *Madras* wrote an explanatory letter to the Viceroy and took it to Canton in person, refusing to deliver the schooner's man; and when he sailed from Macao in March of the new century the matter was dropped. But nothing had been explicitly settled and no-one was satisfied.

In 1802, the American flag was hoisted for the first time over a factory at Canton. This did not improve hopes for a quiet time, since, so soon after the War of American Independence, British and American sailors were inclined to fall into rows ashore, quarrels exacerbated by the seamen's ability perfectly to understand each other's insults, and by their using identical terms, since the great majority of Americans were still of British origin.

King George III's ministers had not flagged in their efforts to come to terms with the Celestial Empire, which continued blandly to stonewall them. In 1805, another letter from his Britannic Majesty was addressed to the Emperor; at the same time the Foreign Secretary launched one at the Canton Viceroy and the Chief Customs Officer or Hoppo. Both fell on stony ground, returned unopened. Acceptance of such epistles would be 'against the fundamental laws of the Celestial Empire'.

In 1806, the Select Committee came to the aid of the merchants in Canton by helpfully setting up a fund there, to be subscribed to by all merchants in proportion to their trade. This would provide an emergency fund against sudden forced levies by the local authorities and stave off individual bankruptcies that resulted from these; and induced a certain limited sense of security amongst the traders along the Pearl River.

Still more helpful was the Emperor's ratification of the proceedings after a murder trial. Seamen from the Indiaman *Neptune* had killed a Chinaman in a brawl ashore. It was impossible to discover who had struck the mortal blow; Captain Rolls of HMS *Lion* declined to allow the most likely suspect to be given up; and settled the matter, he hoped, by indemnifying the friends of the deceased. The trial was held by a court of British and Chinese judges together, in the British Factory. The Britons refused to allow the suspect to be tortured, the payment had taken the sting out of the loss of life, and it was felt that Britain had 'gained a great point by their having prevented the execution of a man not *proved* guilty, in retaliation for the life of the man killed in the affray'. This was 1807: were things looking up? Was co-operation to be established? In the same year, the use of the Chuenpee anchorage at the mouth of the Bocca Tigris was 'tacitly acquiesced in by the Chinese'; and though trade had been halted by them after murder in the affray, it was very soon resumed again. It had become necessary to the Chinese Emperor as well as to foreign merchants, such was the wealth flowing into the country through Canton.

* * *

Despite these promising moves, during the next 20 years things became steadily worse. Through days growing ever hotter, as *Andromache* neared the Equator, William John pursued the weary tale; for to do any good one must first learn, in the hope of understanding. Rows between the Western nations had now, he read, further complicated the South China embroilment. The Portuguese Senate at Macao had in 1807 declined to supply victuals to the *Antelope* schooner; there were complaints to Goa; coolness ensued, and the relationship became colder when three years later, the French, triumphant under Napoleon and having already conquered Portugal, were reportedly about to occupy Macao, so that Admiral Drury with British troops from Bengal landed there to forestall them. Deeply suspicious of this move, the Chinese authorities suspended trade. When the French threat faded the British troops were withdrawn, trade reopened and the Select Committee was superseded.

Hope dawned; but then in 1810 an unidentified sailor, said to be from the *Royal George*, killed yet another luckless Chinaman in yet another shore brawl – trade suspended. Trade reopened, under a promise that the sailor, as soon as identified, would be tried by English law. Hardly had this cloud of dust settled before, in 1812, at the height of the war with Napoleon, America felt the need to chip in, and declared war on Britain; and in 1814 HMS *Doris* captured an American ship on her way from Canton and brought her into Macao. An edict from the Viceroy quickly followed this. Both sides were to 'settle their petty disputes at their own homes', and not 'disturb the tranquillity of the Chinese coasts'. Which was fair enough, except that the tranquillity was purely imaginary – 'the Chinese coasts were beset by pirates in great quantities and of the most ferocious kind'.

* * *

A second formal embassy under Lord Amherst in 1815 had fared no better than Macartney's. Amherst arrived with the same flourish of trumpets, in the form of a Marine Guard, a band, and such a quantity of valuable presents that it required 62 persons to bear them. He was instructed not to kow-tow, but, on approaching the Chinese Emperor's presence, 'to kneel upon one knee and to bow the head, and to repeat the obeisance as often as the locals deemed polite'. The Mandarins who came to meet Amherst had assured him of the Emperor's goodwill, but told him that the Emperor was unwilling to receive him unless he would perform the Manchu kow-tow, mendaciously adding that Lord Macartney had performed it.

Nonetheless, Amherst and his cumbrous party hopefully made their way to Peking, on the chance of a relaxation of this rule, and were lucky enough just outside the walls of the city to receive an immediate summons to the Imperial presence, where the Emperor offered to receive Amherst 'according to his own ceremonial' (which in Georgian times was still quite considerable, involving a low bow and a wide deprecatory sweep of the right arm).

Alas for Amherst! He had somehow managed to become parted from the official credentials, from his baggage, and from his court dress. What, no cocked hat? When the Emperor's message reached him, Amherst was hot, tired, and dusty. He felt 'the indecorum and irregularity of appearing without his credentials'. A Marine Band and 62 presents were not at all the same thing. Naked without his plumes, his gold-laced coat, or his letters from the Sovereign, Amherst declined the golden opportunity of a direct and private interview. The Emperor, piqued at such an unheard-of refusal, promptly sent Amherst packing; his embassy unlistened to, his Marine band unheard. Altogether it had been yet another flop on the road to understanding; and the attempts to bamboozle the Mandarins in an argument about whether and why the British warships that had brought Amherst had left their anchorage off

Tientsin, was likely to make bad blood, and was anyhow pointless as the Chinese war junks – as both sides were well aware – knew better than to attack them.

Reading of these failures, William John determined to do better. Had Amherst been too slow, too argumentative, too pompous? The Mandarins had assured him that the kow-tow was a normal form of politeness which in no way implied that he who performed it was a vassal; yet William could not help agreeing with Amherst that it was a performance 'repulsive to the feelings of a European, particularly the need to kneel repeatedly and press the forehead to the ground'. He himself was not prepared to go through such antics and, of course, if the kow-tow gave the impression that the King of Great Britain was inferior to the Emperor of China, this exaggerated obeisance was emphatically not to be made.

The nub of the matter was that delicate light brown fluid which he much enjoyed himself. Tea was the key to the British interest in the Celestial Empire, he noted: (not until 1838 did anyone think to harvest and export it from Ceylon or Assam). When the Portuguese, as well as the Dutch had first brought tea from China and introduced it to English palates, it had been an expensive luxury available only to the well-to-do, who kept it in specially made and carefully locked small mahogany tea-caddies, with beautiful rosewood inlays, commensurate with the great value of their contents. But slowly tea had replaced small beer as the beverage of the poor; the demand swelled and became so insistent that the authorities decreed that six months' supply must always be to hand in Britain, to guard against accident on its long passage home, or political delays in Canton. These, since 1789, were revolutionary times; and without their regular cups of tea the British also might be led into revolt.

Its sale was quite as vital to the Chinese as was its purchase to Britain. The most hopeful fact in this unpromising situation was, William thought, the undoubted value to the Celestial Court of the money gained by the vast amount of tea exported to Britain. China lived of her own, but in great poverty; and the Imperial Court with its hundreds of concubines and endless officials and other luxuries was hugely expensive. For all his ceremony and grandeur, the Son of Heaven needed by now every penny he could lay his hands on. The Chinese population was estimated at 180,000,000, and her revenue at no more than £8,000,000 annually. The red-haired barbarians had by now become a necessary evil – and could not keep up the supply of silver to pay for their tea unless they were allowed to trade in wools, cottons, and mechanical devices. William believed that if the Chinese, who were natural traders,

who understood trade and conducted it honestly – would only allow
normal trade through all their ports, the Imperial revenue would double
in no time and both countries would be the happier. His great aim was
to effect this.

* * *

The days grew ever hotter and William John's pages ever stickier as
Andromache ploughed steadily southward. On 3 March she crossed the
Equator, and the usual ceremonies were endured at the hands of
Neptune by all the ship's company who had never passed this way before.
It was stiflingly hot, winds were light, the pitch bubbled along the deck
seams, the luckless sheep panted heavily in their pens, and even the
midshipmen became comparatively subdued. William laboured on at his
studies, reading the books and reports of the few Englishmen who had
actually voyaged to China or worked there.

Sir George Staunton, he felt, had only viewed China as an old servant
of the East India Company might be expected to do, announcing that
'the Chinese at length see cause to retract (their rules) in favour of the
British nation'; it was a little difficult to see where he got that impression.
Staunton insisted that Britain should hold on to her trade monopoly;
and as for kow-towing, he wrote, it was 'innocent and innoxious in itself';
he wrongly supposed that Macartney had kow-towed, and thought it a
pity 'to give up the ground so gained'. Sir George Staunton 'may be
deeply versed in Chinese Literature', William commented, 'but in politics he is a Driveller'.

Mr Lindsay, who had put pen to paper after a voyage in the *Amherst* to
China, seemed more of a realist. He thought that her system – 'a
despotic throne over a degraded people' operated 'to the great injury of
the revenue and of the moral condition of the inhabitants.' The Chinese
were industrious, William read, both in farming and in commerce, and
by no means lacking in cleverness, but held down by tyranny and falsehood; and the prohibition of all outside communication held their
minds enthralled. There were frequent rebellions; and Lindsay had
noted the Chinese people's desire for betterment and reform. If it were
felt advisable to co-operate with this desire, it was to be noted that in military matters the Chinese were hopelessly backward; a slight British
force, 'a few small ships of war and a handful of marines along the coast'
could enforce 'a change so much desired'.

* * *

Brooding over the forward policy and the stay-where-you-are policy,
William felt that the right line lay somewhere between the two. As he

read on, he was to move closer to Lindsay's. But now, rolling gently in the tropic swell, he thought that 'such a line of proceeding would be to interfere with the rights and rules and regulations of an independent nation; and it would be cruel and unjust to coerce a whole people'; even if 'it would be to oblige a barbarous government to conform to the rules of civilization, and to restore a system of things established before the conquest of the present (Manchu) dynasty'.

Undoubtedly, the opening of trade would benefit everybody and would be 'in accordance with the wishes of the people of China'. It would restore mutual trade as it had been under the Emperor Kang-Hi, 'only restricted at a modern date by the infatuation of Chien-Lung in the heat of his power and success against the rebellious Tartars'. Another on-the-spot expert, Sir James Urmston, agreed in the main with Lindsay, and 'distinguishes himself by his sound, spirited and manly view' of how best to deal with a nation he described as 'semi-barbarous'. Urmston was for removing our trade depot away from Canton to the offshore island of Chusan; which, thought William John, was obviously the right move; but how, unless by force, or the threat of force, induce the Chinese to allow this?

Was it too late, he wondered, 'the restricted system having the sanction of so many years'? Another point was that while the Company, in private hands, had had control, the whole business had been 'out of the rule of the public'; so that the government could complain but could not act to remedy affairs. He felt, perhaps wrongly, that the reigning dynasty of Manchu Emperors were to be considered as 'Intruders, inimical to the great body of the Chinese'. This idea was then prevalent both in India and England.

There were two possibilities, it seemed; 'either we could go on as we were, trading only through Canton and under endless petty and constantly changing restrictions, and submitting to frequent indignities and injustices, or we could lay all our grievances before the Emperor in Peking and insist upon redress. If none were forthcoming, we should seize the Bocca fortresses at the mouth of the Pearl River, and destroy the forts and batteries along the coast, *first* distributing pamphlets along the whole coast telling the people that this was no war against them or their property, and that all prisoners, officers excepted, would be disarmed and sent home'. Then it might be possible 'to restore the China dynasty on our own terms'. But this was to be no narrow monopolistic notion, 'whatever we ask for ourselves should be equally acceded to all other nations'.

Bending his mind to these available facts, William John suffered with the rest of her ship's company when *Andromache* came to a virtual halt in the baking South Atlantic. The north-east trade wind had died, and for 15 days, between 4 and 19 March, with the sun at its zenith beating down upon *Andromache*, they made negligible progress in the variable winds. 'Very trying for all on board' William commented; and the doldrums gave him an attack of bile, 'or it might have arisen from a good allowance of cool claret . . . I have resumed my old potations of sherry'. He loved claret, and had once been heard saying at his club that he went on with it although he knew it disagreed with him, because he would have no mutiny on board his craft, by which he meant his own healthy frame. Whether sherry in the tropics was any better is to be doubted, but the conclusions he was beginning to form show little evidence of bile, although he did consider that all the historical evidence showed that in all their dealings with China, the East India Company's Directors in London were much to blame – by superseding the local President and Committee members in Canton, they had given the Viceroy the green light to go ahead and impose harsh conditions. But he also felt that in the latest incident, the Committee had been 'too precipitate in stopping the trade, and in loudly resenting injuries which they had no power in redressing'.

'Two points are clear', he thought, feeling hotter than ever as *Andromache*'s idle sails flapped disconsolately overhead. 'From all the discussions and acts of violence which have occurred between the British and the Chinese from their first intercourse in 1634 [when Captain Weddell destroyed the Fort] to the present time – *viz*:

That every Act of Violence on our part has been productive of instant redress and other beneficial results, and:

That every concession made, and every threat used without having it in our power to carry the same into effect, has been followed by insult, oppression and spoliation.'

* * *

On the upper deck, William John would turn to the study he loved best. 'From the 6th to the 10th, a strong easterly current setting to the Eastward was observed by the Chronometers, and on the 11th the waters appeared to have been in a state of rest, or the edge of the two currents, for next day we had a strong current to the west which continued from latitude 2 N to that of 3 South. The easterly current must have been the eddy of Westerly current driven by the trade wind over to the Coast of South America past Cape St Roque.'

By 20 March 'the wind has come rather fresh from the NNW, a curious occurrence in an SE trade. The latter has served us so scurvily that any change will be for the better – short of dead foul.' A certain impatience with the unhastening Captain Chads was still felt. 'We scarce deserve a fair wind, as we neglect to take advantage of it when we get it. This is the first day the royals have been set since we crossed the Line. They all appear dreadfully afraid of *carrying sails.*'

This was the anniversary of his wedding day, and the thought of all the happy years he and Eliza had enjoyed together soothed William John. But how many of the stalwart Georgians who had been at the marriage had gone home since that day 18 years ago at Rankeillor in Fifeshire! – his own much loved parents, Eliza's grandfather, old Lord Hopetoun, masses of Hope aunts and uncles of either or both of them, his own dear aunt Henrietta Napier, his sister Sophia Napier, and latterly Eliza's father, Cochrane Johnstone. This was 'melancholy to think upon', but these had all gone 'in the ordinary course of nature', not to be wept as those dying out of time. And here they themselves still were, bound East, 'with the appointment of a high and important office, which under the blessing of God will I trust redound to the good of the World in general, as well as to my individual fame, and to the benefit of my private affairs . . . I acknowledge with gratitude that "I have had everything given to me richly to enjoy." ' (He was even recovering from gout in the big toe, induced, he supposed, from 'drinking claret after dinner every day for a fortnight, which I *know* I should not have done. It shall be my duty to forswear the French juice henceforth and for ever.')

At daylight on Monday 31 March, they saw the blessed land. 'The South East wind freshened up, and at 5 in the evening we passed the great fort of Santa Cruz commanding the entrance of the harbour of Rio de Janeiro. The view of the Sugar-loaf, Cacovado and the peaked mountains, rocks and hills, the variety of trees with their dark green foliage together offered a most delightful and refreshing scene after a tedious passage of 51 days across the Atlantic.'

Enthusiasm was a little damped by the discovery that it was nearly impossible to find anywhere to stay. Rio was booming, immigrants had rushed in, and prices during the eight years since William John had sailed in in command of the *Diamond* had soared correspondingly. 'Our first object was to find a Lodging, so as to get clear of the ship whilst caulking and refitting. Not a house to be hired for love or money.' One *was* to be had by a combination of the two: a kind young couple, the wife being the daughter of some friends William had made on earlier visits, offered to lend the Napiers their house for the needful week, themselves moving in with friends next door.

Rio de Janeiro harbour was full of ships, notably the *Spartiate*, Flagship of Admiral Sir Michael Seymour; there were also a French admiral and two American commodores. Better still was Captain Robertson, in command of His Majesty's 16-gun *Snake*, who had once been William's first lieutenant and had often stayed at Thirlestane – 'his presence was a source of great delight to us all.'

From their 'very agreeable cottage on Gloria Hill' the Napiers had enjoyed the sights – the Botanic Gardens, the City itself, 'the beautiful ride up by the acquaduct, round the Bosom of Cocovado and down by the Langara to the Gloria'; Maria and Georgiana cantering along beside their father, undiscouraged by the almost continuous rain that fell over Rio during their stay. There was a party given by Mr Young, 'an old Scots merchant', where the Napiers met 'a host of diplomats and other interesting people'; and also, to the joy of Maria and Georgiana, 'a pleasant dance on board the *Spartiate*', given by Sir Michael Seymour. (As one of Nelson's captains, Seymour had taken a French frigate *La Thétis* in a famous single-ship action in which they had banged on at each other through a long moonlit night, before *Thétis* had yielded to *Amethyst* and was towed in triumph into Plymouth Sound; and then repeated the performance with another French frigate as if to assure everybody that it had not been a fluke.) Sir Michael and his wife had 13 children, of whom the fifth son was serving as Flag Lieutenant on board *Spartiate*; this sensible arrangement not yet being frowned upon. The Admiral was to die this autumn, and be buried halfway up the Sugar-loaf mountain dominating this most beautiful of harbours. (His family still pay some odd annual sum like two pounds, thirteen shillings and seven pence to the Brazilian Government to keep the railings painted; and it would be interesting to know if this is ever actually done.)

More formal, though much less fun than the quadrilles, waltzes and Lancers on the upper deck of *Spartiate*, was 'a great Ball in honour of the young Emperor's accession', given, oddly, by the faction that had ousted his father, Dom Pedro. William John thought the new Emperor of Brazil 'a poor sickly tiny boy'. He was seven; and the ball had been opened by his two sisters, 'dancing the Gavotta with much spirit and precision'. In due course they were all presented to this sad little orphaned family, whom they thought yellow and unwell looking, though the little girls had 'some intelligence in their eyes', and all were warmly applauded by the large company. William John wondered whether the presence of this small boy Emperor was necessary to hold the balance 'between contending factions; but perhaps a stronger motive for peace and good order may be found in the fear of a rising of the negroes in case of the spread of republican principles since Dom Pedro's deportation. The affairs of the Republic are managed by three permanent Regents at a salary of about £2,000 per annum' he noted. Dancing had gone on into the small hours, and their father was pleased to see Maria and Georgiana 'enjoying themselves to their heart's content'.

As at Madeira, all too soon the dancing had to stop, and dawn of 12 April saw *Andromache* standing out of Rio harbour, all sails set for the 3316 miles to the Cape of Good Hope. This involved 24 days of mainly harsh weather. Strong winds and a contrary north west current impeded progress and exhausted poor Eliza from the constant knocking about. Even William, more used to being knocked about, was wearied by it, but continued doggedly to study and master the Foreign Office notes on China that had brought him to his wedding anniversary day conclusions.

* * *

Twenty years earlier, in 1814, he read, the Viceroy of Canton had forbidden the employment of Chinese in the British Factory and this had led to yet another brush with John Company, since the work depended heavily upon Chinese labour, and individual Chinese were happy enough to be well-employed and well-paid. In retaliation, the Company had decided that no British ships were to enter the River. The Chinese authorities then ordered HMS *Doris* out of the 'inner waters,' ie the trading harbour at Whampoa, and had seized the Company's 'linguist,' as the interpreters were always called. Here Sir George Staunton had acted diplomatically but firmly, as the Company's chief representative, and in long discussions with the Viceroy persuaded the latter to 'grant permission to the British to address the government in the Chinese language through the Hong merchants, to permit the employment of Chinese, and to allow the men-of-war to ride at the usual anchorage as before'. This triumph had been a little dashed by the Prince Regent of Portugal's decision not to allow the Committee to buy the house they occupied at Macao. The longed-for British trading foothold in China was as far off as ever.

In 1818, some 200 Chinese shops in the vicinity of the foreign Factories were shut down by the authorities, fearful as ever of contamination, not as to disease, but as to ideas. This made it much more difficult, though not impossible, for the foreigners to buy their necessaries. The Free Traders, rather than the Company's servants, had caused this closure: 'the difficulty of conducting the commerce under this system is thus inferred': the Company commented sniffily. The unfortunate Hong merchants, always the scapegoats, were made responsible by the authorities as security for the shopmen.

The Court of the Company after much discussion had voted a handsome sum towards Lord Amherst's expenses and presents two years earlier and had been correspondingly disappointed; though not pleased by the subsequent action taken by Captain Maxwell of the *Alceste*, the vessel which had borne Lord Amherst and his immense suite and their lavish presents to the mouth of the Peiho river in July of 1815. Maxwell, perhaps infuriated by the failure of the mission, which had now gone home in another ship, had, in his own words, 'supported the Honor of the British Flag for forcing his passage to Whampoa when fired upon by 100 guns'.

Lamenting Amherst's failure, the East India Company now expressed their belief that 'no dependence can be placed in the efficacy of any future embassy, though appointed and commissioned by the Crown'. Which was ominous for the mission of William John.

* * *

From this Foreign Office Memoir William drew the conclusion 'that it is evident throughout that the Select Committee have in many instances acted with great indiscretion, making threats and menaces when they had not the power of carrying them into execution, by which they always lost their point.

"The Chinese no doubt have acted from first to last on principles the most arbitrary and vexatious. It would lead one to suppose that the Viceroys and Hoppos were only appointed to make their fortunes at the expense of the Foreign Merchants, and then retire. It is equally clear that if the British are determined to trade on fair principles, they must *use* force, not menace it.' Very little force would be needed, and must be consistently applied. 'The trade is too valuable to them to be relinquished by China.'

Cushioned by this assumption, the trade had been conducted throughout the 1820s very much as before, both sides becoming steadily more aggressive, though only on an individual scale. In 1820, a murderous attack had been made by a party of armed Chinese at Macao on two officials of the Company, Davis and Smith, who had put a stop to a system of extortion by locals on the landing of passengers' baggage. Friction continued in a general manner, and when the American frigate *Congress* anchored at Whampoa, having been allowed supplies by the Portuguese, the Chinese would permit her no Comprador. In the same year the 5th Mate of the merchantman *London* accidentally shot a Chinese. The culprit was sought round the fleet of ships lying at anchor, but when a butcher in one of them opportunely committed suicide, the Chinese were entirely satisfied when *his* body was handed over. The Court of the Company expressed its indignation at this deception; which was odd, as it harmed no-one, and the Company, in its furtive opium operations, had for years been guilty of a far more lethal deception.

Two years later, a boat's crew from HMS *Topaze*, Captain Richardson, was attacked by a party of Chinese and several of her unarmed men were wounded before fire from their ship killed 12 of the attacking Chinese. Upon this, a party of Chinese officers had come to the Island of Lin Tin, where the opium was run, and demanded that the wounded crewmen should be set on shore and handed over. Captain Richardson refused. The Committee at Canton declined interference. The Viceroy insisted, issuing orders to prevent *Topaze* from sailing, and telling the merchants at Canton that they would be held responsible with their lives. After much heart-burning and the arousal of considerable enmity the Viceroy reopened the trade and absolved the Canton Committee of responsibility, but insisted that *one* British life be forfeit, no matter whose.

There was a continued to-ing and fro-ing and even a visit on board *Topaze* by an important mandarin, before Richardson was allowed to leave, on a promise that he would report the matter to his own King, and bring the culprit to justice at home. (But who exactly was the culprit? Surely not the gun's crew who had opened fire to save their mates?) The British Factory then reopened. The interdependence of port and merchants had been re-emphasized; and at least the decision was taken in England to allow no warships to visit China in peacetime, except on the Committee's urgent insistence.

To William it seemed that the Court of Directors of John Company in London had behaved scurvily to 'their servants in China' whose very lives were involved; the Directors conduct 'marked with a character of personal pecuniary interest and meanness which these gentlemen did not deserve, inspite of their occasional indiscretions'. The Directors seemed never quite capable of appreciating the qualities of the local merchants, their courage and persistence often at great risk of life and health, the Directors 'always remembering their dividends'. The dangers and uncertainties of the men on the spot seemed to mean nothing so long as the Directors received their tea and sold their opium, William felt. Yet, of course, the Chinese must be considered and placated. Their relationship with the British was like a cross-purpose marriage where no love was, but which meant too much financially to either beady-eyed party to allow them to separate.

* * *

Nothing is more surprising to one new to the subject than the almost entire lack in contemporary letters and speeches in the late 18th and early 19th century of any mention of the word opium. This life-destroying drug seemingly was not yet looked upon as a peril. Doctors prescribed it almost as freely as they might now prescribe aspirin; and in the form of Dr Godfrey's Cordial it was in general use to soothe teething babies. Opium could alleviate pain; it could tide people over their bouts of depression. The totally respectable William Wilberforce was not the only good man who took it daily for 45 years, – a bottle of laudanum, which was opium in wine, stood on many a respectable sideboard for use in times of tension or unbearable emotion. The addicted poet Coleridge did attempt to lessen his addiction; but there was nothing furtive about his drug-taking, nor was he particularly blamed.

The general British public knew nothing about China beyond the fact that it was a huge country very far away and producing silks, porcelain and tea; a drink to which, over the 18th century the British had become quite as hopelessly addicted as the Chinese were by now to opium. There was no real excuse for this ignorance, since the matter of trade in opium had been debated in the House of Commons in 1832; but a great number of matters debated in the House are quickly brushed under the carpet and forgotten. Idealists were too busy rescuing Africans from slavery to have time to rescue the Chinese from enslavement to a drug.

Men on the spot at Canton and Macao, especially the free-traders like Jardine, Matheson, Innes and others, cannot have been ignorant of the harm they were doing; but they were a six months' journey away from home, and unlikely to spread disquieting news of a trade that so greatly enriched them. The Court of Directors of the East India Company in London were far from ignorant of what was happening; but they were sufficiently humbugging to ordain that ships under their ownership might not transport opium to China, which of course in no way inhibited them from sending it in other ships. In his correspondence with William John, Lord Grey never mentions opium, and Palmerston does so only obliquely. A certain amount of humbug is essential equipment for the successful politician; but the naval officers of the time were under no such obligation to deceive, and they barely mention it either. William John mentions it in a list of other goods imported into China, such as woollens, Sheffield steel, and Lancashire piece goods. Charles Brickdale, a 15 year old midshipman, who thought that fighting one's way up from the sea to Canton was enormous fun, had seemingly no thought of opium anywhere in his consciousness; and Tom Bourchier, a naval captain, who fought in an actual Opium War, thought the whole thing extremely stupid, not because of opium, but because he was against dragooning people into trading by military action. These were honest men, and no humbugs. Yet as far as the opium trade was concerned, they seem unvisited by even a hint of guilt.

If people in England thought about the opium trade at all, which very few did, they felt no more guilt than the Scots felt about the export of whisky, which in immoderation can cause addiction, ruin, and ultimate death quite as effectively as opium. Britons in general who gave the matter a thought would have considered that they were exporting from India the 19th century equivalent of Vallium. Ten thousand chests a year is an awful lot of Vallium? Well, they might have answered, there are an awful lot of Chinese suffering an awful lot of pains.

People live within the ethic of their day, and not within the sad wisdom of 150 years on. The wickedness or otherwise of the large scale import of opium into China was the last consideration entering the mind of William John, waiting vainly for the trade wind in his stuffy small cabin on board *Andromache*, and filling his notebooks with all that could bear on his coming job.

Although the Chinese had been growing and eating opium on a minor scale since the 700s, the habit of smoking it on a considerable scale did not begin till the 17th century. This was said to have spread from America, via a pipe-smoking merchantman. In the early 18th century the Portuguese had found that they could import opium from India and sell it at a profit; the smoking habit spread so rapidly that by 1729 the Emperor Yung Chen, reigning from 1723–35, had prohibited both the sale and the smoking of opium.

In 1773, the British had chipped into this lucrative trade, as did the Dutch and others; but the British were in the strongest position as they had the monopoly of the powerful strain grown in the hot plains of Bengal, which was far preferred by the Chinese to their indigenous poppy. Others, including the Americans, sold Indian and Turkish opium along the China coasts. In 1796, another Emperor, Chia Ching, again forbade the cultivation or importation of opium, so bad was its effect on his subjects. But by now the trade had gained an unstoppable momentum of its own; far too many Chinese were making a great deal of money from it, more even than the British traders who dealt in it or the sea-captains who brought it.

Forbidding their own ships to sail with such a cargo, the East India Company in Calcutta farmed out their opium to 'country traders,' who sold it to Chinese sailors and fishermen and even to local officials all along the Chinese coast. The gold and silver thus acquired was passed to the company's employees at Canton, and used by them for the purchase of tea. In 1729, only 200 chests of opium per annum had been imported into China. By 1830 this had risen to 10,000 chests. In the year 1838, four years after *Andromache*'s voyage, the number had risen to a staggering total of 40,000 chests.

These are the figures of modern research; how much of all this

William John knew is uncertain, probably very little; though he had
been efficiently briefed by the Foreign Office with the sorry record of
the West's dealings with China down the centuries.

* * *

In 1826, the Viceroy at Canton was still out for blood from HMS *Topaze*,
although at a court martial at home in England, her commanding officer had been 'honourably acquitted'. The report of the Directors on this
affair had been cynical in the extreme – 'silence on the part of the
Chinese is a proof that energetic measures are sufficient to hold them in
subservience'.

Hot and cold had continued to blow from both sides, William noted,
as *Andromache* rose and fell in her staggering passage through heavy
gales. Surely a steady breeze of goodwill, with common sense illuminating both sides, was the thing needed? Although, in 1826, a Mr Daniell
and his friends had been beaten up by Chinese assailants in the streets of
Macao, these had been punished; and in the following year the Viceroy
had specifically exempted the British (which at this time included the
Irish as well as Scots and Welsh) when prohibiting all other Foreigners
from addressing the authorities in the Chinese language. Their 'correctness' had gained them this privilege, and the British chief of
Committee was also singled out for his 'moral fitness' by the Viceroy
when deprecating other foreigners who remained in Canton beyond
the permitted season. His countrymen also were allowed the privilege of
remaining, such of them that is, who 'preserved a due regard for themselves'. Were the red-haired barbarians becoming slowly civilized under
Mandarin influence?

This rosy picture became a little blurred when Captain Walker of the
merchantman *Macqueen* 'received a severe contusion from two low
Chinamen in the streets of Canton'; what had he been doing there anyway? The Committee then complained of the presence of Chinese
drinking houses too near the Factories, leading the enforced bachelor-
dom of the foreigners to relieve itself in heavy drinking. But both these
matters were quickly put right by the Chinese authorities, who disliked
above all 'the disturbance of tranquillity' by drunkenness and affrays. All
the same, at Lin-Tin, the row over the *Topaze* affair was still rumbling on
as the 1820s ended; and there were loud murmurs from the foreigners
over the Chinese imposition of further duties and over the poor state of
trade, which in the end caused them to order their ships to remain outside the Pearl River until these commercial rules were altered.

In-fighting had now really begun. The President of the Canton
Committee and the powerful Mr Plowden recorded dissent: trade should

be renewed. Other members were so indignant that they proposed that all British ships be sent to Manila: 'all intercourse to stop until they had gained their point'. Things went from bad to worse as 1830 ended. The President and Mr Plowden were so fiercely opposed to this interdict that their protest took the form of immediately shipping themselves home; shortly before which the Viceroy had published a conciliatory edict, whereupon the Committee opened the trade. Sweetness and light seemed once more the order of the day; the trade stopped opening and shutting like an oyster. Howqua, chief among the Hong Merchants, even invited a Mrs Baynes to accompany her husband to Canton, and a portrait of George IV as Prince Regent arrived from England and was proudly hung in the great dining room of the British Factory at Canton, as if the British were really there to stay and feared no repetition of Chinese insult.

At home, the Court of Directors had thrown a spanner in the works at this point by recalling the recalcitrant Messrs. Baynes, Millett and Bannerman and replacing them by Messrs. Marjoribanks, Davis and Daniell, as a continued protest against local goings-on. The Chinese authorities at Canton were invariably swift to take advantage of foreign dissensions; and, read William, the Viceroy had next issued an insulting edict, commenting most unfavourably upon foreigners in general and forbidding their females to live at Canton. No memsahibs here, for short or long stays. Members of the Committee, seeking to obtain rights of residence at Macao, had then been slammed down by the Portuguese. It was certainly trade under difficulties.

* * *

Things seemed to reach a pitch of tension in 1831, which culminated in a right royal row. A further and still more disparaging edict of the Viceroy condemned the defiant arrival of some of the Committee's ladies in Canton, and condemned as strongly the arrival of a few seamen and some guns to protect the Factory; sailors, guns and ladies were all ordered back to Macao, for which haven they departed with considerable loss of face. Meanwhile, at home, there were increasingly powerful protests from Manchester and Edinburgh over the Company's official monopoly of the trade. The free traders became ever more bold, and were, of course, outside the control of the Company's Committee. The Viceroy issued an edict that if the Company were dissolved 'It is incumbent to appoint a Chief for the general management of commercial dealings, by which affairs may be prevented from going to confusion'. This very reasonable request had produced William John, as that Chief.

The Company had hardly stopped being pleased to report a falling off in French and Spanish trade this year (both were involved in revolutions just then) before they became extremely disconcerted when the Portuguese usurper, Dom Miguele, forbad all foreigners to live at Macao. 'Black Charlie's naval action had put paid to him soon afterwards; but the Canton Committee of the Company were at Macao when they heard that the Hoppo had entered the British Factory with an armed following, had carried off their linguist in chains, and ordered the destruction of British property. The *Louisa* cutter was briskly dispatched from Macao with Smith and Daniell to find out what went on.

On their arrival, Howqua, one of the Hong merchants, greeted them with the news that the Fu Yuen had 'proceeded with violence into the Factory, and removed the dust-sheet from off the King's portrait and sat down with his back to it (perhaps displaying more artistic sense than we know) and ordered the new Quay where the Factories' goods were unloaded (and which had taken three years to build,) to be at once destroyed'. Howqua believed that all had been done upon direct orders from Peking. Daniell and Smith left an address of protest to be given the Viceroy and went back to Macao; not knowing quite what else to do. On 20 May, they were followed down river by a proclamation from the Hong Merchants, containing eight new clauses:-

1. Foreigners were not to remain in Canton over the winter, but to go home to England, or to Macao.
2. Foreigners were not to lend money to the Hong Merchants.
3. Fewer Chinese were to be employed by merchants.
4. Military searches were to be conducted upon all vessels arriving.
5. Foreigners were forbidden to introduce foreign females or to ride in Sedan chairs.
6. Custom House officers were to prevent foreigners from bringing shot-guns or muskets to Canton.
7. Foreigners wishing to come and go between Canton and Macao must request a permit and not come and go as they pleased.
8. Foreigners were to present all petitions through the Hong merchants; if they refuse they may go, not more than two or three at a time, to present them to the Officer of the Guard.

The Committee reacted with fury; issuing a proclamation in their turn that all trade was to cease, from 1 August. They also addressed a *cri de coeur* to the Governor of Bengal, giving up the keys of the Factory and sending a petition to the local magistrate who had refused to present them to the Viceroy. The keys were then returned by Howqua, who maintained that the keys might only be presented through the Hong merchants.

Lindsay, now in charge at Canton, had declined to accept the returned keys, and was heartily backed in this by the Free Traders. But at length these hopeful adventurers discovered that the hated Eight Regulations had been made by the Emperor himself, and not by the authorities at Canton, upon whom they could bring pressure to bear by the well-tried expedient of stopping the trade. Accordingly they climbed down; and on 1 August recalled their proclamation as to the stopping of trade.

The Viceroy did not respond peaceably. He refused to accept a protest about the destruction of the Factories' landing quay – 'the landing place belonged to the Emperor and was destroyed by his orders'. The strongly worded protest directed to him by the Free Traders, led by Jardine and Innes, was rejected by the Viceroy in terms mainly directed towards these two men, 'who being only private merchants are in no wise comparable to the Company . . . If the Barbarian Merchants will not obey orders, the Viceroy will go in person and open a thundering fire'.

Onto this unpromising scene the *Andromache* bore William John Napier steadily south-eastward through the South Atlantic gales.

* * *

In their dealings with China to date, the red-haired Barbarians from Britain had tried grandeur, threat, a Marine Band, thunders from her native oak on the Bogue Forts, a fortune's worth of presents, ineffective menace, good manners, a letter from George III, a letter from the future George IV, a troop of British Cavalry in full fig, Lord Macartney in his cocked hat and feathers, Lord Amherst without his, a posse of footmen in green velvet, a succession of ferociously drunken seamen, promising trade offers, and regular reproaches from the East India Company. All had expended themselves in vain on the great wall of China's indifference. It seemed unlikely that William John, Lord Napier, armed only with determination and goodwill could now succeed.

A slight easing in the wind, a decrease in the violence of the frigate's movements, took William to stretch his legs on the upper deck. Ahead, shadowy but real, was the coast of Africa, a more than halfway house on the way to China.

10

At the Cape and
Crossing the Indian Ocean

At noon on 6 May, three months out from Plymouth Sound, *Andromache* cast anchor in Simon's Bay. Saluting guns boomed out, puffs of white smoke scattered over calm sparkling blue water, and in no time the China-bound party were surrounded by old friends; William John as usual having an ex-shipmate in every port. Young Warren, who had been one of the midshipmen in the *Diamond,* was on board almost as the frigate's anchor splashed into the bright water; he took the Napiers ashore to stay with his parents at Admiralty House, Simonstown. Admiral Warren himself soon appeared, 'the fat old gentleman himself receiving us most kindly and cordially on the jettee' (sic). Even William was glad to step ashore.

'During the last week of our voyage we had experienced some strong gales, with heavy rolling seas, which had rather affected the nerves and health of Lady N.', her husband reported, probably understatedly. Poor Eliza! He had even been fatigued himself – 'deprived of some hours of nocturnal repose'. He and his daughters had stared out with delight as *Andromache* passed the famed Table Mountain and rounded the still more famous Cape of Good Hope, into the peace of what was soon to be called False Bay. 'Nothing could be more agreeable', thought William, 'than to run in a few hours from a tempestuous ocean into a quiet sea, and hence to the bosom of a kind-hearted family who were rejoiced to see us.'

In an hour or two more, William was enjoying a dinner party of old friends and old shipmates from the *Isis* – George Airey, once a midshipman in the *Diamond* among others. Eliza, recovered, was next paying official calls in Mrs Warren's carriage. On the 8th, they set out to view some of the countryside, starting in 'a light coach and four' for Cape Town, admiring Constantia as they made a detour to pass through it, with its 'variety of arborescent heaths and shrubs, particularly the Protea and Sugar Plant in full flower', the enclosures bounded by oak hedges in their autumn colour, the stone pines, 'the pale green silver tree' and the yellow-leaved vineyards in every 'warm and rich defile'. Nobody could have loved the sea more heartily than William John, and none more keenly enjoyed the blessings of the land.

It was beautiful country, and admirable also were 'the numerous little cottages beautifully thatched and white-washed', and the 'more lordly mansions' of the landowners, rising from amongst their green trees, and commanding 'delightful prospects'. Cape Town itself was in more arid surroundings, and William was unimpressed by its 'mouldering barriers', through which their party entered 'under a salute from the Castle or rather mud fort . . . A Guard of Honor had been in attendance but was tired of waiting', and had gone away. But in Mr Drury's Lodging in Plain Street soldiers were gathered to meet them – Colonel Wade, Brigade-Major Cloete, and Captain Beresford, 'and a Highland sentry posted at the door. All these Honours I got quit of as soon as possible', and once they had gone with Colonel Wade to pay their respects to Sir Benjamin and Lady d'Urban (presently to christen the port of Durban), they set out to view the town, which they found 'pleasantly cleanly' with 'a well conditioned people and a thriving population.' Amongst the wide variety of colours and countenances to be seen on every street, they noticed that most of the work was done by Malays, especially everything to do with horses and carriages. Unlike Simonstown, with its Dutch air, Cape Town seemed to William to wear more of the aspect of a Moorish town or a Spanish or Portuguese one. The first arrivals in the Cape, the Portuguese, had clearly laid their stamp on the place, with its low, flat-roofed houses, although the many-paned windows of some had a look of Holland.

Next day, having carried out more social duties and met William's kinsman, John Napier of Tintinhull, who had arrived to settle amongst the relatives of his first wife – a Dutchwoman, the Napiers were free to go further afield, rejoicing at the opportunity.

Then followed a most happy interlude. They hired a spring waggon with canvas roof and sides, fitted with cross benches and drawn by six horses. In front sat two Malays, one driving and the other directing, rather like a helmsman and a quarter-master, thought William; the director 'flourishing with both hands a whip of remarkable length, like a salmon rod and line, so as to reach the heads of the foremost horses', Mr Johnstone and young Hunter rode with them, and Dr Anderson and William John alternated on a third horse. Up behind on the back bench was the steward, Henri Bonjon, 'with a basket of Provender in case of need'. Full of holiday spirit, they made for Stellenbosch along a rough track 'across the sand isthmus to the Eastward, at the rate of five miles per hour and driven with very great care and circumspection so as to avoid as much as possible the numerous holes and deep ruts which abound'.

Stellenbosch proved immensely pleasing, with its rich surrounding vineyards in flat fields, with vine leaves turning yellow and the vines planted and dressed 'in the manner of those in Claret Country'. There they spent a most enjoyable evening and had an excellent dinner with superb local wines. After a comfortable night's lodging they set out for Paarl, the way reminding the Napiers very happily of Ettrick. But the redeeming feature of wild Scotland was wanting – 'the bright sparkling streams which give so great an interest to our glens.' Glad enough they would have been, both man and beast, for a burn or two 'under the glow of an African sun'. Passing on through the Waggon Maker's Valley, with eight horses to the waggon and two fresh Malay drivers, they finally wended their way back to Cape Town – William carrying in his pocket a number of acorns gathered from a huge oak near Paarl, which, he announced hopefully, 'I propose to plant at Macao or Canton'.

'Cape Town', wrote William John, 'is well supplied with all the necessities and many of the luxuries of life, at a moderate price, notwithstanding which I do not remember more exorbitant demands or more bare-faced attempts at imposition than such as are practised upon Passengers by the unprincipled settlers with whom one comes into contact in ordinary affairs.' It was a booming place, its exports of produce had in the first three months of the year 1834 brought in £43,050, 'independent of that from the new Colony at Algoa Bay'; here seven ships direct from England had arrived this year, where not one had come the year before. Invalids from India coming to the Cape to recuperate brought in roughly another £50,000 a year, 'and on their return to their Stations clear the market of young Ladies, many of whom are said to be extremely pretty'.(These exports were, however, non-profit making.)

They paid off the exorbitant Mr Drury, said farewell to the d'Urbans, and bowled out of Cape Town to the sound of a salute from the mud-fort Castle, driving by Wineburg to the hospitable Admiral's family at Simonstown. There they paused for another day, but 'on Monday forenoon the 19th of May, the wind veering round to the NW, we repaired on board, bidding adieu to our kind friends with mutual regrets, we weighed and made sail from Simon's Bay, shaping a course for the Island of St Paul's or Amsterdam, distant 2865 miles'.

* * *

Now, at long last, the bows of the *Andromache* were actually pointed towards China. She sailed steadily to the North of East, sounding at intervals for three days over what was alleged to be the Dutch Bank, 'but got no bottom – the Shoal is either much misplaced or has no existence whatever'. On 5 June, 'intending to make St Paul's Island we ran past it in the night, on account of its being laid down ½ a degree too far to the Eastd. in the Admiralty Chart'. Upon what could one rely? Ten days later, 'we ran over the supposed position of the Fryall Rocks, evidently misplaced on the Admiralty Chart if they have any existence at all', William commented testily. He could be seriously irritated by short-comings and sloppiness over navigation and charts: mens' lives were involved, and good ships as well. It was now very hot. At noon on the pre-vious day they had passed the Tropic of Capricorn, and could be said to be making good progress.

Despite the tropics, William's concentration upon the problems of his coming job did not slacken. Though no intellectual genius, he was also no fool, and very well aware that he had been given conflicting instruc-tions virtually impossible of fulfilment. The King had told him to wear his uniform as a naval officer and act as his representative, and had sug-gested that he might be obliged to use his naval skills. Lord Grey, Prime Minister, had advised a continuous diet of humble pie; harmony and the *status quo* were to be preserved at all costs. Grey cared quite as devoutly about the Tea Trade as any shawled old lady sipping a fireside cup in Aberdeen or Bootle. The traders in China were there on sufferance and must act accordingly; although the *status quo* rarely remained static for more than a month or two at a time.

There had been contradictions in Palmerston's orders to William John. He was enjoined to be moderate and cautious, not to ask for naval help or to menace the Chinese unless there was actual danger, and to respect the laws and usages of Imperial China. On the other hand, he was to go to Canton and protect the merchants, a procedure directly opposed to the laws and usages of China, who liked to use their own methods of protection. No letter asking permission had been sent by the British Government to the Emperor, and Napier was debarred by Palmerston from addressing him directly. He was simply told to go to Canton and start work forthwith, a procedure that would immediately alarm and dismay the Chinese authorities and set them to work at get-ting rid of him by all means, diplomacy being always preferable to force.

The fact that the centuries of dealing between China and the West seemed to prove conclusively that no change could be effected without at least a substantiated threat of force had in no way inhibited the gov-ernment from forbidding William John to use or threaten any. He was 'to convince the Chinese authorities of the sincere desire of the King to cultivate the most friendly relations with the Emperor of China'; which was fair enough, had it been compatible with the order to proceed inland to Canton and treat with its Viceroy on equal terms, thus taking up a position quite unwarranted by Chinese law and custom.

Palmerston had touched but lightly upon the subject of opium smuggling. This, despite Imperial edicts, proceeded with the full knowledge and general consent of the local Chinese authorities, all of whom profited handsomely thereby. *After* they had unloaded their terrible wares, the Chinese war junks would follow the Indiamen down the Bay of Canton, firing briskly and well out of range, and stopping abruptly if the wind dropped and slowed down the Indiamen, who were their supposed targets. This process enabled them to report to Peking that they had driven the red-haired barbarians away from the Celestial coasts in all the ignominy of flight.

'It is not desirable', Palmerston instructed William John, in reference to the coastal traders, 'that you should encourage such adventures, but you must never lose sight of the fact that you have no authority to interfere with or prevent them.' Turn a blind eye, in other words. The one thing on which all at home seemed agreed was that William John was the answer to the perennial problem of what shall we do with the drunken sailor.

Palmerston's final order to William suggested that he should organize a survey of the Chinese coastline for possible safe harbours. Who knew when the Royal Navy's warships might need them? [In the event, it was William John who suggested Hong Kong.]

The King wanted a firm and becoming line taken with the Chinese, the Prime Minister wanted peace at any price, and the Foreign Secretary wished to postpone the firm line until he was rather less busy in Europe. The cocks in that perpetual cockpit, the Eastern Mediterranean, were currently sharpening their spurs.

In London, the job offered William John sounded wonderfully impressive – Plenipotentiary from the King of Great Britain to the Emperor of China; and in London, great emphasis was laid on the fact that he must deal directly with his opposite number at Canton, Viceroy Loo. In his own country, William John seemed just the right sort, a naval post captain who could deal with recalcitrant traders and seamen, and a man of impressive status and tradition, a member of King William's Household, a Scots lord with doughty forbears stretching back into Celtic times, when they had ruled their fief in Scotland with powers of life and death, rather as had the little kings in ancient Greece. None of this would cut any ice in China; Plenipotentiary Napier had, in fact, no power at all.

To William John, the job appealed because, for the first time in his career of service it was one where he could take his family, where he could be 'of use to his Country', (the modest aim of all patriotic Britons of his era,) and where he could live in a free house and save up to endow his little girls, his salary of £6,000 a year being at that time a very considerable amount of money. In five years he hoped to have done enough and saved enough for them all to go home to Ettrick and family and live happily ever after. He meant to go warily, and tactfully, but his confidence was great. People were human beings everywhere, and he had managed to get on well everywhere with them. The Chinese could surely not be so very different?

But they were. Their whole vast empire was necessarily held together by a rigid system, a system permitting no innovation and holding all foreigners in contempt. Bribery, corruption and squeeze prevailed throughout, not surprisingly: the astonishing thing was that so huge an empire held together at all. The Heavenly Realm was isolated from the world and happy to be so. It looked inward, and loved what it saw. The notion of dealing with other countries on equal terms had not yet dawned. How should it? The Celestial Empire had no equals.

As *Andromache* sailed steadily forward through the tropic seas towards the East Indies it was borne in upon William John that he had been sent on a fool's errand. If he had ever heard of the 'fall guy', he was too secure in his belief in the sincerity and integrity of his home government to see himself cast for such a role. He meant to see that the customary rights of the merchants were 'placed on a regular footing, and secured to them by the medium of a Commercial Treaty. It is quite clear to me', he realistically admitted, 'that as long as I have not the means of carrying a threat into execution, I have no other alternative than to submit quietly to every indignity (always under protest).' But he believed that before very long the rising tide of feeling at home, as well as the extreme illogicality of the Chinese position, wanting trade and yet doing everything to hinder it, 'will fill up the measure of their folly and bring down upon them the chastisement of Great Britain, when every point may be gained with the greatest ease, and secured for all time to come'.

A threat, backed up by a few ships and men, would do the trick, he thought, without any actual use of force; and the sooner the better, before any more ill-feeling built up and compelled the use of actual shot and shell. If, in the end, the Chinese Empire would have to be dragged kicking and screaming into the great world, he hoped for the chance to make wiser counsels prevail, and so by-pass the kicks and screams. And it was to be no exclusive British world. 'We should demand no greater privileges for ourselves than for all other nations. Our commercial superiority', William John announced firmly and in the full swing of Industrial Revolutionary confidence, 'is more than sufficient to give us complete command of the market'.

Meanwhile 'it must be my first object to adopt every wise precaution-
ary measure either now or heretofore in use, and to endeavour with
firmness and dignity to regain any privileges which have been lost during
the late quarrels and disturbances, to make every refusal a subject of
complaint to our government until they shall be pleased to avail themselves of the power which has been placed in their hands to humble
these semi-barbarous people and to introduce a new system of operations more consistent with the age we live in and the general progress of
civilization.'

In William John's mind the forward policy had won, however carefully
it was to be conducted. Nor was this all; and here William John, with the
strong 19th century itch felt by most of his countrymen to replace
tyranny with good government, in countries other than their own, trod
upon perilous ground.

'Altho' the military force of China is said to be immense, yet from
their known cowardice, total ignorance of the art of war, even of the use
of the muskett, armed with matchlocks and even with Bows and Arrows,
it is no stretch of probability to say that a very few thousand men would
be sufficient not only to reduce the Chinese government to equitable
terms, but to expel the present Dynasty and to drive them and their
Tartar Adherents, who eat up the country, forever beyond the Wall, and
thus restore the Ming Chinese line of Kings, whose descendants still
foment rebellion and disturbances in the Provinces.' Many Chinese
would surely be delighted to shrug off the Manchu dynasty and their
ferocious Tartar soldiery?

'With such a spirit in the Country and with such an object on our
part, we should experience little difficulty, and our exertions would be
crowned with a Treaty of our own dictation.'

Accurately predicting the extent of Chinese military resistance and
totally unaware of the inner strength of their ancient Empire, William
John laid down his pen and went for a breather on the upper deck.

* * *

In these views of the British mission and the benefits to other nations it
would certainly bring, William John was very far from being out on his
own. That the world would, and most certainly should, convert to
Christianity with the spread of civilization (which was felt to be synony-
mous with Europeanisation) was an axiom of adventurers and
empire-builders for centuries, from the patient Jesuits and the harsh
Spanish conquistadors, from the genuinely devout like William John to
the opium runners such as Jardine or Matheson or Innes. The latter's
equation would have run, Christianity = civilization = TRADE, while

William John's would have run, trade = civilization = CHRISTIANITY; no-one doubted the rightness of the outcome. James Innes was typical, with his well known journal entry during an opium selling trip up the China coast – 'Employed delivering briskly, no time for reading Bible'.

It was true that the fearless Jesuits had long ago penetrated to the court of the Chinese Emperor, but their order was known to have been suppressed and their priests recalled in the 18th century; and in the view of non-Jesuits their principal achievement had been teaching the Chinese how to cast cannon and to despise all other Christians. China was still seen as an immense field for Christian enterprise, for spreading the Gospel. Such a people, so clever, so civilized after their fashion, so wonderfully and feelingly artistic, must be ripe for spiritual development, for gathering into the fold.

It is impossible to understand the characters of earlier epochs without realizing how deeply all were still imbued with the faith of their fathers. There were a very few intellectual exceptions; in the main, everybody believed, everybody prayed, went to church on Sundays and felt themselves candidates for eternal life. God, although often forgotten, was as real to them as the air they breathed. This faith was so sure that they felt no need to discover, let alone admire, or pursue, the fundamentals of religion amongst Arabs, Indians or Chinese: all that they saw was the vast scale of human misery and degradation endured by the followers of such faiths – and the callousness, the disregard of suffering, the huge mortality amongst the children, the brutal treatment of the women, that they practised. For them it stuck out a mile that Christianity, with all its faults, with its frequent humbugs and its Neapolitan slums, was incomparably the best.

Many years passed before the missionary gleam faded from all those blue predatory eyes. In time they were to divert their idealistic side into making life less nasty, brutish and short for the devotees of Islam, Buddha, the Hindu deities, and Confucius, without seeking to unsettle their native faiths. In time, but not in 1834.

* * *

Like most 19th century Westerners, William John did not realize that the Chinese, despite absolute and incalculable Emperors and a corrupt bureaucracy, had a very noble and powerful faith of their own – their Confucianism. In spite of all the ramifications of humbug that had grown up around it over the centuries, in theory and not infrequently in practice, the precepts of Confucius held good. Learned men in China were still able to petition the Emperor and to advance their views. The fearfully elaborate ceremony that was involved in every official contact and which hampered and delayed even the simplest transaction, was descended from the ancient rules of good manners, politeness and patience in one's dealings, however much subterfuge went on underneath. In theory the poor were still to be protected, the starving fed, and the suppliant stranger to be treated with compassion; and sometimes they still were.

Chinese custom and law had evolved into some terrible practices that deeply shocked Europeans and made them feel that the people of China were still all but barbaric. They tortured, they had slaves; and if anyone rescued a luckless fellow from drowning and he subsequently died from his submersion, the rescuer was held responsible for his death, and was lucky to get off with a huge fine and bribes all round. Consequently, when people fell into the Pearl River, as they frequently did, unless they were close relations, no-one raised a finger to save them, nor would as much as throw a piece of wood to them. Ignorance of Chinese law made this seem to Western eyes more brutally callous than it really was. When told the story of the Good Samaritan by missionaries, the Chinese roared with laughter at what they imagined to be a comic tale about a simpleton. The folly of risking one's life to help a stranger and an alien! They were completely at one with the priest and the Levite who had so sensibly passed by on the other side.

When it came to the crunch, the Confucian maxims were not mere words but were based on convictions deeply felt by so many men that they carried great weight. Centuries of solidarity had taught the Chinese that they were right and the rest of the world was wrong, ignorant, and barbarian. This was an extremely potent counterbalance to the faith which the Westerners, above and beyond their desire for trade and money, carried with them through appalling hardships and dangers; strongly desiring to bring to the unconverted world the Christian ethic and all that it involved in the way of freedom for the individual, the rule of law, equal justice, mercy and friendship. All this was somewhat hampered by the Chinese imposition of the death penalty on any among them who even taught the foreigner a Chinese language.

* * *

The Emperor in Peking, Tao-Kwang, was not without information of the great world beyond his frontiers and had become increasingly suspicious of the British – what were they up to in India? They had started with innocent trading posts at Bombay, Madras and Calcutta, and look at them now! Masters of Bengal, most of the Ganges valley, and even of places west. The great Nizam of Hyderabad was still independent, as were the princes of Mysore, Oudh, Gwalior, Sind, and the Punjab; but for how much longer? The British seemed a particularly pushy bunch; great caution was to be observed in dealings with them. The Emperor was aware of his own lack of money and of his fragile hold over his vast domain. Rigid exclusion was his best hope.

In the Bay of Canton, local suspicion was equally strong. In fact, William John's mission was doomed from the start. To add to the basic incompatibility of British and Chinese ideas, and the unlikelihood of their being allowed to treat together as equals, the British Government had made another fatal mistake. With its usual passion for misplaced economy, it had allowed the costs of the mission to be borne in the main by the East India Company whose hated monopoly it had recently abolished, and William John's assistants were to be ex-officials of the Company. This sounded sensible enough, for who else knew the local form or could speak Cantonese? But these facts were instantly known all up and down the Pearl River and along the coast; and as British merchants at Macao pointed out to the Viceroy at Canton and every mandarin and the Hong merchants, the mission seemed just the same old John Company in new form.

'Superintendent of Trade' was the official for whom the Canton Viceroy had asked the British Government, someone who would control the Free Traders and see that they kept to the rules. He hoped for some kind of glorified Taipan, involved personally in trading and making money and therefore liable to pressure and to fear of losing his profits and his job. What they got was William John, no merchant, and as incapable of taking bribes as he was of jumping off the white cliffs of Dover.

'In reporting my arrival to the Viceroy', wrote William John, 'I must explain to him fully the object of my appointment and the extent of my powers, dwelling particularly on his Edict of 1831, stating "the propriety of the appointment of a Chief for the management of affairs in case of the dissolution of the Company." ' But at Canton, Viceroy Loo would be wonderfully unimpressed: 'The Celestial Empire appoints officers, civil ones to rule the people, military ones to intimidate the wicked' he was to announce to the Hong merchants; 'the petty affairs of commerce are to be directed by the merchants themselves; the officers have nothing to hear on the subject'. No Victorian *grande dame* could have turned up her nose more disdainfully at persons connected with Trade, than did Viceroy Loo. William John, while purporting to be an officer and a gentleman, was dirtying his hands in this way; he was therefore irregular and a nobody. The Viceroy could not have been more angularly at cross purposes with William John and his honest determination to put the river trading on a basis more satisfactory in the long run to both sides.

In actual fact Viceroy Loo's statement was a typical piece of what the British regarded as humbug. Viceroys of Canton frequently *had* dealt directly with the merchants who sailed their goods up river to land them on the quay at Canton. That William John should deal indirectly, through the Hong merchants, as Loo was to insist, was to subject his message to endless obstructions and misinterpretations connected with official jealousies or alarms, before being passed on to the mandarins, and to more of the same at the hands of the mandarins before being passed on to the Viceroy, who would in his turn pass it on to the Emperor in a form calculated to please that potentate and increase his own prestige, with small regard to its original contents.

* * *

Happily for him, still unaware of these frustrating facts, William John continued to take sights every noonday and have fun with his chronometer. By 18 June *Andromache* was less than a month from her destination; she passed Christmas Island, and next day rounded Palembang Point at the easterly end of Sumatra, to anchor in Mew Bay. Here was a scenery of high mountains and great trees; the breeze blowing seaward from so much greenery was infinitely refreshing after the hot weeks at sea. They landed to pick up water from the waterfall cascading onto the beach and managed to ship it only with great difficulty 'on account of the swell and lumps of coral. Some of the officers went in search of Game and others of Turtle, equally unsuccessful, being quite impossible to penetrate the dense primeval forests'.

On the 2nd, they were at anchor in Anjeer Roads, across the Straits in Java, where the Dutch had built 'a neat fort commanding the shipping, and with a wet ditch to the land, sufficient to hold the natives in check'. All was done with Dutch thoroughness. *Andromache*'s officers landed to pay their respects to the Dutch Governor, who invited a party to dinner. Here William John and his family had 'the great pleasure of hearing a band of native musicians performing on instruments of percussion'.

The village of Anjeer was 'very prettily situated and contains upwards of 2,000 inhabitants, poor-looking but industrious people gaining their livelihood either by cultivation of small patches of land or transporting the produce by Boat to Batavia. The scenery around the Bay is rich and beautiful – the Country being partially cleared and improved relieves the monotony of an endless Forest'. He was pleased to discover, in a neatly cultivated garden belonging to the Commandant of the Dutch garrison 'a Monument or Obelisk to the memory of my relative Colonel Charles Cathcart who died on his way to Canton, with a very flattering inscription which I copied. It is pleasant to see that since the year 1788 no damage has been done to the Monument; on the contrary, it is kept up rather as an ornament to the Garden'.

The Dutch had, willy-nilly, joined with Napoleon in that long war which had dominated William's boyhood and youth; and this had afforded the British an impeccable chance to seize the Dutch colonies. After the peace, they kept Cape Colony, but returned Java and Sumatra to Holland. Napoleon, brooding on the Island of St Helena in the South Atlantic, to which he had been confined by the victorious British, had expressed the view that the people of that nation were daft: if he had won the war he would, he said, have seized the Cape for France and not allowed the ships of a single other nation to pass round it to the East.

For once in his life William John found himself almost agreeing with Napoleon; we should at least have hung on to this lovely island of Java. Its people would surely have been happier under his own branch of the red-haired barbarians. 'The Governor – whose name I could not learn – appeared a very intelligent and liberal-minded man, (a great deal to say for a Dutchman in these times,) who had been several years in the Island, and it is probable that the experience of Dutch misgovernment had been the means of opening his eyes to a proper sense of circumstances.

'He spake in great horror of a war with the Natives which had continued for six years and only concluded in 1828, during which time they had lost no less than 27,000 men, 23,000 of whom were Europeans, the others allies from the different Islands, some of whom he described as cannibals whom with great difficulty they repressed from the habit of devouring their enemies slain in battle.

'The Dutch Government makes a monopoly of all produce worth exporting, paying their own price, much below the market price, and then making the monopoly profit in Europe . . . Against these monopolies the Commandant argued with judgment and propriety – indeed no military man could approve a state of government upheld by such an enormous expenditure of human life . . . The inhabitants of Java are a quiet docile industrious race, and require nothing but justice and good government to make them the best of Subjects, and their Island the most valuable of all colonial possessions. The Governor, he told us, received a salary of 100,000 Spanish dollars per annum, with a large addition whenever he went on a travelling expedition about the Island, consequently' William recorded with amusement 'His Excellency was never to be found at home.'

* * *

With her crew fed and watered, *Andromache* weighed on 24 June and made the Straits of Sunda. Innumerable canoes had come round the ship selling fowls and fruit; one could buy a chicken for three half pence, or two pence if large, local wages were as little as five pence a day; and one could rent a coconut tree for a dollar a year, so that everyone had been able to stock up, and the lower deck was a-roll with coconuts.

Water was another matter. 'There appears to me to have been great mismanagement in all our attempts to quench our thirst' William commented severely. First of all, they had lighted on the wrong waterfall at their first landing – 'the water proved execrable' – and at Anjeer they had purchased at a dollar a butt some appalling stuff that had run over and irrigated the rice-fields and that gave the crew dysentery. Once through the Straits of Sunda 'we tried our luck again in the waterway of the Banka Islands, and got on board a few tons of the most atrocious stuff of the colour and consistency of Ink'. Away not far to the North West was Singapore, that swampy island off the Malay Peninsula upon which Sir Stamford Raffles had recently laid his creative hand; they might have had better luck there.

Now they were all but through into the South China Sea. 'On Monday 30th June about noon we passed the Equator.' They were back now in the northern hemisphere and there only remained the long haul up the China Sea.

Tragedy was to strike in these last few days. The winds were variable, and the expected South-West Monsoon miserably weak. The heat was intense, 85 degrees in what should have been an airy cabin. 'This day', wrote William on 11 July, 'we have to lament the loss of our Lieutenant of Marines, Mr Sheppard, who died this morning in a raging fever . . . He had been one of several young men who took a day's sport in the rice fields and woods of Anjeer, felt the effects of the exercise and hot sun next day, but would take no remedy, foolishly trusting to a Constitution, which however good in England, cannot oppose itself successfully to the trials of tropical regions, and the less so to the fever endemic in Java. Several cases of bad dysentery from the Anjeer water;' even the surgeon himself had all but died. Too late he had read a note in his medical book to the effect that they should have added lime to it.

'In the evening committed the Body of Lieutenant Sheppard to the deep with the usual honours.' William had been used to sudden death since he was a boy, and was not superstitious. Perhaps others, of less robust spirit, felt a sense of omen as *Andromache* sighted the harsh mountains of China, and four days later, on 15 July, anchored in the Bay of Macao.

11

A Happy Landing

Macao was a rocky peninsula three miles long on the southern side of the Bay of Canton which, to date, the Portuguese had held for nearly 300 years, since its award by a grateful Emperor, and had imbued with a baroque, colour-washed, Iberian charm. Along the peninsula stretched a magnificent harbour of all-but-enclosed water. Macao contained four small forts, by now ornamental rather than useful, and 12 churches, whose bells sounded almost all day. There was a Portuguese customs house as well as a Chinese one, a Governor's house on the waterfront with Corinthian pillars, and an old, magnificently fronted, Spanish warehouse, also pillared – a dash of Greece and Rome on these penultimate shores. Macao contained about 30,000 Chinese to 3,500 Portuguese. The pink-washed and beautiful town was visibly crumbling; a lonely outpost of 16th century Europe that was at once noisy, sleepy, lively and incurably romantic. On a rocky point was a grotto with a bust of Camoens, most famous of Portugal's poets. Banished from his homeland in the 1500s, for alleged subversion, he had written his famous *Luciads* in exile at Macao.

Since the British merchants were also all banned from Canton every March, when the tea crop had been loaded onto their ships, they perforce spent their summers at Macao and had imprinted English hall-marks upon it; crowding into its narrow space a race-course, and a sizable cricket ground. Beyond these, Macao was joined to the mainland by a narrow sandy strip; in this, resembling Gibraltar, as in its much milder heights. The Chinese, incurably poetical, had called this isthmus the Stem of the Lotus; incurably suspicious, they had built a wall across it. In all their 300 years of residence, the Portuguese had never been allowed beyond that wall and onto the Chinese mainland. A small, and rather scruffy, Chinese garrison had been permanently on guard along the barrier. The mainland arm of the bay was crowned with low but picturesque hills.

* * *

Tao-Kwang (Glorious Rectitude) Emperor of China in 1834, though not the man his grandfather Chien-Lung had been, had sat on the Dragon

Throne for 14 years and was business-like, dutiful and righteous; but
things had not been going well for him. Aware of the fragility of dynasties, he brooded perhaps for the future of the Ching. Was he worthy
enough, righteous enough, sufficiently punctilious in his observance of
fasts and feasts? Financial worries, too, raised their ugly heads; his
immense court, with all his concubines and hangers-on, was extremely
expensive. Autumn floods in 1831 had been followed by serious famines
in four central provinces in May of 1832; there had been rebellion in the
south, rebellion in Formosa, an attempted coup in Peking, and worst of
all, in 1833 there had been no rain all spring and summer in Northern
China (there was never any rain in winter). All this could only mean a
lack of righteousness in Tao-Kwang himself, or in his subordinates (who
were, indeed, extremely corrupt).

    In an impressive ceremony on 24 July, just a year before Lord Napier
landed in China, the Emperor had besought the bounty of Heaven, at
the Altar of Heaven outside Peking. Here the Emperor had publicly
searched his soul, and implored forgiveness. 'Looking up, I reflect that
Heaven is benevolence. The atrocity of my sins alone is cause – too little
sincerity, too little devotion . . .' In a robe of pleated yellow satin and a
purple surcoat, Tao-Kwang had made reverent kowtow to the mysterious
ruler of the skies, had prayed long and had sacrificed a bull buffalo
without blemish. Heaven had responded smartly with six inches of rain.
The immediate crisis was averted, but when William John stepped ashore
next summer Tao-Kwang was perhaps still shaken by his narrow escape
from disaster. His confident great grandfather Kang-Hsi (Lasting
Prosperity) had welcomed foreigners to his Court and encouraged foreign trade: Tao-Kwang, less sure, was most unlikely to extend a warm
welcome, or any welcome, to William John or his mission to improve the
terms of trade.

* * *

William John had now to come to terms and achieve mutual goodwill,
not only with the officials of the Celestial Empire, but with Macao's
Portuguese Governor and garrison, and (by no means least difficult)
with the recently unhorsed servants of John Company, and with the
Free Traders, inclined to know no law but their own necessity, and often
at odds with the Company. Of these latter, William Jardine was the most
formidable. He had started his career as a ship's doctor, but had been
unable to resist the lure of shore trading. Like many of the others, only
more so, Jardine was a clever, enterprising and courageous adventurer
who was laying the foundations of a handsome fortune, mainly through
the smuggling of opium. He was sustained, like most of his kind, by the

argument that is forever convincing and forever ignoble – that if we did not supply the Chinese with opium plenty of others would, such was the urgency of their demand.

Jardine's views were much like those which William John had already formed, but more forceful and whole-hearted, since he was bound by no official commission and no native tendency to mildness; and was also deeply involved financially, as Napier was not. Jardine had a considerable following amongst the merchant community, and was wont to express his views very candidly in the *Chinese Repository* or the *Canton Register* in letters signed 'A British Merchant'. Writing in December of 1833, he predicted a crisis. Now was the time that the British Government should, and indeed *must*, appoint a representative of sufficient standing to speak to the Chinese authorities in the certainty that his own nation was behind him and ready to sanction 'vigorous measures'. These might mean war, Jardine admitted, but the traders could not be expected to go on as matters were, 'subjected to a caprice which a few gunboats laid alongside this city [Canton] would over rule by the discharge of a few mortars. The Governor and Hoppo would soon find it was not prudent to provoke those who were willing to be their friends. The result of a war with the Chinese cannot be doubted'.

But actual war, in Jardine's opinion, would not be needed. 'It is well known that the Tartar Dynasty floats upon a smooth but dangerous sea, and that its existence depends upon the habit of tranquil obedience to its authority. Sensible of this, the high authorities view with abhorrence anything that savours of perturbation.'

Therefore, advised Jardine, go ahead and perturb them: it was the only way to gain reasonable trading terms. His views were widely shared. The British traders who made their way to China and did business along her coasts were a tough lot, and they had need to be. The wild winds and sudden typhoons of eastern China made the coastal trade no picnic. 'Gale and sea nothing abated', had reported James Innes, supercargo, in December 1832, in a small ship trading in the Bay of Chinchu; 'as dark as a wolf's throat and the ship riding very uneasily'. There were no charts, there were no lighthouses, no buoyed channels: the risks were great.

'The only thing', Jardine had continued robustly, 'which has raised our character above its abasement and created an influence among the Chinese is the conduct of our men-of-war. They indeed have established a character which makes the Chinese tremble at their approach . . .

'We must practise on their fears. The mere presence of cruisers on their coast would sufficiently alarm them, however friendly might be our conduct, nor is it desirable that it should be otherwise', he added sensibly. 'By bold demonstrations through our cruisers, followed up by negotiations through a commission, we might arrive at arrangements with the Chinese government mutually beneficial, without any violation of justice or any act of hostility.

'We have permitted the Chinese to doze in error when one rude shock would have aroused them to the sense of danger . . . The basis of the new Commissioner's demands should be open trade with China . . . The scrupulous deportment of past embassies should be wholly laid aside . . . A diplomatic Petruchio would be far preferable.'

William John was not temperamentally a Petruchio; and even if he had been, his instructions explicitly forebade him to act like one. Before ever he laid eyes on Jardine or stepped ashore in China, his readings of the story had made him form much the same conclusions; but whatever he thought, he had not the wherewithal, let alone the authority, to take a firm line. Jardine had gone on to admit the difficulty with which the illicit trade confronted the new Commissioner; what would the Commissioner do if the Chinese *did* regard him as a genuine plenipotentiary and then called on him to stop the illegal Coastal Trade? Jardine could not, of course, know that Palmerston had forbidden him to interfere with this.

As against Jardine, Matheson, James Innes, and other holders of these robust views of how to treat the Celestial Empire, a solid body of opinion in Britain, added to some of the local merchants, notably Dent, and the great Parsee firms who traded at Canton, were for a policy of letting sleeping dogs lie, at any cost. They would accept the caprices, the sudden impositions, the threatening edicts, the occasional imprisonments, and all the other impediments and humiliations involved in the China trade, if only they could keep the supplies of tea steadily flowing, no matter how financed. Much of the Indian revenue, by now estimated at a sixth of the whole, depended upon the sales of opium at Calcutta. With this the Indian rivers were being bridged, great roads made, schools opened, and soon enough, the railways would be laid. The Chinese demand was limitless and pressing – and surely opium taken in moderation was not harmful? And if we do not, the Americans, the Dutch, the Portuguese will carry on the trade . . .

Let the flag wave; trade would follow it: and all good things would follow trade. The British had no qualms about the quality of the goods they purveyed – equal justice, the rule of law, the hand of friendship, the practice of democracy. Like most Western Europeans they believed that the opening up of China to trade would make for the conversion of the Chinese to Christianity, an outcome which all, smugglers or otherwise, strongly desired. To them things all pointed the same way – open up

China to Western goods, to watches, clocks, woollens, cotton piece goods, tools, machines, and there would no longer be any need to sell opium to pay for tea. To the British it seemed simple – open up, and we will *all* be happier.

To the Chinese Emperor it seemed quite otherwise. All Westerners were to be regarded with suspicion; and especially the red-haired kind. There was a rumour that they were about to advance into Burma; and where next? Their pernicious and discordant ideas, which the Emperor feared far more than their forces, might at any time come floating over the mountains or be blown in on the sea breezes; perhaps these rapacious redheads even had their bright blue eyes fixed longingly upon the Heavenly Realm itself? But confident as the British were, particularly after their successful ten rounds with Napoleon, not even the Jardines or the Mathesons contemplated making yet another colony out of a vast and ancient empire of 300 million souls, who, unlike the Indians, were not in a perpetual state of battle among themselves, but were under the united rule of one despotic and powerful man.

* * *

Not yet fully apprised of all the possible complications, the Napiers were rowed happily ashore from *Andromache*, looking about them at the blue bay and its surrounding hills and the pink splendours of Macao's waterfront. They had been greeted by a salute from the little forts with their ancient engraved bronze cannon, and the British community, in some numbers, welcomed them on the quay, as they gazed delightedly at the wide sweep of the sea front with its pleasant buildings – the Praya Grande. Robertson, representing the firm of Jardine Matheson, offered the Napiers the use of one of the firm's houses on the ridge of Macao, cool and northward-facing and surrounded by a garden.

William John felt it unwise to compromise himself by acceptance, and they chose a more modest house nearer the sea, somewhere halfway up the hill and facing the harbour.

William John was extremely surprised to find himself borne in a sedan chair to their new abode, being spare, very active, and used to striding up his native hills. Eliza was delighted with the large cool drawing-room, while Maria and Georgiana ran happily from room to room, stretching their limbs in the luxury of plentiful space after five months in the cramped quarters of frigate life.

The sun shone hotly, but an evening breeze soon blew, the bay gleamed in sunset colour, and soon the lights pricked out all along the sea-front; things promised well, and there was even a smell of exotic flowers from the garden. Reporting to Canton, Robertson told his bosses that his lordship was 'a tall, raw-boned Scotsman with light hair'; (veering, in fact, towards being a genuine red-haired barbarian). The daughters, he added, were 'rather good-looking than otherwise'. Unaware of these unglamourous impressions, the Napiers settled down cheerfully to their first Chinese dinner.

Certainly there would be conflicting cross-currents, Lord Strathallan the ex-Chairman from Canton, had assured him of as much; but William was hopeful of being able to steer a straight course.

* * *

William John began betimes in the morning. Acting on instructions, he enrolled John Davis and Sir George Robinson, Bart, both ex-members of the recently dissolved Select Committee of the East India Company, as Second and Third Superintendents respectively. Mr Astell was to be the Mission's Secretary, Dr Morrison the interpreter, and Captain Charles Elliot, a nephew of Lord Minto's, who had travelled out with them in *Andromache*, was to be Master Attendant, with authority over ships within the Bogue, where open sea ended and Canton Province began. All this took a day or two, since some of those selected for the jobs declined to serve.

Once they were assembled, William John read them his commission, repeating to these solemn, intent faces the words he had so often read to himself before. Under the Sign Manual dated 31st December 1833, he was instructed to take up residence at Canton, to protect the interests of the British merchants, and advise and mediate between them and the Chinese Government. In his dealings with the said government he was to abstain from all unnecessary use of menacing language. He was to be moderate and cautious; and was not to ask for naval help 'except when the most evident necessity shall require that any such menacing language should be holden, or that any such appeal should be made'. He was to respect the laws and usages of China.

A further letter from the Foreign Secretary, dated 25 January 1834, had pursued Napier to Plymouth, as had the Sign Manual, and in this letter Palmerston had instructed the Superintendent of Trade to announce his arrival at Canton by letter to the Viceroy, to lose no favourable opportunity of encouraging the Chinese to make a proper commercial treaty, to try all ways 'to convince the Chinese authorities of King William's desire for friendly relations with China's Emperor', he read out.

As to the Coast Trade (smuggling, mainly of opium, into a number of forbidden ports along China's coast), William John was told privately by Palmerston that 'it is not desirable that you should encourage such adventures, but you must never lose sight of the fact that you have no authority to interfere with or prevent them'. The word opium was not mentioned. A final order to William John told him that he should survey the Chinese coastline and choose places from which HM Ships could safely operate 'in the event of hostilities'.

Whether the hearts of his listeners rose or sank on hearing the opening paragraphs of this, there is no means of knowing. Perhaps the double-think involved was less clear to them than it is to us; or perhaps they were so familiar with double-think that this example caused hardly a ripple. If William went, as instructed, to Canton, he showed no respect for the laws and usages of China, which forbade all envoys or consuls. He was unlikely to be able to mediate between merchants and Chinese authorities, when the latter would refuse to see him because he had come to their country without being heralded by a previous letter to the Emperor. He was to behave as if William IV of Great Britain and the Celestial Emperor were equals, when such a notion was so fantastic to the Chinese that it had never even entered their heads – the tributary King William reigned only through the Emperor's own civilized benevolence.

William John was to be as mild, subservient and discreet as the Company's servants had tried to be; giving no offence, staying friends at all times; and yet he was to improve the trading terms imposed by China. He was *not* to threaten, however much experience had shown that this alone induced Chinese concessions. All was to be utterly peaceful; yet he was to fulfil duties which precluded peace; and against future possible hostilities he was sneakily to spy out the land, or in this case, the sea.

Since the Chinese were known to be sticklers for rank, the British Government had sent them a member of the King's Household who was also a lord. Trifling differences in the status of the red-haired barbarians meant nothing to the Chinese. What, no regard for an English lord, a status recognized all over Europe and even in India? Such a thought had hardly entered Palmerston's conception of life on earth. That the new Superintendent of Trade was also to be a naval captain showed that at the back of its collective mind the government also recognized that things must come to fisticuffs sooner or later, and that the situation would shortly demand the threat of force, if not its use. Naval threats, like the opium trade, the Government found 'morally repugnant,' (as well as horribly expensive.) Thoughts of the actual use of force the Government kept well in their places, in the half-formed wish department.

British push, British enterprise, hamstrung by that awkward member, a conscience, yet still an irresistible force, were, once again, about to encounter an immovable object, the immemorial pattern of Chinese life.

12

To Canton and Confrontation

Among the British merchants who had listened to Lord Napier reading out his official instructions from the Government, only one or two voices were raised against his setting out forthwith for Canton. The bulk of them, hoping he would soon obtain better trading terms for them, urged him to go ahead without delay. His chief advisers, who were all old China hands, supported his immediate journey.

William John said goodbye cheerfully to his family; they had all understood from the start that the Chinese permitted no female appendages at Canton. The trip from thence down river to Macao took only 48 hours, and ships and boats passed constantly between them. The new Superintendent of Trade could think comfortably of his family in their airy rooms, or walking the leafy avenues fanned by sea breezes, between the pretty Macao houses colour-washed in green, pink or blue. He would be back with them in a month or two, when the merchant ships, loaded with tea, were to sail on the autumn monsoon.

* * *

Andromache sailed swiftly up the beautiful but typhoon-haunted Bay of Canton. Sharp and jagged-edged islands of rock, naked or with a thin fur of pale coloured scrub, stood up out of the blue water like the teeth of some carnivorous beast. Opposite Macao and due East was the large Lantao Island, beyond which the smaller fishing-village island of Hong Kong, barely inhabited, guarded its incomparable harbour, still as yet unused, with its handy exits at either end. On the starboard bow, Lin-Tin loomed, the pencil-sharp island whose name in Chinese meant Solitary Nail, 2,000 feet high though only three miles long. To this shelter came the opium clippers, unloading their nefarious wares into receiving ships that were like floating warehouses, adorned by their garden-loving Chinese crews with innumerable flower-pots, spilling flowers and fronds, giving these drug-loaded vessels a misleading look of innocence and bloom. Their customers were Chinese smugglers, who arrived in 50-oared Chinese boats with tall masts, paid in silver, and distributed their opium in the same swift vessels, pushing up into lonely coastal creeks and by their speed evading the Chinese customs patrols. The landing and selling of opium was forbidden under pain of death; but was so profitable that there were always willing hands to pull the oars and take the risks.

A less imaginative man than William John would have enjoyed this new scene – the wide sweep of blue water scattered with ships from all over the world as well as with every type of local vessel – junks, sampans perilously bobbing, and high-prowed fishing boats. Occasional near-human cries of the dugong to their young sounded a note of melancholy over the waters; suckling their young, these large aquatic mammals had perhaps, to lonely sailors long since, allowed the dream of mermaids to be born. Soon the water grew grey-brown from the debouching Pearl River; and sad as the dugong cries were, the occasional bodies of drowned Chinese, fallen from sampans and left to float down river to the sea like so much orange peel, or sorry swollen fruit were sadder; sadder still the bodies of tiny babies, almost invariably girls, found surplus to requirements by very poor villagers far up the river and consigned by their parents to be swept down into the obliterating sea.

By midnight *Andromache* came to anchor off the fort of Chuenpee, guarding the mouth of the Bogue, the rocky channel through which the river from Canton entered the sea. Morning brought a war junk, its salute of three guns answered in turn by three from *Andromache*. At noon Napier and his party said farewell to Captain Chads and his crew, not without regret at parting after their long voyage together, and took ship in the *Louisa* cutter, the well-known small vessel of the Company, now sold to the British Government and wearing the White Ensign of the Royal Navy. She passed up and down so frequently without let or hindrance that no thought of a permit entered anyone's head, since she carried no goods and was subject to no customs, being, as it were, the official motorcar with a flag on her bonnet. Proceeding against unfavourable winds, she tacked away up the river to a farewell salute of 13 guns from *Andromache*.

They passed through the Bocca Tigris, the Tiger's Mouth, where the river hastened between high cliffs. So christened by the Portuguese, it had been named the Bogue by the British sailors, with their unfailing instinct for anglicising and de-romanticizing words of a foreign nature presented to them. With its towering cliffs and fortresses on either hand, the Bogue looked a more formidable guardian of the waterway to Canton than it actually was. Altogether five scattered forts commanded the waters en route to Whampoa, 30 miles up river, where the stream widened and formed a harbour, the last port of call with water deep enough for sea-going ships. The menace of the Bogue's forts was diminished by the fact that their long rows of guns were fixed and could only fire at a target directly within line. William John scanned them automatically with his experienced eye as the *Louisa* beat upstream through the hot afternoon. Unknown to the new Superintendent, this waterway was now barred to foreign warships. The Bogue, as William did know, had been forced and its guns silenced by John Weddell in the 17th century as well as by Anson in *Centurion* in 1743 and by the captain of the *Alceste* in 1816. (The spirit of adventure must have run strongly in the Weddell blood, for as recently as 1823, as William John would have known and approved, James Weddell, John's descendant, had discovered and named the ice-strewn Weddell Sea in the Antarctic.)

After Whampoa, they were past the cliffs, and the landscape spread out into an open country of flat green rice fields, dotted with occasional temples, and scattered villages from which came faintly the lowing of buffaloes and the grunting of pigs, the sounds magnified across the water. Now and again pagodas rose like ridged pencils to pierce the morning mists. Distant hills ended the plains on their left; on their right the flatness seemed to stretch away forever into the hugeness of Asia. The river here was a maze of delta waterways encircling a jigsaw of sandy islands; at the dangerous sandbanks of the first and second bars, Chinese pilots were necessary. The country here was so flat that the tall masts of merchantmen were visible for miles. In none of its reaches, broad or narrow, was the river empty of craft, a busy highway of garrulous loud-voiced Chinese, whose comments were fortunately incomprehensible to the occupants of the *Louisa*.

William John's gaze embraced the scene with enthusiasm and sympathy; he kindled with missionary zeal. Somehow, and by peaceful means, to this land where the poor were so poor that they felt obliged to jettison their baby daughters, he longed to bring the joys of Western civilization and a prosperity that would fill the bellies of these thin men with legs like sticks, would open the whole sweep of green country to Western ideas of justice, of equality before the law, to Western values of individual freedom, and thence, by a natural process, to Christianity and the freedom and enlightenment of the soul.

As the cutter drew near the city of Canton, an increasing number of water wheels could be seen along the river bank, with splashing buckets and blindfold buffaloes urged around their endless circuit by imperious small boys. It was becoming too dark now to see much more; in the small but never silent hours, they passed the stilt houses, the sampans of still active boat-girls, and the brothel houseboats of Canton City's approaches.

For all the contrary winds, sailing and rowing they reached Canton at two in the morning of 25 July, and were led to their rooms in the

1. William John, 9th Lord Napier.

2. Enamel miniature of William IV – Painted by Henry Pierce Bone (1779–1855), Enamel painter to Her Majesty & Their Royal Highnesses, The Duchess of Kent & Princess Victoria after the original by Sir William Beechey, RA Principal Portrait painter to Their Majesties.

3. The Western Factories at Canton circa 1850 by an unknown Chinese artist.

4. The official residence of Lord and Lady Napier whilst in Macao, 1834, by George Chinnery.

5. *Lord Napier in later years.*

THE
CANTON REGISTER.

'The free traders appear to cherish high notions of their claims and privileges. Under their auspices a free 'press is already maintained at Canton; and should their commerce continue to increase, their importance will 'rise also. They will regard themselves as the depositaries of the true principles of British commerce."

CHARLES GRANT.

| VOL. 7. | TUESDAY, OCTOBER 7TH, 1834. | NO. 40. | PRICE 50 CENTS. |

CANTON.

The past week has been barren of events; every thing going on quietly; indeed too much so, we learn, for our merchants, who complain that but few of their usual Chinese dealers have yet returned from the country, to resume business at Canton.—The recent arrivals are the SYMMETRY, Riley, from Liverpool and Singapore, the NOSSA SENHORA DA LUZ, Jesus, from Java, and the SETTE DE MARÇO, Mesquita, from Bombay, on the 26th September.

LORD NAPIER.—We regret to say that the accounts of lord Napier's health received from Macao during the week were at one time of a most alarming nature; exciting in the highest degree the sympathies and concern of the foreign community of Canton. It is satisfactory to add however that, by the last intelligence, his Lordship was pronounced out of danger, though still suffering from fever; and from the severity of the attack, it is to be feared a considerable time must elapse, before we can congratulate the community on his being sufficiently restored to enable his giving attention to public affairs.

When his Lordship confided his person to the treacherous conveyance which the government, in consideration of his indisposition, engaged to provide for his speedy removal to Macao (exacting at the same time his open order for the frigates moving out to Lintin) the party were not permitted to proceed, on the first evening beyond the fort in the Macao passage; about three miles from the foreign factories. There they anchored for the night, surrounded by mandarin boats, containing, it is said,

6 & 7. *Extract taken from the Canton Register No 40, announcing the ill health of Lord Napier.*

an escort of about 300 men, the noise of whose perpetually sounding gongs was a complete obstacle to sleep. Other delays succeeded, by which their arrival at Heangshan, which should have been on monday, was protracted till tuesday at midnight; and there in the midst of the bustle and noise of that great emporium, they were compelled to remain at anchor till the afternoon of thursday (about 40 hours) constantly surrounded by mandarin boats and others beating gongs and letting off crackers night and day, notwithstanding repeated entreaties from his Lordship's physician to desist. More wanton cruelty to one suffering from fever, cannot be imagined, and our readers will easily conceive it's effects in aggravating all his Lordships symptoms; not to mention the trifling with his feelings in tantalizing him, from one moment to another, with hopes of being allowed to go on, which they had no intention of realizing. They did not weigh till they heard of the frigates passing the Bogue and the miserable voyage was not permitted to terminate till friday morning; although the state of the wind would easily have enabled their reaching Macao on the morning of tuesday. Thus for three days from tuesday till friday, at the imminent peril of his life, has His Britannic Majesty's Representative, in a state of dangerous, sickness, been held in durance by the Canton government under circumstances of aggravated cruelty and base treachery, which could not have been thought possible even by those most accustomed to Chinese duplicity;—the sad reality of which however must now destroy all confidence in the honesty or strongest averments of the Chinese local officers; and absolutely places them beyond the pale which regulates political relations between civilized bodies of men.

We earnestly hope the British Government will resent this black outrage in a suitable manner; and that a representation to the emperor will be made with a view to bring down the vengeance of their own Government on the guilty parties.

BRITISH CRIMINAL AND ADMIRALTY COURT. Owing to the non—arrival from England of His Majesty's instructions, Lord Napier deferred in the first instance exercising his criminal and Admiralty Jurisdiction over British subjects at Canton. In consequence, however, of the event narrated in the advertisement, which appeared in our paper of the 16th September, his Lordship deemed about that time circulated among the British community a written notice commenting on the same, and expressing his determination, should any occasion henceforth occur, to take on himself the responsibility of exercising his judicial functions, notwithstanding the want of instructions. From that period therefore may be dated the commencement of the British criminal and Admiralty court.

Lord Napier's notice being merely a manuscript document sent round for the perusal of the British residents, the editor had no copy to enable his publishing it; nor should he have felt himself at liberty to insert it in the Register, without his Lordship's authority. But we understand it has lately been introduced into a printed pamphlet, circulated in Macao, by the parties who called for his lordship's protection on that occasion.

We consider ourselves fortunate in being able to present our readers with a spirited account of the actions fought by His Majestys ships in passing the Bogue and Tiger Island Forts;—and though now rather an old story, yet as the particulars have not hitherto been published, we doubt not they will be perused with interest.

We learn that on the ships passing out all the damage was observed to be very carefully repaired, and the paint restored in a manner to resemble old work, so that no traces of destruction should remain.—This is very characteristic of the Chinese mode of deception, and their perpetual effort to save appearances.

A letter of DELTA notices a singular circumstance which we believe to be strictly true, vizt. that on the Hong Merchants applying for Lord Napier's chop for proceeding to Macao, they were compelled by the viceroy and his council to sign a bond that neither his Lordship, nor any of His Britannic Majestys ships shall again molest the Canton Government.

In the absence of the Editor we must admonish a PARSEE MERCHANT to express his sentiments in more decorous language, if he expects a place for them in the Register. Else even the futile threat of publication elsewhere cannot avail in procuring them admission;—a threat, by the bye, which from our knowledge of the Editor's character, we feel assured is most uncalled for;—*the pages of the Register being open to all correspondents who may address it in becoming language on affairs of public interest or who may feel themselves aggrieved by any thing said in its columns.*

We do not perceive that a PARSEE MERCHANT has contradicted any part of the statement in the last Register. If the Parsees have petitioned only for themselves, it is clear the Chinese government has chosen for its own ends to consider them as petitioning for the whole British Trade. And although all must rejoice at the reopening of the trade, we must be allowed to maintain that the same result would have certainly followed without the presentation of any petition. The language of petitioning is no doubt very soothing as a salvo to Chinese arrogance; but many British subjects are we know, of opinion that it would better have been spared on the recent occasion. Although the Parsees did not petition till after Lord Napier resolved to retire from Canton; was not his Lordship, we will ask, more than once importuned with addresses from the Indian community in China, expressing their uneasiness at the posture of affairs, and beseeching him to "relieve them from their most perilous situation",—a sense of which had induced many of them to obtain permits for taking refuge in Macao, whither they were about to start, when their fears were removed by an accommodation taking place? It is but fair to add that in a copy we have seen of the parsees' address to Lord Napier of the 10th September it is stated. "We are convinced your Lordship is acting for the best." The misfortune is their course of proceeding led the Chinese to consider them as disapproving of his Lordships measures; and considering the large amount of property represented by the Parsees, this impression of their sentiments, fixed on the minds of the Hong Merchants, could not fail to weaken the hands of the British Representative.

We admit, with a PARSEE MERCHANT, that all British subjects, of every tribe, are equally under his most gracious Majesty's protection; and they have been wisely admitted to equal *civil* rights; but all are not equally appropriate for every duty. On the field of Waterloo, for instance, it is doubtful how far the Parsees, however well mounted or accoutred, would have been allowed to take the place of the 42nd, the Blues or Scots Greys.

ACTION OF THE BOGUE FORTS.

At half past 12 on the 7th September H. M. S. Imogene and Andromache, under the command of Captain Blackwood, got under weigh to proceed through the Bogue. A stir was immediately perceived among the war junks in Anson's Bay, and the Chunpee and Taykoktay Forts. All of them at first commenced firing blank cartridge, and the two forts followed it up immediately with shot, which from the distance fell far short and astern of H. M. Ships. The Junks, about a dozen in number, got as far as they could into the shoaly recesses of Anson's Bay. As H. M. Ships neared and got within range of the Bogue forts, the wind suddenly shifted to the north, the Imogene standing towards Wangtong Fort on one tack, and the Andromache towards Anunghoy on the other. The Imogene waited until Wangtong had fired several shots, when the last one having nearly reached her was answered, by two; another was answered by two more in quick succession; the Andromache in the mean while returning the fire of the Anunghoy battery with several well aimed shot some of which plunged into the

8. Elizabeth Cochrane-Johnstone, wife of 9th Lord Napier.

Factories, the system of riverside warehouses in which the different foreign merchants lived and conducted their businesses, comfortably ghettoed away from the seething city. William John was up with the dawn, caused the Union Jack to be run up above his quarters, had breakfast, and started work.

The Union Jack had still a mystic property amongst its devotees. When John Weddell had sent out his boats to take soundings and the Chinese opened fire on them, he had captured the Bogue fort and his first action had been to give the flag its due. 'Tooke downe the China Flagge, hung it over the wall and thereon advanced our King's coullours', he had reported. 'Well I know', Captain Elliot was to say later, on a more serious occasion, 'that there is a sense of support in that honoured flag, fly where it will, that none can feel but men who look upon it in some such dismal strait as ours.'

These early and brisk proceedings were a mistake. To William and his compatriots, an arrival in the small hours, however dark, betokened efficiency and a desire to get on with the job. To the Chinese, this stealing in under the shadow of night could only be evidence of felonious intent.

* * *

The Viceroy of Canton was named Loo, and as soon as he heard of Napier's arrival at Macao, he sent an order down river to the effect that the new Superintendent was to remain at Macao until instructions for procedure should be received from Peking. Howqua and Mowqua, the two leading Hong merchants, were the bearers of this order. They travelled by the inland waterways that also led into the Bay of Canton, rather more deviously than the direct river route, and arrived at Macao after the Napier embassy had left. They had been told to find out exactly why Napier had come; but whatever his motive, he must stay where he was, petitioning through the Hong merchants for permission to come to Canton. 'All must respectfully wait until His Majesty deigns to send a mandate', the edict ran. 'Oppose not! A special order.'

Since Napier had been missed at Macao, another emissary was sent to halt him at the Bogue; this also arrived too late, the cutter *Louisa* was already away up the river. To the Chinese their own actions were entirely logical: they had asked for someone to control the traders, but had not bargained for an official plenipotentiary. Those connected with trade passed to and fro without question; but this, to the Chinese, was another kettle of fish. There seemed to be no exact rules to meet the occasion. At Canton, playing for safety, they would await elucidation from the Son of Heaven.

The immense Empire of China was held together, against all the odds in favour of fissure, by strict adherence to the rules and by keeping things exactly as they had been for centuries past. Down most of the centuries, those rules included the rigorous exclusion of foreigners with their incalculable behaviour and their upsetting ideas and innovations. Set plans for trade had been evolved, by which Celestial subjects could manage to live with the despised peoples who had the misfortune not to be Chinese, yet whose trade was very necessary. Ships under sail could not reach South China until the monsoon changed, and were then allowed to trade in Canton during the season March to October. So soon as their cargo of tea was cleared in Canton and taken in lighters to Whampoa for loading onto the ocean-going ships, they must be off. On arrival with their goods at Macao, those ships had always to wait until the Hong merchants had applied for, and received for them, a permit to proceed to the Bocca Tigris. Arrived there, they had to wait in the offing and could proceed no further until another permit arrived to allow them to proceed to Whampoa, where there would be further official delays.

All this seemed to the Chinese to be perfectly rational and in order; to the British and other foreign merchants, who had traversed thousands of miles of ocean to arrive in Chinese waters, it seemed an unnecessary obstacle race; with the Chinese, acting simply upon whim, ideally placed to shift, remove, alter or heighten the hurdles and deepen the pitfalls as the spirit moved them. Although seamen knew the form of old, and the East India Company with its comfortable monopoly had been prepared to put up with it, the free traders increasingly fretted, feeling it all grossly unfair and frustrating. Why should China, whose merchants were so avid for trade, be a law unto herself?

William Napier had left Macao with a clear conscience. He was doing as his orders commanded, delivering his credentials in person to the Viceroy, as manners and efficiency demanded. And as he sailed up river, gazing out over the green fields of the Canton Province, with all those industrious and little-rewarded peasants toiling from dawn till dark, he had felt as certain of his liberating and beneficial mission as any Jesuit pioneer singing his way up a South American river amongst uncomprehending tribes. And who could take offence at a letter in peaceable terms from one monarch to another?

The Chinese could, all too easily, and immediately did. Impelled by the Governor, minor persecution began from the day the new Superintendent landed. 'Howqua and Mowqua', [two of the Hong merchants] William reported, arrived with the copy of a letter enjoining me to retire. I told them I would communicate with nobody but the Viceroy direct.' The two emissaries, beautifully mannered but insistent, continued to declare that he must go back at once to Macao. They were logical; Lord Napier was not a merchant, so that the existing arrangement did not cover his case. He was to wait at Macao, and therefore must now return there, probably for some months, until Peking pronounced. The Celestial Empire was not an organization to be pushed into quick decisions.

William John was a patient man, and not one to take any personal offence at this abrupt dismissal. But as a bearer of credentials from his king, he was not prepared to accept it. He settled down to sit it out. Better counsels might prevail.

* * *

The Factories where the foreign merchants lived, traded, and stored their goods occupied a site near the river, outside but close to the Canton city walls. Between the buildings and the river was an enclosed gravelled square, and a riverside walk whereon the jaded trafficker could stretch his legs. There were the French factory, the Dutch, the American, Spanish, Swedish and Austrian factories, besides the British one. Since recent times, no firearms were allowed, which put paid to the welcome recreation of duck- shooting; more seriously, neither were any women, a circumstance from which the cheerful Chinese boat-girls at least could profit. All foreigners lived very much on sufferance; and mainly because it enriched all sections of Chinese society to have them there. In more relaxed times, the men from the Factories could safely go exploring or duck-shooting along the paths separating the green rice-fields, or rowing a skiff on the wide river; but lately the times had not been quiet.

Though foreigners were known to bring riches, hatred and scorn for them still prevailed to a dangerous extent in the Celestial Empire. Between Canton City and the White Cloud Mountain stretched a wide green valley where lay the Ninety-six Villages, full of furious and savage dogs and of Chinese who disliked strangers as intensely as did their dogs. For Europeans to wander there was suicidal. Even walkers on the walls of the City would sometimes have stones and brickbats hurled at them, and in the streets where polite shopkeepers would bow and smile, by others – less commercial – threatening gestures and insults would be made. It was not surprising that at the end of the season in October, when their ginseng, furs, tin, or cottons were all discharged and the tea duly loaded, the Europeans would sail away down river with relief to Macao.

Canton itself, crumbling and dirty but vigorously alive, sprouted a forest of pagodas, as a modern city might be thickly wooded with sky-scrapers. Hugely wide city walls, breached in many places by the Manchu siege of 1649, were now dilapidated and punctuated by gaps, but still surrounded the square mile of the city and its maze of narrow streets. Canton had always been a Mecca for trade from all over Asia; and in the 7th century the Arabs had arrived, fearless Sinbads in their dhows, bringing their carpets and their spices and (alack the day) their opium; and under the auspices of a resident Imam, a mosque raised its dome, and the accompanying minaret its now ageing spiral.

The English Factory, at which William Napier had just landed, did its best to convey the splendours of Georgian Britain. There was a grand pillared front with a Palladian portico, a vast cool dining-room hung with a glittering glass chandelier. On its wall hung a very large portrait of King George III, brought east by Lord Macartney in 1793 and destined as a present to the Chinese Emperor, and sensibly declined by that potentate. There was plentiful silver, polished mahogany tables, leather-bound books in the excellent library, a good cellar of wine, a store of cigars, and a billiard room. Aware that its employees were in for a thin time, John Company had made a great effort to do them proud.

Business went on on the composite ground floor which joined the Factories. Here there were scales for weighing the silver, hand-pump fire-engines, and an immense communal treasury of gold, guarded by heavy iron doors. Comfort for the exiles prevailed throughout; but it is not on record that anyone in these plush surroundings gave much thought to the multitude of half-starved Chinese without. There were so many millions of them: where could one begin? The Company, however, had not cared to be seen increasing their miseries in public, by actually bringing the debilitating opium to China; that task was left to the Free Traders. Its use or abuse, they would have argued, like a cigarette lobby, was surely a matter for the Chinese authorities, who, as they well knew, were making money hand over fist by it. As to the results upon the addicted Chinese, it is probable that Jardine, Matheson and their colleagues felt no more remorse than did the French who were cheerfully smuggling in brandy along the Dorset coast of England, or the Scots shipping their whisky hither and yon about an eagerly receptive globe.

* * *

William set to work to write his reports in a spacious but stuffy office. The English Factory had the advantage of a covered balcony, cool and lofty, but at this season it was too hot to work anywhere but indoors. With their usual passion for private life, the British had built a walled garden, separated from the rest of the open compound. More admirably, they had planted this with leafy shrubs; and a small formal garden, well laid out, well tended and watered, completed a haven of greenery in an arid world.

Altogether the English Factory was a home from home, and Chinese servants faithfully watered the garden and tended the house during the winter months while the British were away. It was all pleasant enough, except for the pervasive noise, dust and stench of a sun-baked city wafting in from across the wall; and William John was well content with it. Outside this oasis, the huge Empire of China, unimpressed, deeply proud, self-sufficient and static, went about its immemorial business as if no island in the Atlantic had ever arisen   from out the azure main, as their song had it.

Through the heat of afternoon Dr Morrison meanwhile set about translating Lord Napier's letter and credentials into Mandarin Chinese, ready for presentation to the Viceroy. Mr Astell, the Commission's Secretary, was deputed to give this directly to the Mandarins next morning, by the regulation and time-honoured method of a formal appearance before Canton City gate. Here ruled two authorities, one over the Province, the T'sung Fu or Viceroy, and Hsuin or Governor over the city. Both were Chinese. The armed forces were under the Chiang Chun or Tartar general, a Manchu, commanding the Manchu troops of the standing army that had kept the Chinese in subjection since their conquest of the Empire nearly 200 years earlier. No love was lost between Chinese and Manchu, and both authorities were politely at war over their precedence.

Astell was under strict orders from the Superintendent to give the document only into the hands of the Mandarin who would take it to the Viceroy. He arrived with the letter at the Petition Gate in the morning, accompanied by a deputation of British merchants.

The soldier on guard sent a message with the news to his officer, and a quarter of an hour later a mandarin duly arrived. The letter was offered to him, and with great politeness he declined to accept it, on the grounds that someone senior to himself would shortly arrive to receive it.

An hour passed before another mandarin arrived to refuse the letter, equally politely, and with the same excuse. Over the next hour several more mandarins appeared, all refusing to receive the letter on the identical grounds of their lack of seniority, their unfitness for such an honour. Long-nailed hands were crossed and kept firmly within their wide sleeves.

It was noon, and very dusty; and by now a considerable crowd of Chinese had gathered, to mock the patient Astell with rude gestures and loud insults. No-one knew better than the Chinese race that there are more ways than one of putting aliens in the wrong. After more than two hours of midday sun and useless waiting, the Viceroy reckoned that even the cool-headed and China-experienced Astell would be ready to crack; and the ever ready Howqua and Mowqua were sent into action. Bowing, smiling, and polite as ever, they asked Astell why he would not allow *them* to be bearers of the letter? They promised immediate delivery to the Viceroy.

Astell had been long enough in China to estimate the worth of this: he stuck to his guns. At length, another and still grander mandarin arrived, and the hopes of the British delegation rose. This grandee official went so far as to take a look at the letter, held well away from him by a servant; he would not actually touch it. When he saw that it was entitled Letter, and not Petition, he registered astonishment, and declared that this fact put it quite out of his power to receive it, or to accept anything of such a nature.

Finally, the Tartar General's adjutant appeared, with an impressive military following. From him Astell hoped for a rational response. But the adjutant took the line that he could not possibly be expected to know what all this was about. He seemed in dread of a demarcation dispute, and stiffened visibly.

Always patient and polite, Howqua now stepped tactfully into the breach, his hands tucked into his opposite sleeves, his head humbly bowed. Why should not he and General Ha's adjutant *jointly* accept the letter: 'His Honour', Howqua told Astell, 'is greatly distressed that you should have come all this distance in vain. I am sure you appreciate the difficulties in the way of his personally handling the Petition. But I can take it from you, and together we will lay it before the Viceroy.'

During this, General Ha's adjutant had not noticeably registered distress, great or otherwise; nor had he grown less stiff. Astell rejected Howqua's suggestion for the humbug that it was. He declined to hand Howqua the letter, and after a whispered conference, the Chinese withdrew, promising shortly to return. This they did, announcing finally that Lord Napier's credentials were not to be received.

It is to the credit of Astell that after more than three frustrated hours in the midday sun and subject during the entire farcical performance to the increasing jeers of a now large crowd, he was able to take his leave of the General's adjutant with confident politeness.

* * *

In any other country, William subsequently wrote to Palmerston, it would be absurd to fuss over etiquette, but in China the etiquette of all transactions was the breath of life. To him, as an individual, etiquette mattered little; to him, as the King's representative, it mattered very much. The fantasy that the Chinese Emperor ruled over all other monarchs, who existed only as his tributaries, had to be dissolved before any rational discussion could begin.

The merchant community also believed this to be essential. Napier was heartily backed by all but a few of them. One of them, not Jardine, wrote that no-one knowing the Chinese character could doubt that 'it is necessary to do away with this second-hand intercourse'. Napier was acting 'with the advice of his colleagues, men of long experience in China, and the unanimous opinion of the British merchants, and in accordance with the general voice of all persons conversant with the subject', in not consenting to all communication being held through Howqua.

'The Hong merchants, though adapted by their knowledge of trade to fulfil well and even honestly part of their duties, yet cannot be considered a fit organ of communication between the Government officers of the two Nations; from the circumstances alone of the exactions, tortures, and imprisonments to which they are liable, besides manifold interested views of their own.

'The policy of the Chinese Government is to retain them as a scapegoat for their own mistakes, and likewise as a source of revenue, for they are heavily fined on all occasions of imputed error or mismanagement. Every office in the Empire is sold to the highest bidder, the purchaser repays himself by exactions on the persons over whom he presides. Canton . . . is the focus of foreign trade, and the vast wealth that yearly passes through it affords increasing opportunities of extortion to all the officers of its government.'

All this was so; and round one had undoubtedly gone to Viceroy Loo. But William had always been a bonny fighter, and patient with it.

* * *

The edict taken by Howqua and Mowqua to Macao had stated unequivocally that 'the Laws of the Celestial Empire enjoin that with the exception of the merchants and the taipans, their heads, no other Barbarian can be permitted to enter Canton until after a report has been made and an Imperial Mandate received'. Lord Napier, recognizably not a merchant or a taipan, *had entered Canton and now refused to go away*. There was nothing for it but to inform the Emperor of this untoward event. If the Viceroy himself did not, some eager rival for his job most certainly would.

The Barbarian Eye, wrote the Viceroy to Emperor Tao-Kwang, had come to Canton without permission, and attempted to present a letter at the City gates. The envelope or outer covering, with absurdly and insultingly bad Chinese characters, had spoken of its message from 'the Great English Nation'. This showed lack of respect for the dignity and sovereignty of China – the world contained only one Great Nation. Other foreigners always dealt through the Hong merchants in the proper way, the Viceroy continued mendaciously. Despite the fact that Chinese officials at Macao and Chuenpee had seen Napier in a Royal Naval warship and wearing naval uniform, Loo insisted that there was no evidence that the Barbarian Eye really was an official, and no machinery for communicating with barbarian officials even if he were. How had he dared to arrive at Canton without first asking the Son of Heaven for his gracious permission?

The steaming heat of an August afternoon in Southern China settled upon Viceroy Loo. He had dealt with the matter, and could sleep the sleep of the just until further instructions arrived from Peking.

'Next day', William John reported cheerfully to his parson brother Henry, 'came Howqua, Mowqua, Chinqua, Falqua, Goqua, and several other Quas, insisting that I should call my letter a 'Petition' and alter the designation to the Viceroy'. This last he had been very ready to do; seemingly even Dr Morrison the expert had made a slight slip here; but he was not prepared to call his credentials a petition, which they were demonstrably not. All the Quas then departed, promising to come back on the following day.

This promise was duly kept, but the Quas were preceded by a letter, in which the Chinese ideographs that Morrison had used to convey the name Napier in Mandarin had been replaced by two different ones in which the name was expressed in a Chinese character which also meant 'hard labouring vile beast', or 'laboriously vile' for short. Perhaps Morrison would have been wiser not to point this out to Lord Laboriously Vile, but William John appears to have taken it in his stride. Whether he was tempted to reply in kind by addressing his correspondent as Viceroy Lavatory (the term 'loo' being already current in Edinburgh) is not to be known; anyway he resisted it. He did however 'show Howqua his abusive card, of which he pretended to know nothing, although he had sent it himself . . . full of humbug as usual'. Why the change?

'I have been so instructed by the Pilot', Howqua said with dignity.

'What pilot?', William John asked (unaware that more than a century later, Chairman Mao was to be known as the Great Pilot). A polite bow had been the reply to this.

'The fact is' William John went on to his brother, 'the Viceroy neglected to acquaint the Emperor with the changes which had taken place in the trade; the Emperor, again, entertains a gang of travelling newsmongers, who range across the whole Empire and report all they hear and see'. These had reported his own arrival, 'to do what nobody could tell. So down comes a thundering reprimand to the Viceroy; he then attacks the Hong merchants.'

So that, 'for some days past, I have heard nothing about them, except that they have ordered the Chinese boatmen not to take us, or any British or Europeans on the water, which was a favourite rowing amusement, and they have frightened away some of the servants about the Factory, which puts us to a little inconvenience.

'So stand my affairs with them at present; and in a few weeks I expect we may have some advices from Peking.' A correspondent from the Factory was later to remark upon 'Lord Napier's patience and forbearance under most trying circumstances, his disdaining to notice the petty annoyances and insults of the Chinese Government from the first'.

Advices from Peking had not yet arrived in Canton; but if they came they would be addressed to the Viceroy; and if he had not succeeded in getting Lord Napier, 'the Barbarian Eye known as Laboriously Vile' back to Macao without disturbances, it would be the worse for him. The Viceroy accordingly took out his apprehensions on the Hong merchants, issuing through them a series of edicts in quick succession on 28, 30 and 31 July, to the effect that the Barbarian Eye must quickly go.

'But out of tender consideration for the said Barbarian Eye' Loo told the Hong, 'being a new-comer and unacquainted with the laws and regulations of the Great Pure Realm, I will not strictly investigate', the edict kindly continued. The Viceroy would most certainly receive no letter from the Barbarian Eye; the Hong merchants had neglected 'to open the mind of the Barbarian Eye and inform his understanding.

'Nations have their laws, it is so everywhere. Even England has its laws; how much more the Heavenly Realm! Under its shelter are the Four Seas. Subject to its soothing care are ten thousand kingdoms. The said Barbarian Eye, having come a myriad leagues over the sea, must be a man well-versed in the principles of high dignity. I, the Viceroy, looking up, will administer the Imperial wish of cherishing with tenderness men from a distance.'

Meanwhile the Hong Merchants had better watch it. They must 'open and guide the understanding of the Eye', after which 'he assuredly cannot but obey'. If he did not, the Hong merchants would be to blame and could expect to be reported; 'and the laws shall instantly be put in full force'. This was a polite phrase denoting decapitation.

This relatively polite note, urging William John to leave Canton was followed up by two rather sharper ones. Disregarding the many interviews that there had been over the years between the Viceroy and the merchants, Loo pointed out that 'the Celestial Empire appoints officers – civil ones to rule the people, military ones to intimidate the

wicked. The petty affairs of commerce are to be directed by the merchants themselves . . .' No Victorian *grande dame* could have drawn aside
her skirts from any connection with Trade more disdainfully than
Viceroy Loo. Such low matters were no concern of the Celestial Empire
(which in fact was dependent upon foreign trade for a large portion of
the imperial income). Napier must desist and depart from those hallowed shores. 'How flaming bright are its great laws and ordinances!
More terrible than the awful thunderbolt', insisted Loo. 'Under this
whole bright heaven none dares to disobey them.'

In a third edict, permission to conclude his business was withdrawn
from the Barbarian Eye: he must go at once. 'I cannot have him loitering about here': insisted Loo to the increasingly nervous Hong
Merchants. If they failed to get rid of him, they would be punished.
'These are the orders. Tremble heart! Intensely tremble.' A fourth edict
announced that 'the affair concerns the national dignity'. Go he must.
Furthermore, said the Hoppo, or Chief Customs Officer, 'we observed
about midnight the arrival of a Barbarian's ship's boat at Canton bringing four English Devils, who went into the Barbarian Factories to
reside . . . Here is a list of the four Barbarian's names, Lord Napier, who
we hear is a war commander, Davis, Morrison, Robinson'. This midnight
party had been seen to arrive, numbered, investigated – the war commander, in particular, made the whole concern extremely suspect.
Obliterated from the official mind seemed to be the fact that the Viceroy
had actually *asked* the British government to send out a Superintendent
of Trade. The poor Hong merchants by now were, not surprisingly, ready
to fall in with the instruction that they should start trembling intensely.

* * *

The local British traders now told Napier that their normal reaction to
Vice-regal edicts was to laugh heartily and throw them into the waste-
paper basket. Lord Napier had refused to receive the edicts from the
hands of the Hong, who had then given them to the traders and urged
them to impress the contents upon the Superintendent. How serious was
all this? Impossible to tell; and William John decided to test the waters by
the movements of the *Andromache*, due shortly to leave her anchorage at
the Bogue. Captain Chads had told him that 'the Chinese War-Boats contemplate the idea of firing into our Cutter if she continues to pass up
and down the Rivers': and the vessel of a local trader, Mr Markwick, had
also been threatened with attack 'while also following her usual occupation'.

'I am not apprehensive of any annoyance as long as *Andromache*
remains in the River', William John wrote to Chads on 5 August, 'but

whenever you shew your stern to the Bogue, it is then they will endeavour to carry their threats into execution.' Chads had been right not to make his future movements known, and to tell the Chinese admiral that 'any indignity would be resented'. Having heard nothing from the Viceroy for several days, 'I think it likely they are only waiting your departure'. This was scheduled for 6 August and 'I have now only to request that at your convenience you will put to sea, cruise outside the Ladrones [the Philippines] for a week, then run straight up to Chuenpee without touching elsewhere, and give me the earliest notice of your arrival in your old Berth. In the meanwhile I will be enabled to judge of the intentions of these people and when I see you again I will have a letter ready for Sir John Gore'.

'That will bring you back about the 16th to Chuenpee, and I will if possible have the cutter there for you at that time . . . P.S. Of course you won't mention the prospect of return to any body until outside the Ladrones.'

'Tomorrow at daylight I shall proceed in accordance with your wishes', Captain Chads answered. 'The *Imogene* is daily expected, should I fall in with her outside, I shall propose to Captain Blackwood to run up to Chuenpee with both our ships.' If there were to be any trouble, surprise was always good strategy.

On 14 August, William John wrote to Charles Grant, MP . . . 'You will have heard of our arrival at Macao on the 15th ult, and on the 10th I had the pleasure of the duplicate of the 10th Feb., announcing that Government had relinquished the duties – a determination which has given the greatest satisfaction here to all parties but the Americans. The Superintendents are also relieved of a considerable part of their labours, the most distressing part of which evidently have been disputes and references relative to value. I am no longer placed in *opposition* to the merchants but on terms of mutual interest, and during the squabbles which I have had on points of ceremony, carried on thro' the Hong merchants for the Viceroy, I am sensible of having had the support of everyone'.

'These difficulties are not at an end and perhaps may continue for an age – the trade going on as usual. My public dispatch brings everything down to the 9th, but as the *Mangles* has not yet kept her time of departure, I have tailed on the remainder to Lord Palmerston in a private letter to the latest hour. I have also read privately the edicts . . . According to my orders I addressed a Letter of Compliment reporting myself to the Viceroy, and this he refused to accept because it did not come through the Hong merchants and was not called a 'Petition'. I managed to land here inspite of their plans to prevent me, have contin-

ued to reside here in defiance of their orders, as well as against their subsequent earnest entreaties to return to Macao for the benefit of the cool
breezes, which do not blow home in my apartments at *Bottomside*, as the
upper house in the Factory is ingeniously misnamed.'

'The Viceroy, in fact, had made no report of my expected arrival – he
hears of me at Macao, finds me at Canton, and then endeavours to rum-
mage up all the obsolete orders and edicts which have not been heard of
or put in practice for many years. These people are as far behind in ordinary business of the day as they are as a nation behind all others in the
common usages and sciences of a civilized people. The Viceroy finds
himself all astern, does not know how to make up lee-way, and wishes me
back at Macao in order to begin the Business afresh.'

'However if I did go there, either to please myself or to meet his convenience, out would come an interminable edict announcing my defeat
and extolling his own power and authority at the expense of the Honour
of his Majesty's Commission and the dignity and general utility of the
Superintendents. I am, I believe, firmer there than I was before the disputes began, and this offers a very just comment on the power and
energies of the Celestial Empire.'

'The Viceroy blames, and dreadfully threatens his unoffending mes-
sengers, desiring them to tremble intensely for their fate, while the
intruder is left alone.'

In Russia or France it would have involved 'a file of soldiers, to the
guard house with the prisoner in a moment'; and, of course, if threatened with *force majeure* he would go. In England it would have been 'a
constable with an alien act and a steam boat at the Tower all ready to set
him across the water'. Could his own treatment, William John demanded
of Grant, imply that the Viceroy forbore 'from personal patience or a
feeling of respect to a *Barbarian Eye*'? If the actions of the Viceroy were
based on principles of virtue towards a stranger, 'as some suggested that
they were', why did he order every petty annoyance, such as ordering the
boatmen on the river to leave our service, threatening the Compradors
or Purveyors so as to make them leave their trust, fining the Hong merchants whose boats brought up our baggage, and *not* punishing the
Custom House Officers who had broken open those trunks although
offered the keys? The two cases plainly point out the want of energy and
power on the one hand, and the will and the wish to do evil on the
other.'

These things being so contrary, why should not the British Government
'command a commercial treaty and insist upon the laws of nations being
exercised towards those whose interests are so completely blended with
their own?' The Monopolists, who were mostly all for the *status quo*, no

matter how unsatisfactory, assured him that the Chinese authorities could act with vigour when they chose, 'witness the destruction of the Factory Quay!' But this had been done, William was informed, 'in a moment of fury by a man of insane mind', when all the merchants were absent at Macao; and it had been well known 'that John Company would pay for all, and that he would sooner be skinned than lose his trade'.

'Old Howqua, the great Hong merchant', William John went on, 'declared they were in a dilemma at having to agree with so many different establishments, all set up in opposition to things as they were'; and the Superintendent had been glad to hear that the Viceroy 'for all his threatening edicts' had promised him protection: they were all fond of old Howqua, a man of great intelligence and learning, and expert in several languages. Some hopefuls thought that things would now go on as usual, 'the government are sensible of being unable to make it otherwise'.

This was hardly a rewarding outcome of his appointment. 'Are our manufacturers and our merchants and our shipowners to be satisfied with such a modicum of benefit?' The same paraphernalia of endless petty and changeable restrictions, the refusal to allow the merchants their wives or their recreations; no rowing on the river, customs duties altered at whim, squeeze everywhere, and in all transactions rampant corruption, the blind eye to opium smuggling? 'If your Superintendent can sit down at Canton, he may do the same at Nankin, at every City along the Coast', and a cessation of Canton's monopoly of foreign trade would quickly induce them to mend their ways. 'And a gun brig in the offing would be sufficient to protect him.'

Scornful though William John was becoming of Chinese officialdom, he was more and more coming round to the Chinese people themselves. By taking a firm line, the British would be acting greatly for their benefit. Half measures were no good. When the trade had been between a private company and the local Chinese at Canton, things had been tolerable; now the great object was trade between nation and nations. 'I would say to the Emperor, the trade is now restored to the British people, we *desire* you to restore the privileges which were granted by your Forefather the Emperor Kang-Hi (I believe) and which were not finally taken from us till the time of the Emperor Chien Lung, not half a century ago.'

Of course the Chinese might lose out for a year or two, missing the regular East India Company's payments for tea, 'as well as from the enormous increase in smuggling'; but this last abuse was, above all, good cause for the Emperor to listen to reason on the subject of open trade. 'It is evident that *they* will never make the approach, but it is not at all so clear that they may not be frightened into it from the pressure of so

many circumstances, all bearing upon one and the same point.' Which
was that the Emperor wanted the revenue, his local officials wanted the
rake-off, and the Chinese people wanted the trade.

Most of William John's contemporaries complained of the shouting
and insults of Chinese crowds: to William John things seemed quite otherwise. 'My experience, short as it is, in mixing among the people even
of Canton, in their shops and dirty lanes and horrible places teeming
with a naked population, convinces me they are by no means the sort of
people I have heard of from parties in England and even at Macao. I
never met with more civility or so little of a disposition to act with insult
or rudeness than I constantly see among these hard-working and industrious people. There is nothing of the Ruffian Mob so common in
London, Paris, and other great towns, but a disposition to be civil and a
desire to please. I have seen enough of the manner – or want of manners – exercised on petty occasions by some who have been induced
from their situations to value their personal consequence at too high a
rate, to account for many of the little frays that have taken place in times
past and which have been uniformly attributed to the insolence of the
Chinese. I see daily a certain overbearing spirit exercised towards these
people which would not be tolerated for one moment by a dirty fellow in
the streets of London.'

'It is not very difficult to calculate how far any occasional rudeness on
the part of the people may have arisen from the conduct or supercilious
behaviour of a little knot of men great in their own importance, and who
have ruled the roost in this little corner for the last century and a half.'

The Chinese government, who appeared to William not to care two
straws for the well-being of their own people, would be quick to seize the
chance to turn to their own advantage any foreign rudeness to these same
people; especially as the John Company officials would happily sacrifice a
sum of money 'rather than lose the peculiar advantages they enjoyed'.

'The experience of the traders on the Coast confirms not only the
good disposition of the people, but of the mandarins themselves. The
Chief Officers of Government here, purchasing their situations at Court
at great price, use every means and every extortion to complete their fortunes in the little time allowed; and these men being filled and gone,
down comes another set, and the system of extortion descends through
every ramification of the Government down to the lowest menial.'

To give Charles Grant an instance – 'the Mandarins are stationed
with their Boats in houses by the riverside to prevent smuggling. An
English merchant told me yesterday that he wished to embark here at
Canton a quantity of Cassia, the export duty on which was 300 dollars on
a given weight. Such a duty was enormous – therefore, instead of paying

such sum to the Customs he paid 100 to the Mandarin, who put it on board the merchant's vessel by his own mandarin boat in the very middle of the day . . .'

'I would impress it on the minds of HM Ministers, with all due respect, that a reform of the trade *at home* must be followed by a reform in the trade *abroad*. It will be quite impossible to carry on when principles diametrically opposed to one another – although a general system of smuggling may fill the temporary gap – but which being in itself vicious in principle must often be attended by vicious results. It is impossible to trust the untried spirits of Liverpool and the Clyde. Such men as Jardine, Innes or Dent may manage quietly enough, but they are peculiarly prepared for the purpose. At any rate, smuggling is not to be desired.

'And now, my dear Sir, I daresay you think I have fallen into the hands of Jardine, or Innes, who set the Chop House in flames: [because he was set on and wounded in the Custom House and had failed to get redress by legal complaints] but although I am on the best of terms with those gentlemen, and they readily propound doctrines which can only be squeezed out of some others, yet you may be assured that I lay my errors at the door of no man. My opinions are the results of my own observations, and although common to many, are entirely my own.'

'On my first appearance I could discern with half an eye the run that was made by either party "to mark me for their own." ' He had had plenty of advice, and 'many insinuations thrown out for and against individuals, but I have determined to look upon myself as the adviser and not the advised, and keep all busy people at a proper distance. I could not have believed the paltry enmities I see even among some who should have souls above it. To reconcile them is utterly beyond a hope. Those who lorded it once are put down, and those who have got the upper hand are rejoicing in their strength'.

'The Chinese say that *none of the Company's Servants* ought to have been included in the Commission and I believe they are right, indeed I am sure of it. The Free Traders have ever said the same and continue to say so now – they have a little enmity to gratify.' William John himself hoped that these Company men would go to India and stay there – 'I would fain see no more of them'.

'I have now given you a little of my own mind in plain terms and, of course, I trust in your discretion in making use of it', and he was, 'believe me, my dear Sir, ever yours very sincerely, Napier.'

* * *

To the Chinese Viceroy all this looked very different. To Napier he seemed 'willing to wound and yet afraid to strike'; and this seemed a lamentable weakness in one with such wide authority. Loo believed in getting one's own way without striking, but was none the less determined to get it. He aimed to win through with no disturbance of tranquillity, for to disturb tranquillity was to embark on open-ended trouble, and was a cardinal sin in the Chinese calendar of offences. Any fuss would be reported to Peking at once and would bring down the dangerous displeasure of the Son of Heaven.

In a sad postscript, William John recorded the sudden death of Dr Morrison, the interpreter, 'an inward disease had been preying upon him for a considerable time'; one of those many Asiatic plagues against which the Europeans had as yet no defences. 'I have appointed his son, who is an adept in the Mandarin tongue.' Both the other two Mandarin speakers were away – 'Gutslaff is absent on the Coast, converting and healing, while Jardine is trading'; and William hoped to have further information from them on their return.

Having made plain to Grant the feeble handling of affairs of the Chinese authorities, William John urged him not to alter his opinion on this, 'should you hear of my being hoisted out *vi et armis* [by force] at any future period . . . I would stake my existence that with 20 armed men in this Factory I would defy the whole disposable force of Canton'. There were said to be 10,000 troops there, but the whole régime was a house of cards; the Viceroy and the Mandarins seemed like old women in their fears and hesitations, changes of mind, and constant petty malice. 'Their Social System comprehends in practice an abominable system of morality, and would not stand a shake for a moment.' Events were to prove him right as far as Canton was concerned; a few years later it was easily captured from 30,000 Chinese soldiers by a British force of less than 4,000. But, meanwhile, he had neither the authority from home, nor the power to hand, to administer the necessary shake himself, which he believed could be effected by the mere threat of force, without any use of it.

13

Eliza in Macao

At Macao, Lady Napier was calmly unaware of any impending trouble. 'My Dear Henry', she wrote to her clergyman brother-in-law on 19 August, 'William tells me that he has a few lines from you by the *York*, sailed the 17th April from Liverpool, and that you mention our dear boys as well on the 20th March. Anne also tells me that they cannot be received at Meinengin till September. I trust therefore that arrangements were made for their remaining at Thirlestane for some time longer, so as to allow only a few weeks for their journey and visits to C. [Castle] Craig, Runnymede and to you before their departure for the Continent. I hope they have written to us by other ships which have not yet arrived, as this vessel came direct.'

It is, however, not very much good being told by others that one's children on the other side of the world are all right; one needs desperately to be told this by themselves. 'Be sure', Eliza urged their uncle, 'to enforce their writing *very frequently*, it is such a comfort and pleasure. Last night was such a happy one. Could you but have seen how we all rushed upon the packet of letters sent down from Canton, and with what eagerness all were read! I have begged Caroline to forward to you a long letter written on our passage from the Cape here, and finished a few days before our arrival at Macao; this will give you an idea of our progress, and save me much writing, for I have a great deal to do in that way'.

'We are all quite well, the heat was very great for the first fortnight, as high for three days as 90 in a large airy drawing-room, and never below 84 at nights, but since then we have had strong gales and thunder and lightning to clear the atmosphere, and much cooler weather, 80 generally, and the nights not unpleasantly hot. Every evening we have a breeze, and can always walk between 6 and 8 o'clock, which is a great comfort; and in this consists the difference between this place and India, at least Bombay, Calcutta and Madras. There, one never can walk at all, almost. After this month we look for a decrease in heat, and by October expect it will be very agreeable.'

'At Canton it is still hotter, and from its confined situation it is far more oppressive. At this moment matters are at a stand there. The Viceroy has refused to receive William's letter as it is not couched in the form of a *petition*, and will hold no intercourse with him, except through the Hong or Security Merchants – this he will not hear of. In revenge, they stop the trade which punishes themselves equally with the British, and at this particular time it is a measure of but little importance for the floods have destroyed the rice and prevented the tea from coming down to Canton, so that the vessels could not get their cargoes at all events for some weeks.'

'You cannot think what absurdities the Chinese descend to in order to express their hatred of the Barbarians. William's placid temper and calm good sense despises all such trifles; yet as they are part of a wide system of exclusion and insult there is a point at which they must be resisted . . .'

'William is in excellent health but he is hard worked and cannot leave that horrid confined Prison Canton for some time, the Chinese having ordered him away would be sure to say he had *run away*.'

'This peninsula and island called Macao is one of very many points of land and islands by which the whole coast is indented. The land is high and bare, but green, intersected by many valleys and presents many picturesque points of view, so that a very eccentric old artist, a Mr Chinnery, told me he had been here nine years, and although he takes a sketch every morning at 6 o'clock, yet he has not exhausted his subjects.'

'This settlement is far from being wholly Portuguese and they have no treaty to shew that the sovereignty was ever yielded to them, that essentially exists in the Chinese Government, and they have within the last few years encroached on all points. Macao contains 4,500 Portuguese and some say 40,000 Chinese, altho' this renumeration seems to be somewhat exaggerated. They crowd together, however, in the most piggish and miserable manner, wear only old sheets, gaining a poor existence by fishing. I have been but little in the Chinese part of town, the lanes are narrow and filthy and the people, though by no means uncivil, crowd around one out of curiosity. The shops are not worth visiting, everything comes from Canton and the Europeans have sometimes nearly been starved out of Macao by the Chinese cutting off supplies.'

'A few years ago – that is, about 25 years since, the English could ride about 14 miles into the country; now they cannot extend their limits beyond three or four miles, and the extreme circuit wall is not quite seven miles, but I believe Gentlemen sometimes in winter land on the barren islands and scramble about, though not without risk. Of course there is a great sameness in our walks, but there is sufficient expanse for me, and there is a hill very near us called the Peena where we go of an evening to enjoy the fine view.'

'The English and Portuguese live along the beach, we are in one of the best houses, close to the water, and the sight of the harbour is always a subject of interest. The small vessels coming from England generally communicate with the shore and pass about five miles out en route to Canton River.'

'There are two or three houses situated a little behind this, in gardens, these are the most desirable, being a little retired and yet commanding a view of the sea, but these are permanently occupied, and I do not know where we shall settle. Good houses are scarce and very expensive and there are no good sites for building. In the mean time, we may remain here if we please, the Tenant, Captain Grant, being in England. The rooms are very large and airy and we are fortunate in having it. A spacious house is essential to health in such a climate.'

'I have nothing but Chinese servants, they are civil and quiet, but indolent, and require continual hinting. Their cooking is good but we have little variety. Fish, poultry and pork must be varied day after day. Good beef is to be had in the winter, I hear, and people get sheep from Bengal; if fattened here it is very dry and hard.'

'The society here is very limited indeed. We all dine at half past three o'clock and walk out at six, when we meet each other and occasionally drink tea together. In the winter the hours are later, so then there are some dinner parties. Sir George Robinson's wife, Mrs Davis, Mrs Daniell and Mrs Jackson are all pleasant people in their various ways, and gentlewomen, but the first two ladies will go home, I believe, next spring.'

'Hitherto, the Gentlemen of the Factory have always had their wives here, and till the last few years there were scarce any merchants. Now the Company is dissolved the Society must deteriorate still more, because the private merchants, though respectable men, are not educated ones, and if they bring their wives they have probably risen with themselves. Mrs Daniell, however, remains, as Mr D. is principal agent for the E.I. Company, and she is a very handsome and ladylike person. She was a Miss Legatt. He is agreeable too, and very well connected. Mrs Jackson is his sister, a pretty young creature married to a man a great deal older and in very bad health – he is going to the Cape for a change of air.'

'There are one or two Portuguese families who are wealthy; the Pereiras are highly respectable and very rich. The Governor, (Suarez d'Andrea) has a very small salary indeed, not above £600 a year, and therefore lives very retired. He has some wretched looking soldiers, and they group – some black, some brown. He is rather a liberal man and has done a good deal to clean and improve the town, building a quay along the beach etc., but his funds are small and the workmen are slow. He has been *very* civil to us, and William wishes to pay him every respect. In fact, he is *the* authority here, but hitherto the E.I. Company and the Portuguese Government have never been on good terms, forgetting that the English are only here on sufferance.'

'There are two or three decent Americans, a Mr Sturgis from Boston is very intelligent. Monsieur Gerneant is the French Consul, and has the agreeable qualities of his countrymen in society, but my favourite is an old Gentleman, a Mr Beale, who has been here *38* years. He once had £100,000 but speculated and lost all, and now never can realize enough to go home. He lives very near, and has a most rare and beautiful collection of birds and plants. He has the only living specimen of Bird of Paradise that ever was brought from its native place – Amboyna – he has had it several years. Nothing can be more perfectly elegant than its form and movements. What we see in England as the Plume, as supposed to be its tail, are feathers growing from the side of its body.'

The Reverend Henry Napier, like many another bachelor parson in the early 19th century, was a passionate gardener, naturalist and bird-lover. 'Mr B. has some parrots that would make you die of envy', his sister-in-law told him; 'their body the richest crimson with bright green feathers in the wings, and the upper part of the legs purple.' Macao might be a little short in the exquisite manufactures of the Orient, but not in its natural wonders.

'Besides the persons I have mentioned', Eliza went on, 'there are the Captains of what are called the *Country Ships*, that is, traders between this and India, they are here during four months of every year and bring their wives, these are not all fine ladies, and being respectable, though not refined, I said I should be happy to receive them and return their visits. It is absurd in a place like this to be *exclusive*, civility is easy and intimacy need not follow.'

'Captain and Mrs Nash Nevill (?) are Scotch people, she is a good specimen of a sensible well-conducted countrywoman of ours. Two parties have been given to us here and I have seen *everybody*, and extend to all utmost limits, including Portuguese – the numbers are not above 40.'

'And now, dear Henry, I think I have told you all. We are perfectly well and the Girls have surmounted the first attack of mosquitoes from which they suffered dreadfully. If you please I wish you to send this to Charles to read, I cannot write the same thing over twice, and he will be anxious at first to know what kind of a place we live in, and I am not sure whether William has written since our arrival. I do not in general like letters to travel, therefore unless I mention my wish in that way do not allow them to go out of your own hands. This I intend for the *Spartan*, having written to Scotland [Anne Carmichael] and Runnymede [the Reids] by the *Magnolia*, it is uncertain which will reach England first.'

'And now, God bless you, my dear Henry, I hope to hear from you when you have seen my boys, believe me, ever yours most affectionately, E.Napier.'

14

Plenipotentiary without Power

The very sudden death of Dr Morrison had affected William John deeply. During the long hot evenings in the confinement of the Factory they had become firm friends – like minds engaging in endless discussions. Dr Morrison had been a learned man, a fellow Scot, a fellow Presbyterian, deeply interested in religious and ethical concerns, and translator of the Gospels into Cantonese. He had been much respected and liked in the small community where he had worked; and to add to William John's isolation at Canton, both Davis and Robinson, his two assistant Superintendents of trade, had gone down to Macao with Dr Morrison's body and were staying there to attend the funeral of so good a friend.

On the 14th, the day of Morrison's death, William John had written a long private letter to Palmerston in addition to his official dispatch. He told the Foreign Secretary of how he had asked the Captain of *Andromache* to bring her back, as in view of the threats 'I thought perhaps some violence might occur'; and also of how the Hong merchants had requested on the 10th that all the British merchants should meet two days later at the Consoo House. William had then called a meeting of all British inhabitants at Canton; in consultation they had decided that this was simply a ruse to split them up, cashing in on their known divisions. A polite letter declining the invitation was concocted, altered slightly, and then passed unanimously.

The Hong merchants, evidently under pressure from on high, had then sent on all the Viceroy's edicts to the three principal merchants – Jardine and Co., Dent and Co., Framjee Munchagee and Co. [the Parsees], 'desiring them to enjoin the Edicts upon me, a duty with which, of course, they at once refused to comply'. He and Davis had written a reply which again, with a few alterations, had been passed unanimously. Clearly the Chinese plan was 'to create a schism' and to encourage some merchants 'to force me to retire by threatening to stop the trade'. William John sent on copies of the edicts to Palmerston as he thought they might amuse him. The Foreign Secretary was a famous enjoyer of jokes, and as much in need of a laugh as the next man.

But the main thrust of his letter was a serious one, and its point was to emphasize that 'there is no disposition on the part of the Chinese

139

authorities to enter into commercial relations with His Majesty's Government'; which disposition had been hopefully mentioned in Palmerston's dispatch of 25 January, sent to William John at Plymouth.

He now tackled Palmerston on the contradiction involved in his orders – 'I am in the first place instructed "to ascertain how far it may be practicable to extend the trade" – but I am only to do so by "encouraging certain dispositions which may be discovered". The disposition discovered by the Edicts is *not very encouraging*', he pointed out, in the best understated vein, 'and in case of putting to hazard the existing opportunities of inter-course, I am not to enter into negotiations with the Chinese authorities, but if an opportunity of a negotiation should *appear*, I am to lose no time in reporting the same to HM Government, in doing which I must lose at least ten months and perhaps the opportunity of effecting good for ever'.

Without disrespect to HM Government, 'and as little towards your lordship, I ask if that paragraph does not instruct me to do one thing – a very material thing – and then deprives me of the means of doing it? Suppose now the Viceroy relents and admits me to a conference, and I then may have the opportunity of improving our commercial relations at this port by urging any claim or praying the removal of any difficulty without first reporting to HM Government? I cannot help thinking that the whole of this paragraph has been framed without a just considera-tion of the real state of feeling of the Chinese and their authorities, and without due reference to the history of past times.'

He may have thought, but did not say, that they had made him a plenipotentiary without any real power to do a deal or to advance the cause of better trade.

'When was it ever known within the last Century that the Chinese Authorities evinced a disposition to encourage foreign trade? On the contrary, all the privileges formerly enjoyed by the British have been cur-tailed from time to time, till we are at this moment tied down under dreadful restriction to the mere port of Canton.'

Certainly our trade had increased, but not with any favourable wind from the local authorities, 'but through the enterprise of our merchants and seamen and the great desire of the people to obtain our manufac-tures and to participate in the general advantages of trade. The House of every Chinaman in these extensive suburbs is a shop of one sort or another . . . and in fact every man is a merchant, yet does one of these edicts speak of 'the petty affairs of commerce', as if commerce were of no concern to the Empire.' At the same time, it was well known that the Emperor himself relied upon the Canton trade to keep the machinery of the empire running; and certainly all in authority in the Canton region profited hugely by it. The humbug of the whole thing, so glaringly

obvious to the British, seemed nowhere to enter into the official consciousness – or was not allowed to enter.

The principle that the Chinese Empire had no need of trade had
been so long upheld and so often voiced, William John went on to
Palmerston, 'that it is quite impossible to suppose they will ever show any
desire to join with His Majesty "in measures likely to promote the happiness and prosperity of the two Kingdoms". The Chinese authorities
spurned such an idea as "our gracious King's desire of cultivating
friendly relations for the common good of both people." ' Such a notion
was entirely foreign to their way of thought, as Commodore Elliot was
presently to discover, some years later, in April 1837, when the crew of a
British ship rescued a dozen drowning Chinese seamen at great risk to
themselves – surely this must create a feeling of good will? Thinking this
a good occasion for friendly overtures, Elliot wrote to the Viceroy at
Canton telling him of the rescue, of how glad he had been to save
Chinese lives, and expressing the hope that this would kindle warmth
between the two nations. He was roundly set down. The merchants who
had effected the rescue, the Viceroy pointed out, were only in the Bay of
Canton on account of 'the all pervading goodness and cherishing kindness of the Great Emperor'.

'How can there be what the Barbarian Superintendent is impertinent
enough to term "bonds of peace and goodwill" between the Holder of
the Dragon Seat and the ministering servants to whom he distributes his
bounty? This "petition" of Elliot's had used "crude and loose phraseol-
ogy", omitting the respectful expression "Celestial Emperor" and
substituting, absurdly, "your honourable country". This was appallingly
disrespectful, "and the ideas that animate it are ludicrous in the
extreme".' End of episode.

More than the 43 miles between the Bocca Tigris and Canton separated the turn of mind of a Captain Elliot, RN (retired), from the turn
of mind of official Canton.

Confucius had laid down kindness to barbarian strangers, but not
the acceptance that it might be reciprocal. Barbarians, as all knew, were
incapable of kindness.

But all this was hidden from the minds of those in power in far away
England, enchanted as they were with Chinese good taste, with the
porcelain, the sandal-wood boxes, the cunningly wrought jade, the
exquisite manner of it all.

***

To William John Napier, up against it and on the spot, there appeared to
be but one solution; he urged it upon the Foreign Secretary. Mr Ellis had

told him that 'there are 40,000 men in garrison in Canton continually. Four edicts have been let off against me for landing without a red chop or permit, I have been ordered off, and entreated to depart, there has been a suggestion that the wiling arts of my wife should be brought to bear against my obstinacy, yet with all this, and the 40,000 men and the flaming bright laws and the terrible thunderbolts they have not yet raised pluck enough to take me by the neck and heels and send me down the river'.

In dealing with the 'utter imbecility of the Government and the favourable disposition of the people', William John could not believe that 'HM Government will be ruled by the ordinary forms prescribed among civilized nations'; and would Palmerston 'expunge this paragraph which according to my reading can never be acted upon'! William John's original orders had forbidden recourse to Peking, however desirable it might seem, but now Palmerston had directed him at least 'to find out the best means for such a communication'. Davis, the Second Superintendent, had advised direct communication – only so would the Emperor receive the message in anything approaching the form in which it was written.

Meanwhile, William John would let the Foreign Secretary have his own views at once, 'recommending HM Government to consult immediately on the best plan for commanding a commercial treaty, or a treaty which shall secure the just rights and embrace the interests public and private of *all Europeans*', (in which category Americans were at this time comprehended: they and the Dutch, French, Portuguese, Spaniards, Swedes, Austrians and others all traded with Canton) – 'not of the British alone, according to the principles of international law. It will be as easy to work for the civilized world as for ourselves, and it will be as easy to open the whole coast as any particular port'.

The whole coast was, in fact, already open, he told Palmerston, in the sense that the smugglers of opium and other goods traded all up and down it in defiance of the law, with the active connivance of all ranks ashore; though a local mandarin would sometimes put up a show of resistance, for the look of the thing. In a sense the Chinese people were already in revolt against their Emperor, who strictly forbade foreign trade and above all the importation of opium. The merchant adventurers such as Jardine and Innes, and the many others who operated along the coasts, argued that since the Chinese did not accept international law, there was nothing to be said against breaking it along their coasts. How much better, thought William John, to put the whole thing on a regular basis, with legal trade, and fixed customs duties! The pretence of the whole system was sickening, and harmed Chinese and Europeans alike; but all the men in power in China were on the side of a system which so greatly suited them. One impeached Chinese Governor of Canton was found to have salted away the then fabulous sum of £300,000,000.

In commanding a treaty 'it may possibly be advisable to go to Peking on the occasion, or perhaps only to send from the mouth of the Pei-Ho river or from any other point along the coast. Sending an Ambassador is the more courteous, but the presence of an Embassy presupposes room for debates and long delays, for alterations and amendments in plans proposed. Now, I would say we should propose nothing but what is fair and just to all mankind, and avoid entering into minute details. Demand the same personal privileges for all traders that every trader enjoys in England'.

'Having once acquired the right of settlement at every port, let the trade go on according to the established rules of the Chinese Empire, good or bad, reserving always the common right to represent and negotiate where wrong prevails.' No more disgraceful incidents like the torture and strangulation following the surrender by his captain of the innocent gunner of the *Lady Hughes*, at Chinese hands, in order to save the bacon of the East India Company. 'Our first object', William continued firmly, 'should be to get a settlement on the same terms under which any Chinaman, Pagan, Turk or Christian sits down in England'.

'No doubt this would be a very staggering proposition in the face of a *red chop*, but say to the Emperor – adopt this or abide the consequences – and it is done'.

'Now "abiding consequences" immediately presupposes or anticipates all the horrors of a bloody war against a defenceless people. The Monopolists would cry out [loss of trade] and pious people would affect alarm. But I anticipate not the loss of a single soul, and we have justice on our side'.

'The Chinese are most anxious to trade with us – the Tartar Viceroys are helpless savages who cannot comprehend this', William John pronounced unfairly, since he had not hitherto actually met one. He also greatly misunderstood the immensely touchy sense of their own world-wide significance that dwelt within every Chinese Emperor, Mongol, Manchu, or whatever, when writing 'If the Emperor refused our *demand* remind him he is only an Intruder and that it will be his good policy to secure himself on his throne by gratifying the wishes of his people. Remind him that the British traded to the ports of China before his dynasty escaped from the wilds of Tartary, and that even one of his early forefathers (Kang-Hsi) not only opened all his ports to

foreigners but invited them to settle and spread civilization within his
Empire.'

* * *

Like the Chamberlain Government at the outset of the Second World
War, William John advocated the dropping of propaganda leaflets – on
the coasts if not from the air. 'The Chinese all read and are eager for
information; publish among them and disseminate far and wide your
intentions both towards the government and themselves. Disclaim any
view of conquest or of holding partial possession beyond a certain time.
Disturb not the passage of their vessels, nor the tranquillity of their
towns; only destroy their forts and batteries along the coast and the
riversides without interfering with the people – such to be carried into
effect of course only in case of the obduracy of the Emperor. Three or
four frigates and brigs, with a few steady British troops would settle the
thing in a space of time inconceivably short. Not Sepoys', he added pre-
sciently, for it was to be the cruelty and rape perpetrated by a few sepoys
[Indian troops] who had become separated from their British officers
that would most enrage and alienate the Chinese peasants in 1840.

'Such an undertaking would be worthy of the greatness and power of
England', William John assured Palmerston, 'as well from its disinter-
estedness towards other nations as from the brilliant consequences
which would naturally ensue.' Ships would soon be returning from the
Coast, and from these he hoped to hear confirmation of all the facts he
had learned locally. His views might perhaps be thought speculative,
'but I feel assured in my own mind, from no little enquiry among all parties of people professing opposite opinions as to the power of the
Chinese, and from other sources and considerations, that the exploit is
to be performed with a facility unknown in the capture of a paltry West
Indian Island', where the British had been always up against trained
French, Dutch, or Spanish troops.

'Should your lordship prefer making *gradual* propositions by an
Embassy', let them for goodness sake give up the hopeless idea of trying
to impress the Chinese Emperor into friendship by their grandeur. 'I
would recommend none of that ostentatious nonsense practised in the
instances of Macartney and Amherst – leave all presents behind, all
musicians and idle amateur gentlemen, literary and scientific, and go to
work in a manner determined to carry what you mean.' Here again he
misunderstood the Chinese, who loved music, presents, literature and
science.

'This is a vigorous measure, which might possibly "alarm the preju-
dices" of the Celestial Empire were I to make my ideas commonly known

among the Hong. They are now only thrown together for more special consideration, and till I have your authority to proceed upon more active principles your lordship may rely upon my forbearance towards a Government of old women, which is too contemptible to be viewed in any other light than that of pity or derision.'

This communication might have startled Palmerston, but that in the six months since the Napier Commission left home, the government of Lord Grey had fallen, and Palmerston was out of office and never received it. It fell on deaf ears, was far too definite and alarming, although the terms proposed by William John were infinitely more gentle and fair than those imposed by a later British Government after two bloody wars in which a great many Britons and thousands of Chinese had lost their lives.

Once started, William continued to make his point as convincingly as he could. In his central thesis, that the Chinese would never open their ports to trade unless under threat or duress, he was perfectly right, as events were to prove. Whether they *should* have to do this, was another matter; except that, as William John maintained, it was in their own interests as well as everyone else's that they should. In the end the Great Pure Realm was to be broken asunder by forces infinitely less merciful than a bunch of British officers brought up on the Gospel according to St John.

* * *

'What advantage or what point did we ever gain by negotiating or humbling ourselves before the Chinese government?' William demanded of a Foreign Secretary who would never read him. 'The records show nothing but subsequent humiliation and disgrace. What advantage or what point again have we ever lost by acting with promptitude and vigour? The Records again assure us that such measures have been attended with complete success'.

'Two centuries have elapsed this very year, I think, since the bold Captain Weddell came from London with three or four merchant ships to propose a trade. The Mandarins at first deceived him, but on a better understanding of his case they demanded an interview with the Viceroy. This was refused, and the Chinese batteries opened upon his ships. In this predicament, the gallant Weddell hauled as near the enemy as he could, beat down the walls about their ears, landed and took the forts, embarked their guns, took their Admiral prisoner, sailed up to Canton, renewed his application and had an audience of the Viceroy immediately . . . From that time down to the action of Mr Innes last year, success has ever attended determination' and he went on to tell the tale of how

Innes had won redress. The pattern had continued; and when Weddell had carried out his action 'the Tartars, a war-like people, had just over-run the country. Their descendants now, although continually re-infused and invigorated from the Steppes, are a wretched people unfit for action or exertion. Last year some hundreds of these Tartar troops required to march against rebels in the province were found so enervated by every species of vice that it was impossible to move them'. Were Chinese ener-gies and hopes to be held in check under the rule of such men?

England's energies, her valour and her discipline, thought William John, had increased 'beyond even what they were known to be before; it would only be needful to *mention* an army and a fleet of ships to the Emperor, and a reasonable arrangement, beneficial to both could be arrived at'.

The child, we are assured, is father to the man; and William John, since childhood and during his most impressionable years, had lived in an atmosphere most accurately described by his friend and contempo-rary, Captain Frederick Marryat. The great Joseph Conrad, praising this earlier sea-writer, said of Marryat's characters 'there is truth in them, the truth of their time, a headlong, reckless audacity; an intimacy with vio-lence; an unthinking fearlessness; an exuberance of vitality which only years of victory can give'. Much water had flowed under William John's bridges since his days with Marryat in *Imperieuse*; but something remained of them; perhaps in awareness of this, he went on to say, 'Now my lord, I am perfectly aware that it may be said that I recommend such measures from early professional associations, and with the hope or view of participating in the spoil'.

'I declare that I am the most peaceable of men. I have no delight in war. I would neither make a prize or divide a dollar. I am convinced that a commanding attitude, along with the power of following the threat with execution, is all that is required to extort a treaty which shall secure mutual advantages to China and to Europe.'

'If the Government is willing to extend the trade with a high hand, (which I take to be the only way of doing it,) it is an easy matter to feel the public's opinion through the medium of the press by discussing the policy of such measures – you may be assured the Country will carry you through.'

He went on to describe his own situation as delicate. He had been ordered to present his letter to the Viceroy, who had refused to receive it; he had done his best to obey but had not succeeded, and now 'the trade is put in jeopardy on account of this difference'. The Viceroy's refusal was particularly absurd because previous officials in his position had frequently held interviews with visiting officers or chiefs of

Committee at Canton, from the impetuous Captain Weddell in 1734 down to Sir Theophilus Metcalfe and Captain Chavell, RN in 1816, not to mention various merchants since.

'Viceroy Loo rakes up obsolete orders, or perhaps makes them on the occasion; but the fact is the Chiefs used formerly every year to wait on the Viceroy on their return from Macao, and continued to do so, until the Viceroy gave them an *order* to wait upon him, whereupon they gave the practice up.'

From the general tenor of the edicts he had issued, it was plain that the Viceroy would not have seen Napier even if he had 'degraded the King's Commission so far as to have *petitioned* through the Hong merchants'. If Loo were now to send an armed force to order him to the boat, he would go, in 'a retreat with honour'; but Loo's object was to strike through others and perhaps close the trade. This would have serious consequences for the merchants, 'also to the unoffending Chinese', but the Viceroy 'cared no more for the comfort and happiness of the people, as long as he receives his pay and plunder, than if he did not live among them'. William John himself was in a different position; 'I cannot hazard millions of property for any length of time on the mere score of etiquette'.

'If the trade shall be stopped, which is probable enough in the absence of the frigate, I may possibly be obliged to retire to Macao to let it loose again. Then has the Viceroy gained his point and the Commission is degraded.' But, William John went on to argue that whether he retired by force of arms or because of the injustice to the merchants, the Viceroy had 'committed an outrage on the British Crown and should be equally chastised'. Because unless he were in some way chastened, the present impossible state of affairs would inevitably continue.

'The whole system here is that of subterfuge and the shifting of blame from the shoulders of one to the other.' When the Hong were told to enforce an edict on the Superintendent and he refused to obey, it was the wretched and blameless Hong who were threatened and told that they must 'tremble, intensely tremble'. When there was an edict from Peking against smuggling, it was the luckless coolies who unloaded the stuff and ran the boats who were arrested and strangled, and not the mandarins who gave the orders and pocketed the profits.

To William John, coming fresh to all this, and with no time or wish to accommodate wearily to the local ethic, it seemed impossible to arrive at any *modus vivendi*, let alone to improve the situation without bold and decided measures. Everything about the Chinese authorities ran dead contrary to his clear-cut notions of right and wrong, his sense of reality, his downright Scots integrity.

'Act with firmness and spirit', he counselled the home government, 'bully the Emperor and he will punish the Viceroy as the Mandarin did the wood-cutter who had wounded Innes'.

On 15 August, the Hong merchants, instructed no doubt by the Viceroy, 'put a stop to the shipping of Cargoes on British account', because William John had declined to receive the Edicts at their hand.

15

'A Man of Solid and Expansive Mind'

In mid-August the cheerful pen of Midshipman Charles Brickdale of HMS *Imogene* was in action. Though only 15, he knew well what all this was about, and why his frigate was lying off the Bogue in the Bay of Canton. 'If we had a row with the Chinese here we should have all the Old Women on our backs when we got home for taking their tea from them' he told his brother at home in Norfolk. 'The Chinese authorities at Canton had treated Lord Napier very badly. in fact they would hardly receive him at all.'

Now a message had come from Lord Napier to Captain Blackwood of *Imogene* to proceed upstream to Canton. 'You must know', Brickdale went on, 'that they will not allow men-of-war to go above a place in the river about 23 miles from Canton where the river is not more than broad, and they have two or three other forts below it, and we were in hopes that we were going to slash past these forts and give them a broadside if they fired a shot and then go up to Canton but there was to be no such luck for the only *Warlike Action* we did was loading our guns. We went Peaceably up . . . directly we anchored the fort close to us fired a gun which was answered by all the forts up the river . . .'.

'We have had no fresh provisions yet and no chance of getting any. Remember me to Papa and Mamma, my Brothers and Sisters, Miss Holland, Grandpapa, the Uncles and Aunts.'

On 18 August, they had been still 'laying at the Bocca Tigris with nothing to eat except *salt grub* when on the morning of the 20th of August a message came down to me'. Lord Napier had sent for *Imogene*'s captain, Blackwood, to come up to Canton in the cutter, with a boat's crew to protect the British Factory, and lives, in the event of trouble. 'We went up very fast as we had the wind and tide in our favour. When we were about 18 miles from Canton the cutter ran ashore, the Captain got very angry as there was but one boat on board the cutter.' This the Captain took, and met 'a dreadful squall' which wetted everyone through, and most of the dry clothes they had with them; 'so everyone was obliged to share garments, like prize money. The midshipmen for there were four of us were luckier, we had a pleasant bathe and the only disagreeable thing was that there was nothing to eat and nothing to drink for we only had two fowls between us for 24 hours, however the boat came down again for us'.

At Canton, Brickdale found the Inn outside the city walls 'a very nice one kept by an Englishman', but he was soon staying in the Factory with Mr Astell, 'he was very kind to me. The part of Canton that I saw consisted of very narrow streets with shops on both sides. I went inside the *Celestial City* gate I would not have such a door to my *Pigstie* [sic]. We did not go more than a few yards inside but far enough to see it was a beastly dirty hole – I do not think that they would have touched us if we had gone further.'

After these comments on the Great Pure Realm the midshipmen were back on board the *Imogene* after five days ashore. 'The Captain stopped up at Canton as Lord Napier was going to have a conference with the Mandarins (that is Chiefs)', Brickdale explained.

* * *

Three powerful figures from the Emperor at Peking were shortly expected at Canton on a visit of inspection to the province and the city. Events here had been moving at speed, after the long deadlock of early August. On the 15th, the Hong merchants had notified the British merchants that the trade would be stopped, 'because their honourable officer' instead of obeying with trembling the Viceroy's order to return to Macao had stayed put, and so 'we dare not hold commercial intercourse with the gentlemen of your honourable nation'. Next morning, the 16th, William John addressed a meeting of all the merchants, whom he had summoned. He had two propositions, one of which was the formation of a Chamber of Commerce, with a committee, some of whom were to be Parsees, 'so that the affairs and interests of the British Merchants might be put into a course of regular management', and of communication between himself and the Hong merchants on all matters connected with the British Merchants' interests.

He went on to tell Palmerston of what he called 'a very painful subject' – the lack of unity among the merchants. It had been made known to him before and since his arrival, was known even in England, even by King William, that there was 'dissension and animosity existing in the British Mercantile community of Canton'. This did no-one any good, least of all themselves, and he had been expressly commanded to advise and protect them. Let anyone with a grievance come to him at any time, night or day, he told them, or write him a letter, and he would receive them without bias. He hoped that now that they had their longed-for freedom of trade, they would use it properly; for their own sakes, for HM's sake, 'and also for a slight feeling on behalf of myself and my

present position, that all disagreements should be arranged, and cor-
diality be the feeling amongst the British merchants of Canton'. He
hoped they would not feel able to say that he had refused any of them
justice.

He felt that the trade had been stopped because of the absence of the
Andromache; but now both she and *Imogene* had been sighted off the
Bogue, this would have an effect on the Viceroy. Meanwhile, the
Committee should be formed and should present a united front – 'a
more imposing attitude'. Some mutterings of an inharmonious nature
were now heard from the back of the gathering; but Napier went on to
suggest Mr Fox as Chairman; he was voted in, with Mr Goddard to draw
up a working scheme for the Committee and Mr Boyd to be Secretary.
These had at once concocted an answer to the Hong merchants, and the
meeting ended with 'a declared intention of acting with unanimity on all
future occasions'.

As William John told Palmerston, there had been no government
edict stopping the trade, and the Hongs would only delay it, a matter
which bore more hardly on themselves than on the British.

The Hong replied with equal promptness, pointing out the difference
between this particular envoy, an official, and all the previous taipans or
head merchants, under which system, lasting for over 100 years, there
had been 'mutual tranquillity'. (This brushed aside all the affrays, shoot-
ings, stranglings and trade stoppages which had characterized the
century.)

There were two things to be considered, thought William John, 'the
Honor of HM's Commission and the Interest of the Merchants. I conceive it my duty to sustain both, but not one at the expense of the other'.
He had spoken earlier of 'a point of etiquette', but it was not really all so
simple as that. To give way would be to accept a humiliation to the
Crown, since, acting in its name, he had been denied the privilege
enjoyed by his predecessors who held no such commission, and to allow
'a cruel and criminal measure on the part of a petty Tyrant to annoy the
merchants on the score of a dispute which had little to do with them'.

Stopping the trade for any length of time would have wide repercussions at home, as Midshipman Brickdale had so graphically pointed out
to his brother; and William John told Palmerston that 'if after a fair trial
of all justifiable means, I find the merchants are likely to suffer, I must
retire to Macao, rather than bring the cities of London, Liverpool and
Glasgow upon your lordship's shoulders, many of whose merchants care
not one straw about the dignity of the Crown'. But he did not intend to
leave without publishing in Canton the full reasons for his leaving,
describing 'the base conduct of the Viceroy', and attributing his own

departure out of compassion for the British, Chinese, and other foreign merchants in this stoppage of their means of livelihood.

'I can only once more implore your lordship to force them to acknowledge my authority and the King's Commission, and if you can do that, you will have no difficulty in opening the Ports at the same time.'

He would stop here, as the *Mangles*, carrying mails, was now at last getting under way. 'Her merchant passengers will of course report every falsehood for the purpose of raising the price of Tea – which will alarm all the old Ladies in the Country'. But he believed the crisis would be short-lived. 'The *York* American ship', he continued, drawing his mind away from tea, 'has this day delivered to me Mr Backhouse's Circular of the 29th March on the subject of the Dollars, but nothing more of an official character.'

William John had two causes for hope, besides a third supplied by a naturally hopeful disposition. One was the expected arrival at Canton of 'Shing-Yiu, a Manchu Tartar and Chief Member of the Censorate Board at Pekin. He comes with a Commission to enquire into the affairs of the Province'. This surely must shake Viceroy Loo into reasonable behaviour, coming as Shing-Yiu did from the source of all power, the Emperor; who could and would send disgraced Viceroys into exile on the cold and comfortless northern borders of his realm, as well as confiscating all their wealth. One could understand where the Viceroy acquired his desire to make others tremble exceedingly. 'I shall make an attempt on Shing-Yiu as soon as he arrives.'

The second cause for hope was more calculable. The tall masts and chequerboard hull of HM Frigate *Imogene* had appeared at the Bogue and she had anchored off Chuempie, 'for the purpose of protecting the trade', announced her commander, Captain Blackwood. 'The *Andromache* has returned with her and will take letters to India. I may be able to turn the arrival of the *Imogene* to good account', William John commented hopefully.

* * *

Mr Maurice Collis, in his interesting and lively book, *Foreign Mud*, finds this letter to Palmerston 'shrill in tone, as if Napier were beginning to lose his head . . . He did not remain cool, he became more and more heated, till he found himself in an untenable position'. He also writes that neither Napier nor Palmerston 'had taken the trouble to obtain expert advice, nor to read the State papers relating to China'. Collis describes Napier as now coming wholly under the influence of Jardine, that ruthless and enterprising opium smuggler, a realist who favoured a forceful policy towards China as the only way to improve trade, as did many others. But Jardine, in actual fact, was still away from Canton and up the coast; and William John had always been his own man, and so remained; he had formed his own opinions before ever he laid eyes on William Jardine.

All this while the Viceroy, aiming for a good impression upon Shing-Yiu, had not kept his beautiful brushwork pen idle, any more than Napier had kept his quill. An earlier edict had declared that 'If the said Barbarian Eye throws in letters, I, the Viceroy, will not at all receive or look at them'; he had then outlined the terms on which the foreign merchants were allowed to live and trade at Canton – 'all these are points decided and fixed by certain laws, which will not bear being confusedly transgressed'. Yet here was Lord Laboriously Vile, still confusedly transgressing them; some explanation for his presence would have to be made: perhaps a very mild and gentle admonition would impress Shing-Yiu and at the same time do the trick where Napier was concerned.

On 18 August, the Viceroy issued a fifth proclamation more conciliatory in tone, and less peremptory. Perhaps, in a bout of nervousness, Loo had decided to pretend that Napier was probably not an official representative. 'Whether the said Barbarian Eye Lord Napier be an officer or a merchant there are no means of ascertaining', he wrote, despite the fact that the Chinese officials at Macao and at Chuempie had seen Napier wearing the King's uniform and disembarking from a King's ship. But as he had come to the Celestial Empire for commercial purposes, 'it is incumbent on him to obey and keep to the laws and statutes'. Loo had begun his letter grandly and unexceptionably with a Confucian precept to the effect that arrivers in strange countries should ascertain what their laws were.

In not reporting why he had come through the proper channels, the Barbarian Eye had shewn 'a want of decorum. If things had been decorously managed by him at Macao, this would have 'rendered change needless'. The Barbarian Eye had indeed tried to present a letter, which the Viceroy, acting correctly, would not receive. 'There never has been such a thing as outside barbarians sending in a letter . . . A duly prepared petition should be in form presented', and a proclamation awaited. Why, unlike the merchants, had Napier failed to understand 'the flamingly luminous ordinances and statutes'? There was nothing slighting in saying – 'Obey and remain, disobey and depart'. And Viceroy Loo here praised the Hong merchants for stopping the trade – 'this manifests a profound knowledge of the just principles of dignity'.

But the Barbarian Eye, the Labouring Vile Beast, had disobeyed, and this perverse opposition would have made it correct to stop the trade at once; but the Viceroy, 'considering the said nation's king has been in the

highest degree reverently submissive', [King William would have been
startled to hear this] knew that, in sending Lord Napier, this reverent
king 'could not have desired him thus obstinately to resist'.

'The duties paid by the merchants from afar concern not the Celestial
Empire the extent of a hair or the down of a feather', the Viceroy continued, with the usual magisterial mixture of poetry and untruth. 'The
possession or absence of them is utterly unworthy of one careful
thought.' (The duties and trade profits in fact made up an eighth of the
whole Imperial revenue.) 'The goods sent by Britain, "the broadcloth
and camlets" are still more unimportant and of no regard. But the tea,
the rhubarb and the raw silk of the Inner Dominion are the sources by
which the said nation's people live and maintain life.' (Even to Viceroy
Loo, it must have seemed the least bit odd to think of this robust nation
sustained entirely upon tea and rhubarb and dressed exclusively in raw
silk.)

Riding blandly on the wave of these two massive misstatements, the
Viceroy graciously went on to say that he would not cut off this livelihood
for the fault of one man, new to the Country and acting in ignorance. 'I,
the Viceroy, looking up, and embodying the great Emperor's sacred,
most divine wish to nurse and tenderly cherish, as one, all that are within
and without, feel that I cannot bring my mind to bear it. Besides, the
merchants of the said nation dare dangers, crossing the sea for myriads
of miles, to come here from afar. Their hopes rest entirely on the attain-
ment of gain by buying and selling.'

These poor fellows were now, it seemed, being coerced against their
will; were they to be so threatened by one man's obstinacy? 'They cannot
but in such case be utterly depressed with grief. In commiseration I,
again, give them temporary indulgence and delay.'

Would Napier now, 'with an unruffled mind, consider thrice'? If the
whole system of trade was so unreasonable as he seemed to think, 'how
could all the barbarian merchants yield to it the willing submission of
their hearts'?

The barbarian merchants, who had been heartily kicking against the
pricks of Chinese extortion and caprice for at least the last 50 years, must
have read this sentence with a certain grim amusement. The Hong merchants, who would not have dared to act without the Viceroy's consent,
continued meanwhile to halt the trade. The Emperor's tender compassion appeared somehow not to have infected them.

'Let the Co-Hong once again enjoin the Barbarian Eye with an unruffled mind to consider thrice.' Surely the Superintendent was here to
supervise; 'if he talk not reasonably how can he gain the submission of
the multitude?' In strong contrast, the Viceroy himself, had 'never

treated a man contrary to propriety, how can I be willing to treat tyran-nically the requests of men from afar?' But this was a question of national dignity – this could not be 'transgressed or passed over'.

'I hear that the said Barbarian is a man of very solid and expansive mind, and placid speech: if he considers, he can himself doubtless dis-tinguish right from wrong. Let him on no account permit himself to be deluded by men about him. Let him answer through the said merchants, and the trade shall continue.' But if the Barbarian Eye did not want his nation 'to have there the liberty of the market, the trade shall be imme-diately stopped and eternally cut off'. Napier's King would then know that it was all *his* fault and that the Celestial Empire was in no way to blame; and perhaps the Viceroy here cherished a hope that this tiresome Laboriously Vile might too be banished by his monarch to a cold north-ern border (which was where William John lived by choice anyway).

* * *

Pending the arrival of the great men from Peking, from whom so much was hoped by the Barbarian Eye, and so much dreaded by Viceroy Loo, the former embarked on a progress report to Lord Grey, or rather a lack-of-progress report, and a plea for substantial support.

16

The Visit

During his brief stay at Canton, William John had felt himself becoming involved with China and the Chinese; and was now about equally in sympathy with the Chinese people as a nation as he was disgusted with their rulers and their system. He now besought the Prime Minister, with real feeling, to do something about the impossible deadlock in negotiation between himself and the Chinese authorities; thus going against all his instructions not to disturb a legendary tranquillity desired as keenly by Lord Grey as it was by Viceroy Loo. The difficulty was that Grey knew so little of what actually went on. Distance lent enchantment, and in his mind's eye the British Prime Minister perhaps saw only the bending willows and the swooping swallows, the lotus and the peonies, curved-roofed pagodas mirrored in still lakes, the peaceful long-robed figures drinking tea. (The Prime Minister liked a cup as much as anyone.)

In fact, Lord Grey was now no longer Prime Minister, since his government had fallen in July. He was probably away in Northumberland, happily fishing, or further north, walking up grouse this August day. And temperamentally disinclined to take firm action.

Writing on the 21st, William John begged Lord Grey to bring real and visible pressure to bear upon the Chinese Emperor, since to make sensible progress at Canton was beginning to seem impossible. Although even the Chinese had described Napier as a clear-seeing man with a calm manner, Maurice Collis finds in this letter assurance that 'the noble lord was becoming very confused'.

He repeated to Grey the conviction he had already expressed to Palmerston 'that the time had come to extort from the Chinese Government a Treaty which shall embrace the public and private interests of all civilized nations who may be induced to trade with that people'. The Chinese *people* were 'most desirous to trade; their Tartar Government being alone anti-commercial'. And this Government, he insisted, upon his present evidence was 'in the extreme degree of mental imbecility and moral degradation, *dreaming* themselves to be the only people on the earth, being entirely ignorant of the theory and practice of International Law'.

As they lived under rules and conceptions totally different from ours, it was virtually impossible to come to any sensible arrangement with them. They were simply 'not in a position to be dealt with or treated by civilized nations according to the same rules as acknowledged and practised among ourselves'; living as they were on the capital of a magnificent past.

'The trade of European nations was not limited under the last Dynasty, as it is at present, neither was it the policy of the first and greatest of the Tartar Race' [of Emperors]. Trade had been confined only since the reign of Chien Lung: 'Emperor Kang-Hsi encouraged trade with other nations and invited the learned of Europe to settle in his dominions'. Much harm in this respect, thought William John, had been done by the Jesuits, in their determination to persuade the Emperor to exclude all other kinds of Christians from his realm. 'But it was not till 1786 (I think) that Kien-Lung confined us to Canton.'

Since then the trade had been narrowly confined to a Company of Merchants and the Chinese Government, who 'had combined to play into each other's hands to their mutual advantage, without any reference to the comfort or convenience of the Chinese people. The restriction of the trade to one point was conformable to the interests of Monopoly; and the arrogance and senility of the Government have been matured and upheld by the mean concessions of the Company upon any case of aggression', and William John's mind reverted to that fellow-seaman, the innocent gunner of the *Lady Hughes*, delivered over, in the cause of tranquillity, to torture and strangulation.

The Company, by nervously falling in with the local ideas, had taught the Chinese to believe that the entire British nation was indeed 'dependent upon China for food and raiment'. Nor had the cautious merchants dared to contradict the Chinese notion 'that the Emperor was the only Monarch in the Universe'. [This impression was long-lived and likely to die hard: 'there is only one eternal God in Heaven and only one sovereign on earth' the Mongol Emperor Mong-Ke had crisply informed King Louis IX of France, via Friar William of Rubruk, in the 13th Century; and Mong-Ke's grandfather, Genghis Khan had stated categorically that 'Heaven has ordered me to govern all peoples'.] The conviction had become a part of the souls of Chinese and Manchu successors alike on the Imperial throne: but naturally seemed a nonsense to loyal and thrusting Europeans born in the 18th Century. How could one deal with the Chinese as equals, as normal human beings unless they could be dragged, perhaps kicking and screaming, onto the same planet as the rest of humankind?

The local merchants were 'open-mouthed for extended trade'; and so

presumably were their opposite numbers at home in England. If it came
to enforcing a treaty 'is this the most favourable time or not'? Acting on
instructions, he had come to Canton to report himself by letter to the
Viceroy; and although the Cantonese authorities had expressly asked for
such an official, this uncivilized being had expressed himself 'debarred
by the dignity of the laws from communicating with an outside barbarian', and threatened to cut off all trade if he did not leave immediately.
The Viceroy had gone on to describe his own leniency as due 'to the
virtue of the reverential submission exercised by the said Nation's King'.
At the same time, the Viceroy had not 'the spirit to send a Corporal's
guard and banish me from the Factory, remaining as I do in spite of five
Celestial Proclamations'.

'One could not be angry with such a government; what one could do
"with a determined purpose, and a strong arm if necessary" was to make
a finish of such nonsense and bring them to their senses', and though
the British merchants had their differences, all were agreed that this
could most easily be done. A visit from three powerful mandarins from
Peking was promised, and William John considered that all the Viceroy's
high-handedness might be in order to impress the high-ups with his
efficiency. However that might be, his own immediate job was to come to
a settlement that would allow our merchants 'to ship off the goods
already paid for'.

'That being done, it depends upon the Viceroy to go on openly as
heretofore; if he does not agree to that, the smugglers will do the business for him.' Their activities robbed the Viceroy of his dues; he would
hardly want the legitimate trade to suffer at such hands. Both Napier
himself and the higher authorities were at one in believing that smuggling was no way to do business. As for himself – 'if the worst comes to
the worst I can only retire to Macao, but the consequences will be disgraceful'. It would be a slap in the face for the British, and the extortions
would go on as usual, at local caprice. Nothing would have been settled.

Here William John made a firm request for a new policy, backed from
home. A show of force was the only way to effect a fair arrangement that
would benefit all. Would Lord Grey send 'a messenger to Calcutta overland to order a British force with some small craft to act along the
Coast'? He had already suggested this to Palmerston – 'we should soon
bring matters to a close. In the meantime, I will endeavour to unite the
merchants in the plan of being quiet until I can hear from your lordship
whether I am to submit to every edict or whether the Government will
assert our ancient rights of commerce.'

As things were, 'the greater part of the trade is carried on by smuggling'; what trade remained could be halted for a while 'without any

great loss or handicap'. He had long felt that such a dishonest muddle should not be allowed to continue indefinitely.

The said messenger, after talking to the Governor General of India in Calcutta could 'proceed on here by one of the Clippers or fast sailing traders during any season of the SW Monsoon. His arrival there in May will allow abundance of time to prepare a little armament to enter the China Seas with the first of the SW Monsoon, which on arriving should take possession of the Island of Hong-Kong', [the first official mention of this place] 'on the Eastern Entrance of the Canton River and admirably adapted for every purpose'.

Grey, he went on, might think this all high-handed; but William John reminded him that, in 1831, the previous Viceroy had issued a proclamation to the effect that a Superintendent to take general charge must be sent on the dissolution of the East India Company. Britain had complied; and what had happened?

'Considering that they have refused me every privilege as formerly enjoyed by the Chief of the Factory, of personal communication and correspondence, I feel satisfied that your Lordship will see the urgent necessity of negotiating with such a government while having in your hands at the same time the means of compulsion. To negotiate with them otherwise would prove an idle waste of time.'

'Now, if your lordship will send me a messenger in advance of an armament, I would recommend that I should be instructed to give immediate notice at Pekin, and all along the Coast, of the demands about to be made, so that no *sudden* appearance of Force might intimidate the people; but that they might look to the arrival of such a force as the happy means of their emancipation from a most arbitrary system of oppression', William John went on hopefully, greatly underestimating the solidarity of the Chinese, together with the fact that people who have always been oppressed are unfamiliar with any other way of life, and tend to be nervous of it. He shared to the full in his contemporaries' missionary zeal for good government conducted in the interests of the governed.

This preliminary notice would also 'give the Government time to reflect and "tremble" at the consequences of refusal'. It might be objected that it would also give them time for defensive preparation, which was perfectly true; but he thought the preparation would not be much more effective than those for the recent campaign at Salt Hill [where some Eton schoolboys had rebelled and set themselves up in the local inn, from which shortage of food had obliged them before long to trickle back to school].

'You read of a standing army of above 1,000,000 to defend the

Empire. It is an absurdity.' For sending against a rebellion the Imperial
authorities at Canton had been able 'to muster only a few hundred
wretched creatures last year, and one half of them were utterly incapable of taking the field. Governor Lee and his troops were defeated,
and he was, of course, superseded by the present man, Loo, who paid an
enormous bribe to the rebels and thus restored order. What can an
army of bows and arrows, pikes and shields, do against a handful of
British veterans?'

* * *

Not much, as the event proved. The Chinese by no means lacked
courage, but in warfare they were clueless; the Manchu bannermen,
once all-conquering, were now enervated by long peace and had no
modern weapons.

'The batteries at the Bogue are contemptible, and not a man to be
seen within them. They have no doubt a long muster roll of the Military,
but the Governor draws the pay, and if he wants a force within the batteries, the plan is to drive in the peasantry from the surrounding
country.' William John had little belief in the bond between the Chinese
and their Manchu conquerors. The Hong merchants themselves were all
Chinese, and expressed dislike and helplessness in the face of the
Manchu.

Losing the trade was, of course, a bad business for the British merchants, but he felt sure they would put up with the temporary
inconvenience for a positive benefit. 'Meantime, I will endeavour to
carry on according to the principles already recommended by your lordship, which are certainly most fitting when one has a reasonable people
to deal with.'

'Lady N. and my two daughters are, of course, at Macao and in good
health. I was never in better health myself', William John added stoutly,
'thank God, altho' the heat is dreadful at times and not a breath of air to
enter our close built apartments.' These were to be his last few days of
good health.

On that same day, the 21st, William John sent another short line to
Palmerston, since the *Mangles* had still not left the river. He told the
Foreign Secretary that *Imogene* and *Andromache* had anchored at
Chuenpee, and that a body of Hong merchants had at once appeared, to
know why? And when were they going away? To which William John
had replied that if conducted to the Viceroy's presence he would explain
all. Howqua and Mowqua had looked pleased; but had come back crest-
fallen on the following day to say that his Excellency would have no
communication with Lord Napier, who was again ordered to depart. If

he himself, the Viceroy asked, had landed in England, would he not be expected to obey the laws of that country? 'On the principle of reciprocity I heartily concurred; were he in England he would be received and treated as a Gentleman, and I required no more here.' To this the Viceroy had replied with his fifth edict.

'I have requested Captain Blackwood to detain the *Andromache* in the meantime.' She was due to sail for India on 1 October, so that keeping her for another few weeks would mean that the Monsoon would make no difference to her on her passage to Madras. 'I have written to Lord Grey on the subject of an armament from India, and requested advice overland as soon as possible.' With no authority to take decisions and no power to enforce them if he did, he could only play this tricky situation by ear, and from day to day.

* * *

The very next evening brought the fresh development for which he had been hoping. On the evening of 22 August the Superintendent received through Howqua and Mowqua a request that Lord Napier would receive a visit at 11 o'clock the next morning from the Mandarins from Peking. Pleased at this development, and in his sanguine heart seeing it as a sign that the obstructive front might be yielding, William John told the two Hongs that he would receive the Mandarins in state in the main Hall of the British Factory.

Despite the heat, William John next morning put on his full dress, an affair of gold epaulettes, a high stiff collar with its double row of gold lace, and a dark blue frock coat of woollen material, better suited to the reception of potentates on a warship's upper deck in a stiff English wind than to a tropical interview behind closed doors. At nine o'clock, the Hong interpreters, known as 'linguists', arrived at the English Factory, followed by servants carrying ceremonial chairs. These they placed in the hall of reception, three for the Mandarins, facing south, which was the correct and customary direction of the compass ordained for a successful meeting. Two rows of chairs, facing east and west, were put at right angles to the Mandarin row – these were for the Hong merchants. Napier and his staff, it was assumed, would spend the conference humbly standing before the great ones.

William John would have none of this, because the Chinese chairs for the Hongs, so placed, turned their backs upon the portrait of King George III (which he had vainly asked the government to have removed, fearing just such a difficulty). The experienced Mr Astell assured the Superintendent that the chair manoeuvre had been a calculated insult, to which it would be unwise to submit. So William John had a table inserted, with himself in the middle, facing south, as Chinese custom demanded, with a chair for a mandarin on either hand. Astell was to be opposite, with the other Mandarin on his right hand, and Johnstone the Secretary and the other Superintendent, Robinson, on his left. The Hong merchants were to sit in a row a little back from the table, and facing the portrait of King George III.

Howqua and Mowqua arrived shortly after this and viewed the arrangement with palpable dismay. They feared to be squeezed for British misdemeanours; surely for such a trifling concern as the disposition of the chairs Lord Napier would not like to see such old friends to British commerce victimized? The Chief Superintendent was known to be good-tempered and reasonable, would he not put the chairs back?

Assuredly not, William John said, in his usual calm and level tones.

As it was by now 11 o'clock, the British and the Co-Hong sat in their appointed seats, where they remained unvisited until 1.15. Howqua, who must have known the form, made no attempt to explain to William John that punctuality was not the politeness of Mandarins, and that indeed it was part of their prestige never to arrive until at least two hours after the appointed time. Such a thing was inconceivable to William John, brought up in the Navy where the practice is to arrive 45 minutes before anything can possibly happen. Irked by the high collar of his full-dress, breathless in the noonday heat, and probably very hungry, his urbanity had been, perhaps, a little worn down by the time the Mandarins, gorgeously dressed in flowing silks and followed by a crowd of attendants, finally put in their appearance.

William John, Astell, and the other Englishmen rose and bowed, motioning the Mandarins to their seats. Whatever these thought of the arrangements, their manners were too good for comment. They sat down, protesting that the honour done them was too great. William John then asked the Mandarins, through Morrison, whether the hour at which they had asked for a meeting had not been 11 o'clock? Yes, Mowqua replied for them. William John then proceeded to take them to task: they were no longer dealing with merchants of a private company – he himself was 'an officer appointed by His Britannic Majesty'; rudeness to him was rudeness to his King. Good manners to envoys was a civilized practice recognized world-wide.

The Mandarins remained true to their silks. They made no reply, though doubtless amazed at the audacity of the Barbarian Eye.

William John then asked to what he owed the honour of this visit? The Chaou-chow-foo, the Chief of the Peking Censorate, then explained that they had been sent by the Viceroy to demand the reason for Lord

Napier's arrival in Canton? What was his business, and when did he propose to leave?

William John then read them the Chinese Edict of 11 January, 1831, asking for the appointment of a Chief who understood business, to come to Canton to manage commercial dealings and prevent confusion. He then produced his commission, given him in accordance with the said Edict. Had they forgotten their own Edict? He referred them to their official records, where it would certainly be found.

As to his duties, these were all in the letter that the Viceroy had so far refused to receive; would the Mandarins either convey it to him, or open and read it themselves, on condition that it was placed in their government archives? As to returning to Macao, he would go when it suited him.

After this there was some desultory conversation, perhaps while the Mandarins pondered their next move. One of them then pertinently observed that the King of England ought to have written himself first to the Viceroy. Not so, said William John; his King could only correspond on equal terms with the Emperor.

The Mandarins were probably staggered by this outlandish notion; and at this point in their meeting, here in this far distant country, in the stifling afternoon, in his stifling uniform, for the first and last time in his life, William John pulled rank. The Chinese, the people of Howqua and Mowqua, who, however now subservient, remained always suave and dignified, were one thing; the Manchu were another. The Chinese had been spinning silk and exchanging philosophical concepts when the people of William John had been painted bright blue and roaring down the hill, naked claymore in hand. But these Manchu lords, now dressed in exquisite embroidered silk, had barely 200 years ago been greasy nomads, eating melted butter and fermented mare's milk, living in reeking tents, and raging over their desolate landscape on horses far too small for them and putting to the sword every man, woman, and child who stood in their way. Nine hundred years ago William John's forebears had been living in stone castles and worshipping a living God; 300 years ago they had still been owners of large tracts of Scotland, living in their castle outside Edinburgh, writing theological works on the Trinity and inventing logarithms and the decimal point. He would stand no further nonsense on this score.

None of this, of course, found utterance. In his usual level tones he told his hearers that he was 'a hereditary nobleman in his own country, was of much higher rank than any mandarin present and on a perfect equality with the Viceroy or Governor, and a proper channel for such a communication as he had been sent to make'.

There was a brief pause. Could he not tell them his business verbally, the Chief among the Mandarins asked? Certainly not – he must officially present his letter, insisted William John. Why not through the Hong Merchants? This point had once again to be firmly resisted.

The meeting then adjourned, and refreshments and wine were offered, and partaken of in what seemed total amity. Everyone smiled, bowed, and as far as was in them owing to the language difficulty, joked. They all parted seemingly as good friends, the Mandarins hinting at an early return. Just as he left, the Kwang-Chou-Lei, or chief military officer, said in jovial tones that it would be very unfortunate were the two nations to come to a rupture. Not at all, William John replied, equally jovially, to this veiled threat; on our parts we were perfectly prepared, but the general might be assured of His Majesty's most gracious desire of maintaining the friendliest intercourse with the Emperor of China.

Privately William John thought that the Mandarins had only come because of the two frigates anchored at the mouth of the river. Why the Viceroy sent them remains unknown; perhaps he thought these dangerous persons from Peking might be obscurely discredited and lose face, if they too failed to deal with this determined envoy. All that is certain is that The Chief of the Censorate went away from his visit to Canton laden with so much gold that the price of it rose sharply on the Canton market. It is only guesswork that a favourable report on his merits as an official had been bought at a high price by Viceroy Loo.

* * *

'In any other country' Napier told the Foreign Secretary, 'the disposition of the chairs would have been a matter of trivial importance', but in a country like China, 'where actions are entirely governed by etiquette', it had been important; and was so considered by the other Superintendents, who told him that the Mandarins' yielding in such a matter 'affords to them the strongest proof' of how needful it was 'to conduct business with firmness and determination. The slightest concession is sure to be followed by subsequent embarrassment and defeat'. [The Chinese, in other matters so inventive, had come lately to chairs, upon which Egyptians had been sitting for at least 5,000 years. In their hearts they remained seated on mats on the floor; the exact title of Chairman Mao was 'Mat-master Mao'.]

* * *

On 27 August, William John sent off a cheerful report by the *Spartan*. He now heard that the Hong merchants had stopped the trade 'in a pet', and contrary to the wishes of the Governor, who had had it forced upon

him by the Kwang-Chou-Foo, who was said to have since departed for
Peking. The Viceroy's edict of 18 August had only threatened to stop the
trade, and then spoken of indulgence and delay. The majority of the
Hong had been against the ban, he heard, 'but old Howqua, who rules
the roost, and who has no commercial dealings with the British has all
the others under his thumb as his debtor, so carried the day'. These tales
were possibly true; Howqua had nothing to lose under the trade ban,
and most to lose by being squeezed from on high.

All the same, it seemed as if some of the younger Hong were anxious
to find some way of going back on the ban without loss of Viceregal face.
'In all respects', the Foreign Secretary was told, 'events have been decidedly in our favour', and the fact that his request to the Viceroy to send a
high military officer to see him had been followed two days later by the
proposal of the visit from three Mandarins of high rank had been
promising. He was sending an official report, but in this private letter he
did not resist telling Palmerston of how half-drunk poor Mowqua had
become 'on Constantia and Cherry Brandy' during the discussion over
the chairs. It seemed oddly 'vacillating and undecided', after all those
refusals to see him, for the Viceroy suddenly to send three Mandarins to
confer with 'an outside Barbarian'. It was 'an occurrence which has
astonished the shopkeepers beyond measure. They – poor devils – would
be happy to trade with us on any terms'.

William's sympathy with these uncomplaining and heavily oppressed
people was increasing every day. They asked little of life, and got less
than that little. He very much wanted to be in direct contact with them,
and the people of the Canton countryside in general, because he felt
they had been entirely foxed by their rulers as to the benevolence of
British intentions towards them. Accordingly he was getting Morrison to
draft 'a letter for circulation among the mercantile community in general', pointing out that the reason for his presence in Canton was in
answer to a Chinese request; he had been refused reception, and for that
reason he was not going away.

The big news, he told Palmerston, was that the Kwang- Chou-Foo had
been suddenly dismissed from office, to be replaced by the Chaou-Chow-
Foo, and that the Hoppo, or Revenue Commissioner was also on the
move. 'He is known as skin-flint in his own language, the greatest extor-
tioner ever sent from Peking.' The Hoppo's dismissal was unexplained,
'he appeared a stupid laughing old man, who was not possessed of two
ideas. The Chaou was the orator, and an impudent fellow for the occasion; the military Kwang a fine looking coarse-featured old man and
extremely desirous of accommodating matters. But it was quite impossible to *send messages* on important business – these men are all the most

dexterous liars imaginable, and I had no security that my business would have been properly reported'.

Meanwhile the Chinese population, as yet little affected by all these high-up changes, were celebrating a religious festival with their usual enthusiasm: the night sky was splendid with soaring fireworks. Across the river and from Canton itself came joyful shoutings, and the warm, still, nights were blazing with festal lights. 'The whole community including Mandarins and Hong merchants are much taken up with feasts and oblations dedicated to the Devil by way of propitiating him to show mercy to such of their friends as have fallen within his clutches. The illuminations on board the vessels on the river are magnificent every evening, and all sorts of orgies are there performed.' The Chinese people, in themselves, so splendid but so oppressed, deluded, and a prey to grinding poverty, with their pitiful earnings squeezed out of them, were beginning to arouse in William feelings alarmingly paternal. 'Surely it would be an act of Charity to take them into one's hands altogether, and no difficult job.' His heart kindled with a vision of plump Chinamen, their legs no longer like a couple of crutches, their bodies as well-fed and well-cherished as his own tenants in the green glens of home.

Meanwhile, he had organized a suitable festivity for his own people. 'Our lower stories have all been afloat by the floods within these last three days, so it was only yesterday that I could make out a dinner in Honour of His Majesty's Birthday. I believe every Englishman in Canton dined with me but one – and a principal one too – who has not yet got over his party feelings.' (Dent, perhaps?) 'Everything went off in the greatest harmony', William John concluded happily.

Next morning, on the 28th, he was happier still. The bag of mail was closed, and the *Spartan* on her way downstream, but she could be overtaken. At noon he opened the bag to tell Palmerston that the ever active Howqua and Mowqua had just been to request that Lord Napier 'would receive four Mandarins on Saturday next'. He had, of course, agreed, but the coming of four more bigwigs must surely mean that things were on the move, the refusal of the Viceroy to see him might be 'tottering, which will soon lead I hope to an amicable adjustment of our difficulties'.

But Lord Napier's next Chinese visitors were to be of quite another kind.

17

Forcing the Bogue and a Pause at Whampoa

It is to be doubted whether the Napier Commission would ever have won through to an interview with the Viceroy of Canton, however patient and good-humoured its leader was, because too great a loss of face would by now have been incurred by the Viceroy in granting one. He was uninterested in precedents set by former Viceroys and even more deeply uninterested in change. William John's next move made it certain that no interview would ever be given.

On 29 August, the Superintendent's attempt to communicate directly with the Chinese people was posted up at street corners in Canton. It was brought swiftly to the Viceroy's notice that in it the Chief Superintendent had spoken of 'the obstinacy and ignorance' shown in stopping the trade, 'whereby thousands of industrious Chinese must suffer ruin and discomfort through the perversity of their government'. This well-meaning attempt to explain to the locals the friendly nature of British intentions towards them was a mistake – the fatal innocent error in the frequent assumption by English gentlemen that those with whom they had to deal were governed by the same ethic as themselves, and that one had only to tell the truth of a situation and others would surely see it. Quite another truth was about to be revealed – when you are 40 miles from the safety and freedom of the sea, and guarded only by 20 marines, though it may be safe to drop leaflets from the air, it is unsafe to have them posted up in person.

To the Chinese authorities this was the sin of sins, the sin against the Holy Ghost. The Mongol invasion had been fostered by traitors within, so had the Manchu invasion; the same subversion was at work when rebellions from Ming claimants broke out, as they not infrequently did. For Viceroy Loo this proclamation was by far too much: the posters were to him simply an incitement to subversion. Confucian tenderness to strangers quickly went by the board. Loo reacted with fury, issuing an indignant proclamation himself on 2 September. It did not mince matters.

'A lawless foreign slave, named Laboriously Vile, has issued a notice.

We do not know how such a barbarian dog can have the audacity to call himself an Eye. If he were so in fact, though he were a savage from beyond the pale, his sense of propriety would have restrained him from such an outrage. It is a capital offence to incite the people against their rulers and we would be justified in obtaining a mandate for his decapitation and the exposure of his head as a warning to traitors.'

A second edict followed on the same day. The Viceroy told of how he had sent the Mandarins to see Lord Napier to find out why he would not send his credentials through the Hong merchants. These merchants, perhaps through fear, had not made the Viceroy's orders sufficiently plain, for the barbarian mind was slow and dull. 'The Barbarian Eye has listened to what was told him as though entangled in a net. He is stupid indeed, blinded, ignorant. To make him see reason has been impossible, so misled and extravagant a man is he. There can be no quiet while he remains here; I therefore formally close the trade until he goes.'

'The said Barbarian Eye, Vile Labouring Beast, has cut himself off from the Celestial Empire. It is not at all what we, the Viceroy and Governor, could have desired. The barbarian merchants of all other nations are permitted to trade as usual. Let all with trembling awe obey. Oppose not, a special Edict.'

An embargo was now laid upon all ship's boats proceeding from the English ships at Whampoa to the Factory at Canton, where all British merchants were to be isolated. Upon pain of death for disobedience, all in British employment – their brokers, agents, interpreters, porters, servants and boatmen were withdrawn. No Englishman, from either Whampoa or Macao, might enter the Factory; to enforce this a chain of boats was drawn up along the riverside so that exit or entrance by that means was impossible. Round the landward sides of the Factory a double rank of soldiers was drawn up; and on its walls were posted notices accusing the Barbarian Eye of every known or imaginable form of sexual perversion and threatening him with an extremely unpleasant end.

The old-woman image which Viceroy Loo had seemed to William John to present to the world had emphatically been discarded.

On the day before this edict came out, William John's secretary, young Alexander Johnstone, had begun to see signs that the Chief Superintendent was under attack from an enemy more dangerous than any Chinese Viceroy. It was just a fortnight since Dr Morrison had died of fever, from one of those unknown viruses to which Europeans in China, and particularly newcomers, were especially prone; perhaps it was the same deadly virus that now laid siege to William John. As he kept no journal after his landing at Macao, it is impossible to say what his plans had been; but his proclamation to the Cantonese people had perhaps been intended to explain to them why he now meant to leave Canton and go down river. But whatever he had intended, he could not now retreat in the face of what had openly become the enemy. Increasingly ill every day, William John now felt it incumbent to stay put and fight it out. He was an extremely healthy man, and had no doubts about recovery.

* * *

On 4 September, Sir George Best Robinson, Bart, the 2nd Superintendent, recorded, they were all sitting at dinner (a meal which still took place in the later afternoon) 'when the room was suddenly crowded by the Chinese of different classes in our service, and those connected with the establishment of the East India Company, compradors, cooks, coolies etc., who ran upstairs in great alarm, saying the mandarin soldiers had surrounded and were about to enter the Factory'. Going down, 'we found a line of them drawn up in front, and a great number assembling in the public square, part of whom were landed from boats, which were then moved in front of the garden and stairs in such a manner as to prevent all egress. These vessels were furnished with spears, lances, swords, etc., and both chains and iron manacles were displayed. The doors were closely beset, and I considered we were about to be made prisoners'.

'All the Chinese having left the Hong, there remained His Majesty's Superintendents, and the Europeans attached to their establishment, eight or nine persons. It was intimated to me by many Chinese that threats were uttered on the part of the mandarins, of unroofing our houses, preventing all supplies of provisions, and seizing, or at best, closely confining to the Hong, the Chief Superintendent – to prevent his escape', Alexander Johnstone, also present, made a statement confirming all this, adding that he had seen the Viceroy's edict being pinned up on the wall, and heard threats to set the Factory on fire.

After which, dinner was resumed, presumably, and finished. William John, who could at least no longer complain that the Chinese authorities were unable to make up their minds also made up his, in consultation with his staff. The rabble of soldiers without were threatening, and though he had never been much concerned for his own skin, he had the lives of his colleagues, and the treasury in the Factory to consider. It had become the fashion among the foreign community to be extremely mocking of the Chinese and their threats, but aside from the *Lady Hughes'* gunner, an Englishman called Francis Scott had been executed by the Chinese authorities, a Frenchman had been publicly strangled in 1780, and the American seaman, Terranovia, had been surrendered to them and strangled in 1821, only 13 years ago. Maybe the noisy demonstration and the threats of execution amounted to nothing much: maybe they did. Whether he was by now very feverish or whether he thought it a necessary precaution – as did his advisers – William John sent a message to Captain Blackwood that he should, 'remedy these inconveniences, and afford protection to the EI Company's treasury, request that a guard of marines might be landed at the Factory, and also that HM Ships *Andromache* and *Imogene* might pass the Bogue, and take up a convenient position at Whampoa, for the more efficient protection of British subjects and their property'. He added emphatically that the ships were *not* to fire unless fired upon. It does not sound a very fevered message.

The night was not made more peaceful by the discovery of a Chinaman who had climbed up the verandah with a view to arson; another was heard trying, and failing, to scale the wall. By midnight, the question of pilots was exercising William John's mind, since he realized that no local pilot, so necessary in the river, was going to risk the death penalty imposed by the Viceroy on anyone working for the British. The difficulty was that the cutter *Louisa*, the only shallow water craft, was still at Macao, where she had borne the mourners in Dr Morrison's funeral.

Robinson, despite his best efforts, reported that he could not find either man or boat to carry William John's message telling the frigates to wait the arrival of Elliot and the cutter *Louisa*, since she would have difficulty in winning past the Bogue forts unless in company with the frigates. Robinson then 'proposed to Lord Napier, with whom I most fully and entirely concurred throughout and in all respect, that I should myself be the bearer of his letter to Captain Blackwood'. (The first letter had gone down the river in the schooner *Hawk*, property of Jardine Matheson and Co.)

Aided by Mr C Markwick, and at some risk to both, Robinson stole out in the early hours and boarded the schooner *St. George*. Arriving at Whampoa, Robinson was delighted to obtain the services of Mr. Wilson, second officer of the merchantman *Fort William* to pilot *Imogene* up the river. Robinson and the pilot both arrived on board *Imogene* off Chuenpee at midnight on the 5th, much relieved to find that the marines had already been sent off. Robinson then sent the *St. George* on to Macao, to warn the local shipping of what was going on at Canton, and to hasten the cutter *Louisa* in joining the frigates. These large ships themselves were not summoned to Canton, since the river depth above Whampoa would not allow of their passage.

Back at the Factory, Alexander Johnstone had 'thought it necessary to keep watch during the whole night until the arrival of the marines'.

These, brushing aside any attempt at opposition, moved up river briskly and made their way into the Factory on the evening of 5 September. It was reassuring to have them, but as Johnstone pointed out, they made another 23 mouths to feed, as they had only carried two days' rations. Luckily, William John, with considerable foresight, had brought a quantity of 'salt provisions from Europe' with him, and the neighbouring factories smuggled in supplies, so that hardship in this respect was not great.

'All this day and until the 21st of September', Johnstone wrote, 'the premises by day and by night were constantly surrounded by soldiers, and the part of the Hong which looks upon the river was closely barricaded by boats lashed together.' One of the marines, bored by being cooped up by the surround of jeering Chinese soldiers, had managed to crawl out and disappeared into the town of Canton, from which he returned with a flapping chicken in hand. But the guards, enraged by this kind of insouciance, tore the poor bird from him, so that he regained the Factory with nothing left but its head, clutched in his determined hands. Johnstone noted that William John's health had rapidly declined since the 1st of the month, and that he had not improved it by 'constant attention and application to business, day and night'. Neither was it helped by 'the want of wholesome food and exercise, with the thermometer frequently in his rooms at 90'. By the 9th, his fever had mounted dangerously, but even if he decided to go, to whom could he hand over? Davis was an elderly scholar, and Robinson was now on board *Imogene*. How give up now, asked William John, when it was his own impasse?

* * *

Down in the Bay of Canton, and still with 'no fresh grub', the days had passed slowly for the ships' companies of *Andromache* and *Imogene*, still anchored off Chuenpee, though Captain Blackwood was back on board, which made activity more probable. But on the 5th, things began to look up for Midshipman Brickdale, and for others who shared the lively bloodthirstiness natural to his age. On that day, he told his parents, 'some orders came down from Canton of a warlike kind, for we sent up eight marines and a mate and *Andromache* sent eight marines and a Lieutenant and a mate as guard to Lord Napier'.

'We also prepared to force the Bocca Tigris', Charles Brickdale went on to his parents, 'that is to say we knocked out the Bulkheads of the Captain's cabin and mounted two of the guns that were on the upper deck in their proper place etc.'

After this there had come a disappointing lull. 'We should have started next day but the Government cutter was down at Macao and if we did not protect her past the Forts they would not have let her come up afterwards so that we did not start till Sunday'.

'Unfortunately the sea breeze which had set in strong almost every day that we had been here did not set in till 11 o'clock and then foul and very light.'

'We weighed in company with the *Andromache* and cutter (we are senior officer so of course took the lead) and stood across towards the right bank of the river. Having stood over far enough we tacked and stood towards the Old and New Forts on the other bank.'

At this point, warning shots were fired from the fort at Chuenpee, under which the ships had hitherto been lying. 'They fired some blank guns and the junks of war that were laying near it did the same, however we took no notice of that. They fired a few shots after that (not blanks) but they fell a long way short of us.'

Imogene and *Andromache* were now four miles into the defile proceeding with deathly slowness up the calm water. 'The Chinese', Charles Brickdale explained, 'fire without parley or warning shots. We tacked again and the Old and New Forts began firing at us so we made the signal to the *Andromache* to commence action. She was still on the starb'd tack standing over towards Whangtong so that she commenced firing her starboard guns at the old Fort with great execution; we were then engaging the Fort at Whangtong with our larboard guns. As we had continued to advance the Whangtong Fort fired two shots which we returned with the focsle gun and as the fort continued to fire we returned it with two of our main deck guns (in fact we were very forbearing only returning shot for shot).'

'The action then became general, both the forts firing away at us and the *Andromache*. The New Fort behaved very cowardly, I do not think they reloaded their guns once, if they even fired them at all. The Whangtong behaved a great deal better, loading their guns as fast as they could and firing.'

'We stood close over to the New Fort and then tacked, we were then in a position to be raked by the Whangtong Fort, so that we kept up a constant fire on the Whangtong, and the *Andromache* on the New Fort, which was a very pretty sight.' An even prettier sight was provided by Captain Elliot, sitting on the deck of the unarmed *Louisa* cutter with his umbrella up, though whether to shield himself from the blazing September sun or from the splashes of the shot falling all round the *Louisa* it was impossible to say.

Making towards Whampoa was not easy. Any ship attempting to force the narrow defile was obliged to tack backwards and forwards, during which she would come under point blank range from successive batteries. *Imogene* and *Andromache*, with the wind now almost dead against them, were no exception. After passing the four first forts, two on each side of the defile, (the first two with little opposition) they would be faced with a fifth, on Tiger Island, looking down the defile towards Wantong, where the river was less than half a mile wide.

In fitful breezes, under a thundery sky, they passed with slow pace through the deep defile, but had now to pass the narrowest part of the Bogue. At one o'clock the wind shifted into the North, slowing both vessels. There was so little help from the wind that when abreast of the fort at the end of their tack they had all but lost what little way they had on. With 14 guns on each side, these being 32 pounders, protected only by their wooden bulwarks, the frigates had to encounter probably 30 heavy calibre guns in stone casemates firing from each fortress, and should have been entirely at their mercy.

But the cannon in the forts were fixed in the stonework of their loopholes, and so could only hit a target directly to their front. The Chinese called this defile the Lion's Mouth, but to make it less than a paper lion would have needed the importation of foreign guns, or at least of foreign gunners to show the Chinese how to traverse their guns, and to date this had not been done.

It took the frigates an hour to pass upstream out of gunshot from the two forts, even with the aid of the now flooding tide. At 2.15 the wind dropped completely, and it was necessary to anchor. Here, windless in the hot green landscape, between hills that were now lower, the ships were obliged to stay until the afternoon of 9 September. Ahead lay Tiger Island.

Midshipman Charles Brickdale had never been in action before, and was naturally excited. Those at home were going to hear all about it, because although it would not mean much to Grandmamma or Miss Holland or the Aunts, it would to the men of the family, and it would make them realize that he too was a man. 'I will tell you the damage we received. We had one shot that carried away our larboard main shrouds, came close over the hammock netting and passing through all the people on the Quarter Deck went over the starboard Quarter without doing any other harm; another shot came through on the Quarter Deck about five feet above the Deck, passed through the whole group of men that were standing there hauling a rope in, grazed the Main Mast and went overboard having wounded one man with a Splinter.'

'There were two shot struck her about three feet above the water's edge of which one went through and broke the whole of the mess things belonging to two of the men's messes and fell down on the Lower Deck and was picked up there, the other one struck the Ship's side.'

'There was also a shot that cut one of the chain plates away and it is very lucky that it did or else it would have gone through onto the Main Deck and most likely have killed a great many men.'

'The *Andromache* had only two shots struck her and nobody hurt. We had several minor ropes cut away by shots, however we thought ourselves very lucky considering that there were nearly a hundred guns playing at us.' These were the first shots in a long, sad war of West versus East, but a cheerful 15 year old was not to know this.

'We had another fort to pass for which we wanted a fair wind as the passage was not more than 700 yards broad and we expected to pass within about 50 yards of it.'

* * *

For two days the frigates lay idly, anchored on a river ruffled only by its currents, while matters at Canton came to be dominated by the increasing illness of William John. By the 9th, his fever had mounted dangerously, but Dr Colledge could not persuade him to give up and go to bed to recover. If he were to take this advice, to whom could he hand over? Robinson was still on board *Imogene*, becalmed in the river, Davis was not yet back from Macao, Elliot was equally wind-bound in the *Louisa*.

William Jardine, now back at Canton, had started his career as a ship's doctor, before turning merchant adventurer and opium smuggler, and Dr Colledge now called him in, to add weight to his own advice.

William John was certainly a trier. The more Irish the situation became, the more set he became on persuading his opposite number to see reason. They had asked specifically for a Superintendent and then refused to see him when he came; they promulgated new laws without making them known and then punished people for disobeying them. But he was still a believer in sweet reason, and on the 8th he had sat down to answer the Viceroy's edict of September 2nd, which had by now found its way to him.

The heat was oppressive, a sullen heavy blanket hanging over the South China plain. The temperature in the Factory stood all day at 90, dropping at night only to 84. William John's temperature stayed steadily in the hundreds, high at each sultry dawn, soaring again in the evenings. He sat determinedly at his desk, writing and copying.

His letter was addressed to William Boyd (newly appointed secretary at the merchants' meeting) for forwarding to the Hong merchants, since there was now clearly no other means of communication. This had always meant that no message was ever delivered as pronounced to the Viceroy, since the Hong were always too terrified of him to let him have it straight. And in insisting that communication had always been held exclusively through the Hong, the Viceroy was not stating the truth. 'During the last 200 years, constant personal intercourse has been maintained between the Viceroy of Canton and the British subjects resorting thither', so that the allegation in the edict 'is not founded in fact', and having consulted the records, William John produced chapter and verse:

'List of times when the Viceroy has received officers or merchants:
1637   Captain Weddel
1734   The Supracargoes of the East India Company
1742   Commodore Anson
1759   Mr Flint and the Supracargoes
1792   A Committee from England
1795   The Supracargoes
1805   Mr Roberts and Sir George Staunton
1806   Mr Roberts, and later on in the year Mr Drummond and Mr Elphinstone
1811   Sir George Staunton
1816   Sir Theophilus Metcalfe and Captain Chavell, RN
and on many other occasions the Chiefs of the Factory on their annual return from Macao to Canton. Therefore, the allegation of the said Loo and Ke is not founded on fact.'

As to who he was and why he was there, the Kwang-Chou-Foo and Chaou-Chou-Foo had both seen him in the King's uniform at their reception, and would have seen his credentials and known why he had come, had they taken his letter to the Viceroy, 'and had His Excellency given him the same reception as had been usually accorded to others'.

So far, so polite; but the Superintendent had heard news that made him hot with more than climate and fever. It seemed that the Viceroy's latest ploy was to pretend that Lord Napier had no standing at all, was not an envoy, not an officer, not really anything; and one unlucky individual had been executed for maintaining that he had seen his lordship arriving in a King's ship, and another, a linguist, had been tortured and imprisoned. The letter continued in some anger and ended with a short but unmistakable lion's roar.

After the Viceroy had pronounced his 'indulgence and delay' in not enforcing the ban on trade, William wrote, the merchants 'in full reliance on the honor of the Viceroy', had continued to buy and sell as before, and then, on 2 September, Loo had declared all these transactions null and void as from 16 August – an act of 'unprecedented tyranny and injustice', and his order that ships should not come up river meant that those on their way to unload their own goods and pick up their cargoes of tea, for which they had already paid, were now to be held up.

William John protested against the stopping of the trade, and warned that 'it is a serious offence to fire upon the British flag'. On the orders of the Viceroy this had now happened – 'they have opened the preliminaries of war, they destroy trade, and incur the loss of life of unoffending people rather than grant to me the same courtesy that has been granted to others before me'.

Loo and Ke knew very well that Napier had been sent there by his King at their own request, 'Why do they vainly contend against their own actions, to the destruction of trade and the misery of thousands?' He would, William John assured Loo, repeat the entire course of events to the Emperor in Peking, and also the actions of the new Kwang-Chou-Foo, 'who has tortured the linguists and cruelly imprisoned a respectable individual, Sun-Shing, a security merchant, for not having aquiesced in a base lie', [that Napier had arrived in a merchant ship.]

His Imperial Majesty, William John stated confidently, 'will not permit such folly, wickedness and cruelty to go unpunished; therefore tremble, Governor Loo, intensely tremble'! Loo seemed to have no idea of what a great and powerful monarch the King of England was, William John went on. King William was 'respectfully subservient to no-one. He rules over an extent of territory in the four quarters of the world more comprehensive in space and infinitely more so in power than the whole of the Empire of China. He commands armies of bold and fierce soldiers, who have conquered wherever they went, he is possessed of great ships of war carrying even as many as 120 guns, which pass quietly along the seas where no native of China has ever yet dared to show his face.'

William John feared the Hong merchants would be afraid of passing on such a letter, but he added that if he had no reply from the Viceroy by the 15th of the month, he would publish it on the streets and circulate copies among the people, 'one of which may peradventure find its way into His Excellence's presence'.

William John concluded with his small roar. 'The Hong merchants are already aware that there are two frigates now in the river, bearing very heavy guns for the express purpose of protecting the British trade, and I would warn them again and again that if any disagreeable consequences shall ensue from the said Edicts, they themselves, with the Viceroy and Governor, are responsible for the whole..'

Three days later, on the 11th, the Viceroy did reply, by the simple process of brushing aside almost everything that the Superintendent had said. On that same evening, William John was so ill that Dr Colledge told him that unless he at once downed tools and went to the coolness of Macao, he would not answer for the consequences. Through a season which the doctor described as exceptionally hot and oppressive, the Chief Superintendent had worked hard and long, and enough was enough; go he must. His life was in danger.

* * *

An unbroken stillness hung over the river on the baking morning of 9 September. *Imogene* and *Andromache* were still whistling for a wind. 'Unluckily we could not get any wind till the 9th', Midshipman Brickdale lamented from mid-river, still some ten miles from Whampoa. 'I feel quite convinced that the Governor of the Forts in their official letters said that they damaged us so that we were obliged to remain two days to repair; at all events the report up at Canton', (he learned later) 'was that we were *dreadfully damaged aloft* and had *several hands* killed and wounded. We got under weigh about two o'clock in the afternoon with a light breeze and stood across the river, which we were obliged to do to get into the Channel.'

'When we bore up to run past the Fort they might have raked us very easily, however they kept their fire till we were close, the Captain gave order to *double shot* all the guns for the first round and it was a time of very great anxiety running close and expecting every moment to have a shot at us.'

'At 2.30, the Fort commenced firing the first shot and we immediately commenced a very heavy carronading which we kept up with great spirit the lads cheering away finely. Our distance was about 300 yards, they fired all the guns at us as they bore but they fired so badly we only had one shot struck us which came through the Forecastle Hammock netting and took the head off a fine young man called Plat who was Captain of the Forecastle gun and killed him instantly the Splinters also wounded a man called James Trod who was stationed at the same gun', and Brickdale's punctuation fled from him in the excitement.

'Our efforts were all supported by the *Andromache* so that at 2.35 the Fort ceased firing but we continued firing till our guns would not bear which was at 2.45' – they had carried on in case the Fort on Tiger Island opened up again on *Andromache* or the following cutter *Louisa* – 'having kept up a continual fire with our guns double-shotted we fired about ten Broadsides'.

'The *Andromache* had a shot entered into one of her ports which killed one man and wounded three. We thus (after their having had fair warning) forced the passage of the Bocca Tigris which the Chinese thought impassable, with two small ships and a foul wind. If the same forts had been manned with Europeans they would have sunk us over and over again.'

'We anchored the same evening about four o'clock, we were 'about three days getting up to Whampoa as the Channel is very intricate and we were obliged to put marks down in one place, we also got on shore twice but we got off both times in a very short time.' Before they left deep water the bodies of that fine young man Platt, and the seaman from *Andromache* were committed to the deep, heavily weighted, with the burial service read in full, the bared heads, the usual honours.

'We got up to Whampoa in the evening of the 11th and have been laying here ever since.' 'It is gratifying to me', Captain Blackwood of the *Imogene* wrote to Charles Brickdale's parents, 'to express to you my continued satisfaction at the correctness and propriety of your son's conduct. His behaviour whilst under fire and engaging the batteries of Bocca Tigris and Tigre (or Piper) Island was all I could wish.' He had done well; and certainly they would have no cause to complain of him as a correspondent.

* * *

Viceroy Loo was by now very angry; an anger largely compounded of fear that these untoward goings on in the Pearl River would reach the ears of the Emperor. 'The great ministers of the Celestial Empire', he repeated in his edict of the 11th, 'are not permitted to have interviews with outside barbarians' (unless they came bearing tribute). 'The affairs of the former Ming dynasty need not to be brought into discussion.' As to any interviews granted by 'the great Tsing dynasty', these had only been given 'in cases of receiving tribute', Napier's list of chapter and verse when these conditions had *not* been operative, Loo passed over in dignified silence. All that Loo was doing, he pointed out, was obediently maintaining the national dignity. 'From the first I have not been commencing what is strange, or sounding forth my loftiness'.

Failing to get an answer about why Napier had come, or who he was, Loo had even sent officers to the barbarian factories, to make personal enquires. 'On the part of me, the Governor, it was the utmost, the extreme of careful regard and perfect kindness.' This had still brought no response, and 'with extreme pain of mind' Loo had ordered the ships' holds to be closed.

'The said Barbarian Eye has not learned to arouse from his previous errors'; and furthermore he had 'alarmed the local population' by bringing in the 20 marines. As to his 'commanding the ships of war to push forward into the inner river' and allowing them to fire their guns, this is still more out of the bounds of reason'.

'The soldiers and horses of the Celestial Empire, its thundering forces, guns and weapons are assembled on the hills, one and all are there; and if it were desired to make a great display of conquering chastisement, how could the petty little warships afford any protection? Besides, all the merchants trading here, I, the Governor, treat most liberally; what need is there of protection?'

'By such ignorant and absurd conduct, entering far into the Important Country, he is already within my grasp. Arrangements have been made now to assemble a large force, ranged out both by sea and land. What difficulty will there be', Loo wanted to know, 'in immediately destroying and eradicating?'

But, Loo added, he was slow to act, 'because I consider that such movements are not according to the wishes of the said nation's King, nor are they according to the wishes of the several merchants'. Here was a last chance for the Barbarian Eye 'to repent of his errors, and withdraw the ships of war'. If so, 'I will yet give him some slight indulgence'. If not, The Viceroy would find it 'difficult again to display endurance and forbearance'.

There was a rumour going the rounds that had not yet reached William John, to the effect that Loo was for yielding, and Ke for fighting; but this hawk and dove distinction had declared itself but faintly. The Viceroy concluded his edict on a cryptic note. 'I apprehend that when the Celestial troops once come, even precious stones will burn before them: on no account defer repentance till afterwards.' This, the experts said, meant that the troops might be dispersed by a heavy bribe, but only if it came to hand right now. The edict ended on an altogether unexceptionable note. The Hong were to make all these things known to the merchants, commanded the Viceroy, 'with even temper, reasoning upon it'. Even now, with a little common sense and some financial adjustments, the much desired tranquillity might be resumed.

* * *

Pacing the deck of the frigate *Imogene*, now anchored at Whampoa, Captain Blackwood had no notion of being within anyone's grasp, and temperamentally disinclined to tremble exceedingly at the behest of any man. He wanted to send Robinson and Davis back to Canton, where they belonged, and he would have liked consultation with the beleaguered Chief Superintendent. He decided that a party of seamen and marines in boats could probably fight their way through to Canton if the British Factory were actually in immediate danger, and British

lives at risk. Otherwise the losses involved would be unacceptable, the
risks too great. The frigates themselves could hardly proceed more than
a mile or two further up the river, where they ran the risk of being
grounded.

The concrete blockships that the Chinese were reported to have sunk
in the channels on the approach to Canton were beside the point, as the
frigates were effectively blocked by the shallows; and the blockships were
unlikely to halt the progress of the small boats in which any move on
Canton would have to be made. But owing to his slow progress, due to
contrary winds since leaving the Bay of Canton, the Chinese had had
time to amass numbers of ships in the river between Whampoa and
Canton, and he could see for himself that the nearby shores and hills
were swarming with Chinese soldiers. He had been summoned upstream
to protect British lives and property at Whampoa and told not to fire
unless fired upon; the placid waters of the harbour were crowded with
British shipping. Their need for protection seemed greater than the
danger at Canton. The experience of Robinson and Davis was useful;
they reckoned, probably correctly, that the Viceroy might threaten but
would not attack the English Factory, or permanently upset a trade from
which both he and his master the Emperor derived such vast sums of
money.

Having but problematic alternatives, Blackwood in *Imogene* and Chads
in *Andromache* sat tight and enjoyed the scenery, keeping a sharp look-
out for fire-boats, or other signs of Chinese hostile activity.

The harbour at Whampoa was as far into China as most Britons got,
and was the place from whence they formed their impressions of the
Celestial Empire – full marks for picturesqueness, five per cent for worthy behaviour. Chinese callousness to their fellows in misfortune
particularly struck home, being so wholly out of accord with the
European tradition by which one rescued everyone from drowning,
friend or foe, in war or peace. All the same, in many ways Whampoa was
a seaman's Paradise, especially after the very long sea voyages which
brought them there. It was here that the sea-going ships unloaded their
wares into smaller craft for transfer the remaining 13 miles to the walls
of Canton; and here they waited for the tea and silks, the cassia, the
carved sandalwood boxes, the jade and the ivory figurines they had
come so far to find. Whampoa Island was long and green and full of
wine-shops and welcoming Chinese girls; the fact that a European ceme-
tery, tenanted at an alarming rate, had been laid out ominously nearby
appeared to deter no-one.

Long before an incoming vessel could come to anchor, the strong and
cheerful boat-girls in sampans would be alongside, vigorously plying the

one oar over their sterns, proffering much needed oranges, lemons and fresh vegetables; offering to wash, iron, mend, and otherwise service sailors' clothes, and to supply any other wants that a long, lonely and hazardous journey had aroused.

Against a background of rice fields and low hills, Whampoa Roads presented a lively spectacle. Dozens of tall-masted clippers, and other ships less speedy, lay there amongst Chinese junks, shaped like goggle-eyed Noah's Arks, many-oared Chinese 'centipedes', smaller, stockier boats with rush-matting awnings housing large families, leading their close-knit lives almost permanently on the water, peopled by yelling children with intelligent black eyes, and propelled by a single oar fore and aft. Occasionally a beautifully painted Mandarin boat, with shield-hung sides and a dragon prow would pass swiftly on its master's errands; and always amongst the fishermen and the trading boats piled high with pots, or lanterns, or paper toys, were the seething mass of indefatigable sampans, their shouting crews plying their varied wares for trade with the incoming ships, with their chequerboard hulls, squared yards and spread awnings, tall as cranes and graceful as swans amongst a busy crowd of ducks.

Fishing vessels clustered on the shore of Whampoa village; from the trees behind it rose a tall pagoda. Between the two monsoons that regulated the arrival and departure of the trading ships from afar, the waters of Whampoa Roads knew hardly a dull moment. Yet another salt-encrusted vessel would ride in from Chuenpee, and every so often, when wind and tide were right, a tall clipper laden with tea would shake out her white sails and make off down the river for the open sea and home.

From all these delights, the British sailors were for the moment barred, though the occasional daring boat-girl might be shipped forward, at the risk of ultimate destruction at the hands of local authorities. But on the whole, the wonderfully disciplined Chinese steered clear. Few welcome oranges were smuggled on board under cover of darkness. There was nothing to do but await the event. Under an interdict, and cut off from further orders by the ban on communications, they could only lie at anchor and bide their time. The wind, if any, was dead against the cutter *Louisa*, in which any further movement towards Canton must be made.

'I do not believe that anybody knows what the end of this affair will be', Brickdale told his parents. He had heard about the stoppage of supplies to the British Factory, but thought it rather pointless, 'as the Chinese allow the other people in the Factories to have as much as they please, so they go and dine with them'. He had also heard that Lord Napier 'had arrived without any letter to the Viceroy' but, more accurately, he had learned of the attempt to discredit him by insisting that he had arrived in a merchant ship and that 'one of the Chief Chinese Tea Merchants who would not say what they wanted him to, was tortured until he did'. Brickdale had gathered that the Chinese authorities had wanted Lord Napier back in Macao till they heard from the Emperor, 'but this his orders will not allow him to do'.

'We can do very little more than we have done.' Echoing (it is probable) Captain Blackwood, Brickdale concluded sensibly, 'if we even fight our way up to Canton the only thing we can do is to fight it down again which would not be much use'.

As far as reaching Canton was concerned, Blackwood was stymied. On the quarterdeck of *Imogene*, as the hot afternoon hours rolled towards yet another sunset, he could survey a scene of beauty, the many anchored ships reflected in the windless river, the hills fading into a shadowy purple. From its small conical hill on the island of Whampoa, the nine-storeyed pagoda stood up against a paling blue sky, and may have seemed to Blackwood pleasantly reminiscent of the pictures on the pretty porcelain in his mother's cabinet at home.

18

Withdrawal and a Fevered Journey

Immobile they might be, but it was with immense relief that on the morning of 12 September watchers on the roof of the British Factory at Canton saw the tall masts of *Imogene* and *Andromache* at Whampoa, clearly visible across the flat rice-fields that lay between the city and that port. The mere fact of their presence was a tonic to the British, with their surround of Chinese soldiers and others, seeming never to tire of loud insulting yells.

Howqua, chief Hong merchant, now made a friendly approach. He wanted 'to chin-chin Lord Napier, to forget all that is past, and to begin afresh'. Possibly he also wanted to see just how ill the Chief Superintendent was; this could be an important factor in the negotiations. William John, firmly quelling his fever, suggested that as soon as the trade was opened, the frigates should leave the river. To this the Hong merchants, after some parley, agreed. William John then sent the necessary message to Blackwood, and this was allowed to pass without let or hindrance.

Once the messenger had departed downstream, Howqua reappeared, forever polite and smiling, but expressing his regret. He had unfortunately 'made a mistake'; the Government would not ratify such an arrangement. The frigates must first move, and *then* the Government would reopen the trade. The hopelessness of dealing through the Hong was all too clear.

At this new manoeuvre, William John's hopes of coming to a satisfactory arrangement, if he still had any, finally died. All that he had thought and had been told, about the impossibility of communicating through the Hong merchants, was finally confirmed. On the 14th, ill and feverish, he wrote to Mr Boyd to tell him of his decision to leave for Macao. 'In answer to Messrs Whitemans' petition of 7 September, the Hoppo had undertaken to reopen the trade as soon as he himself left for Macao; 'I have now to request that you will be pleased to move the proper authorities to order up the British cutter now at Whampoa, that I may take the earliest opportunity of giving effect to the same'.

'It is undiscovered what is the subject reasoned about', the Viceroy replied next day to Boyd through the Hong merchants. If the Viceroy knew what Napier had come here for, he would put it to the Emperor, and all must await the Imperial reply. 'As to the Ships of War entering the Port, it is a thing long prohibited by the Laws. All the nations know of it. How is it that on this occasion the Ships of War have presumed to break into the Port, throwing down the Forts?' As to sending for the cutter, what did 'giving effect to the same' mean? Having gained his point over the sending away of the frigates, the Viceroy could afford to be polite, and was.

'As the Kwang-Chou-Foo does not understand my letter, I have to request you will afford him the following explanation', William John replied patiently, on the same day. His difficulty in reasoning or explaining his mission to the Viceroy lay in the latter's refusal to see him, even after 'I showed his Excellency from many examples that Englishmen of rank had been admitted to private communication with his Excellency, and it would have been but courteous of him to have placed me on the same footing'. As to the law against warships coming up the river, 'it would have been both wise and politic had the authorities provided me with a copy of such prohibitions', as the Governor had earlier complained that 'I was quite ignorant of the laws of the Celestial Empire'. He did not add that the knowledge of such laws could not be very widespread as no-one in the Factory, that is Morrison, Dr Colledge or the equally experienced 3rd Superintendent Robinson had told him of them when the moment for decision had come.

As to the ships themselves, *Andromache* would be sent at once to India, and would carry the Viceroy's replies to his letters; and the Admiral in the East Indies would act according to their tenor. The other frigate would stay at Whampoa to carry him and his staff down to Macao.

'I hope this is plain enough for the comprehension of the Kwang-Chow-Foo', William John ended, rather less patiently. Having gained his point, why could not the fellow act generously? But the Kwang-Chou-Foo had no intention of letting it rest there.

On this same evening, the 15th, William John wrote to the whole body of British merchants.

> 'Gentlemen – My letter to Mr Boyd of yesterday would prepare you for the present. I now beg leave to acquaint you that I now no longer deem it expedient to persist in a course by which you are made to suffer. I therefore addressed Mr Boyd that the authorities might provide me with the means of doing that which all parties desire, namely, to retire, and admit the opening of the trade.
>
> When I consider that the subject of dispute is not of a commercial nature, but altogether personal, I shall retire with the satisfaction of knowing that your interests are not compromised thereby, indulging

the hope that the day will yet arrive when I shall be placed in my proper position by an authority which nothing can withstand.'

Reculer pour mieux sauter [Retreat in order to leap better] was William John's hope: he believed he would soon be back, followed by effective force and operating, next time, with Factories on an island in the open sea. He had even selected a suitable one, Hong Kong, where only a few fishing families eked out an existence, to date.

'I considered it my duty', he went on, 'to use every effort to carry His Majesty's instructions into execution, and having done so hitherto without effect, though nearly accomplished on two occasions, I cannot feel authorized any longer to call on your forbearance.

I hope, Gentlemen, soon to see trade restored to its usual course of activity; and that it may long continue to prosper in your hands is the ardent wish of

Gentlemen, your obedient servant, Napier.'

* * *

"Much fruitless negotiating took place regarding the cutter" the official dispatch recorded. 'Why not send both ships of war out to the Outer Sea immediately, reporting at the same time their day and hour of sailing?' asked the Viceroy. He would then issue orders to the military forts (who were actually in no way to be able to stop them) to let them pass. As to *Imogene* remaining at Whampoa to take Lord Napier to Macao, why not send this ship also outside the Bogue, there to await him, and send the cutter up to Canton to fetch him down the river? If the cutter came up to Canton, when will the warships then sail?

It was clear that the authorities could not wait to get quit of the frigates: a reply, said the 11 Hong merchants who signed this communication, was urgent.

On the same day, the 16th, William John replied that the *Andromache* was staying at Whampoa 'on account of the more near communication; she will sail as soon as I hear the Viceroy's reply'. *Imogene* would stay at Whampoa to take him on board from the cutter, and would wait for him there.

'The frigates came up the river for the purpose of affording greater security to the persons and property of British subjects, after the most barbarous and cruel edicts of the 2nd September, which yet remain in operation', [the edict which had suggested his beheading]. 'The Authorities have to blame themselves for acting in that base manner towards the representative of his Britannic Majesty, and if the prohibitions did actually exist, they ought to have been communicated to the Superintendent officially beforehand.' [The ships had, after all, lain at Chuenpee for some days previously.]

'The frigates did not fire upon the Forts until they were obliged to do so in self defence', William John concluded firmly. Ill he might be, but defeated he was not.

If both ships were to sail at once 'to the Outer Seas at Lin Tin', then the authorities, the Hong announced, would allow the cutter up to Canton to take the Superintendent (who was still being laboriously vile) to Macao.

But no sooner was this undertaken than permission for the cutter to come to Canton was withdrawn.

From the letter of reply sent by the merchants to Lord Napier on the 16th, it was clear that they had *not* all been of one mind, a circumstance that the Viceroy had naturally exploited to the full. 'While very sensible of the sacrifice of feeling which your lordship has thus made', Boyd wrote, 'it appears due to ourselves and to the principles which have actuated us, to observe that considering the Honor of our Nation as suitably placed in the hands of His Majesty's Superintendent of Trade, and being convinced that the well-being of the trade is indissolubly bound up with that honor, we have studiously refrained from weakening the effect of your lordship's measures by an ill-timed interference in giving way to expressions of fear or discontent, or offering advice unasked respecting a negotiation of which the full bearings were not before us.'

'That unanimity so desirable in such discussions (more particularly in this country where our only power is reason and moral influence) shou.d not have existed on the present occasion, is to us a source of deep regret.'

'We feel most grateful to your Lordship for your persevering efforts and zeal in asserting our country's cause under privations of a most unusual nature, terminating at length in the sacrifice of your Lordship's health. We return our thanks for your Lordship's good wishes for the prosperity of the Trade.'

'With sentiments of high respect and ardent wishes for your speedy recovery . . .' It was signed by the British Chamber of Commerce, John Slade signing for Jardine Matheson and Co, by John Slade for Robert Turner and Co, by Arthur Saunders Keating for John Templetons and Co, and by James Innes and William Sprott Boyd, and for Lloyds by Nicholas Crooke.

On 18 September, Dr Colledge did what he had long wanted to do, persuading William John to go to bed and let him take over the prolonged but very necessary negotiations for his return to Macao. He was by now very ill; though his fever seemed to be of the recurrent kind, with intervals that seemed to point to recovery if only rest and fresh air and fresh food were obtainable.

'Lord Napier's continued indisposition rendering it desirable that his Lordship should not be harassed by a continuation of the negotiation now going on with the Chinese authorities, and that his departure from Canton should not be delayed, I beg to inform you that I have undertaken, with his Lordship's concurrence, to make the requisite arrangements with the Hong merchants,

Thomas B Colledge,
Surgeon to H M Superintendent.'

Lord Napier, he added in his report, had stipulated that a suitable vessel be allowed or provided to take the Marines back down river to rejoin their ships, and that the frigates 'should not have to submit to any ostentatious display on the part of the Chinese Government'. There was to be no nonsense about the passage downstream of either of these. Nor was there: the Viceroy's argument was not with them.

Delighted to have achieved all that the Viceroy wanted, and hoping to have saved his own pocket in the process, Howqua now reappeared in the British Factory and spoke with his usual immaculate manners. 'Mr Colledge, your proposition is of a responsible nature, and from my knowledge of your character I know you intend honestly to carry it out. Shake hands with me and Mowqua, and let Mr Jardine do like wise.' Little suspecting what was to follow, 'we all joined hands', wrote Dr Colledge.

Having persuaded William John that the cutter was not going to be allowed to come up to Canton for him, and having reassured him as to the plan for the Marines and his insistence that the frigates should pass the Bogue without insult to their flag, Dr Colledge had now to insist to the Viceroy 'that a suitable conveyance for his Lordship and his suite should be supplied, befitting in every respect his rank and station'.

* * *

Early on the morning of the 21st, the Marines and their Lieutenant set out downstream in two boats. Armed and disciplined, red-coated and impervious, they passed the jeering boat-people with their throat-cutting gestures and the river banks still crowded with the Emperor's 'thundering forces', unconcerned and unmolested, for the Viceroy did indeed desire peace. What they felt is not to be known, since for feelings we depend on letters that survive. The trip to Canton must have made a welcome change from ship life, but they cannot have much enjoyed the

short commons and close confinement of the British Factory, or its surround of mocking Chinese soldiery. Confident as they were, they may
well have rejoiced in their sortie to tear down some of the notices posted
up on the Factory wall, officially declaring that their King's representative, the Barbarian Eye, was a sodomite, a mother-rapist, a child-abuser,
given to bestiality and to all other vices and perversions known to the
human race. The Marines may even have hurled them, crumpled up,
into a few of those besieging faces, when no-one in authority was looking.

The Marines rejoined their ships on the evening of the 21st, and
these at once set sail. By the evening of the 22nd they had gained the
open sea, passing the Bogue without insult, (either the Viceroy was keeping his word, or the forts had run out of ammunition). This rapid
progress effectively disproved the official Chinese version that the river
had been rendered impassable downstream from them, and called the
bluff that the frigates had been boxed in.

'On the evening of the 18th', reported Secretary Alexander
Johnstone, 'His Lordship, leaning on my arm, being then scarcely able
to walk, proceeded in the dusk of the evening for fear of being
molested . . . through another Hong to the house of Mr James Innes,
who kindly offered the use of it to him as being the coolest in Canton.'
After the days of delay, Dr Colledge knew that Lord Napier's only chance
of recovery lay in a swift return to the cool sea breezes of Macao and the
comfort and rest of home. Three days in a cooler room than his own in
the Factory had enabled William John to sleep, and his fever was a little
abated. He was, however, weak as water, and had almost to be carried, on
the evening of the 21st, with a helper on each side, as he and his party
made their way to the Chinese boat that had been provided. It was not a
very bad vessel, but neither was it very good. He, Dr Colledge,
Johnstone, two servants and a linguist were all the party, and all, wrote
Johnstone, 'were under the impression that in two days, or three at the
utmost, his Lordship would arrive according to Custom at Macao'.

With relief William John stretched out on the bunk, with relief they all
felt the air of movement , and saw the lights of Canton dwindle down the
dark river.

Their relief was short-lived.

* * *

Some hypocrisy is inseparable from government; and humbug the occu-
pational disease of statesmen. Inseparable, come to that, from ordinary
life: we all pretend to be better or worse than we actually are. But this
world-wide game of 'Let's Pretend' has its limits, and the Celestial
Empire in the 19th century exceeded them. Not that they were unique

in their involvement in humbug; merely surpassingly self-deceived. Between the humbug of an alarmed Viceroy of Canton seeking to hang on to his lucrative job and the humbug of a British administration seeking to retain office by passing a vote of thanks to an Admiral Gambier for victory in a battle that he had done his utmost to stop happening, and from which he remained distanced throughout by a dozen miles, there is a difference in degree but not in kind.

Such a disturbance in tranquillity as all that banging of guns on the river had caused could not, the Viceroy knew, be kept hidden from the Emperor in Peking, whose vast administrative network kept him well informed of what went on in the Important Country, the Great Pure Realm. Many were the Viceroy's jealous underlings, and rivals eager for his job. He wrote without grave apprehension, for although tranquillity had not been preserved, he had gained his point and sent this intrusive Barbarian Eye packing down the river, and not without a well-orchestrated ignominy, calculated to abase the foreign devils and exalt the prowess of the Celestial Empire.

'Your Majesty's servants', he began, 'kneel and report . . . that the English ships of war, and Barbarian Eye, have all been driven out of the Port, and that the naval and military forces have been returned to their stations: on which report, they, looking upwards, entreat that a sacred glance may be cast.'

'An English Barbarian Eye, Lord Napier, having presumed without previously having obtained permits to enter the River of Canton, having also irregularly presented a letter, and having, in disobedience to repeated orders plainly given, continued obstinate and perverse, I, Your Majesty's Minister Loo, closed, according to law, the holds of the said Nation's merchants' ships.'

After which the said Barbarian Eye had 'ordered two barbarian ships of war to push in suddenly through the maritime entrance up to Whampoa'. So that, naturally, guards had been instructed, naval vessels summoned, and 'in narrow and important passages', soldiers had been stationed; the whole carried out 'in perfect security and good order'. What with 'the spars ranged out, across and all around, with guns and muskets as if it were a forest . . . soldiers stationed and encamped on every place on shore . . . their military array imposing and alarming, the ships of war at Whampoa remained subdued among the vessels. They did not dare to advance one step. Nor did one person dare to ascend the shore'.

'The Barbarian Eye, when he found that the passage by water was intercepted, became timid and fearful'; and had then pretended that the frigates were only at Whampoa '"to protect the barbarian trading ships", in order thus to show that he had no other purpose'.

'When our soldiers accumulated daily, the said Barbarian Eye became still more alarmed and fearful'; and he had then sent 'to beg that a Sampan boat might be given him that he might leave Canton'. The foreign devil had been, it seemed, on his knees begging for so much as a row-boat in which to make his exit.

But the Ministers, although 'the said Barbarian Eye had come up to Canton without having obtained a permit, and that the ships of war had also sailed into the Inner River, which acts, although in no way heavy offences against the laws', the Viceroy admitted, 'were yet committed in wilful opposition . . . showing an extreme degree of daring contempt'. If the Ministers had allowed Napier at once to leave Canton, 'thus coming and going at his own convenience, how could it be possible to display a warning example, or to show forth his fear-stricken submission?' So they had again sent the Hong merchants to question Napier 'with authoritative sternness'. What exactly had he been at? Plain answers, or else 'exterminating should assuredly be brought into operation . . . no alternation or indulgence'.

This strong line, Loo told the Emperor, had resulted in Napier's acknowledgement of his ignorance. 'Now he was himself aware of his error, and begged to be graciously permitted to go down to Macao'. He had also begged permission for the warships to leave. Despite all this repentance, Loo and his colleagues considered that 'from first to last he had not told plainly' on what account he had come to Canton. His saying that the entrance of the ships of war had happened by mistake (?) was 'but a glossing pretence . . . when the soldiers opened from their guns a thundering fire upon the ships, these had had the daring presumption to discharge their guns at them in return'. Rafters and tiles in the forts had thereby been 'shaken and injured'.

[This last, it was to be felt in Macao, was a daring admission, a great leap forward in accuracy: when Sir Murray Maxwell in the *Alceste* had battered the same forts into silence, the then Viceroy had reported it as 'an exchange of salutes'.]

'How came they thus to be bold and audacious?', Loo demanded; and he had 'further commanded the Hong merchants to enquire with stern severity'; a tone of voice of which, when confronted with the barbarian characters in the flesh, neither Howqua or Mowqua were capable. [Since there was a law against teaching the barbarians any Chinese language, upon pain of death, all conversations had to be carried on in the most absurd pidgin English, for which these extremely learned and cultured Chinese were held in a needless derision.]

And next, Loo went on, had come Colledge, the said barbarian merchant. [Dr Colledge was much incensed when he read this, his proper prefix and his superior medical status having been brushed aside.] This individual, Loo wrote, had said that 'Lord Napier had really come to Canton for the purpose of directing commercial affairs', and therefore, considering himself an officer, is called Superintendent, and wished to have correspondence with the civil and military officers of the Celestial Empire. He had pleaded self-defence over the return fire of the ships – 'the error is deeply repented of, and the damage done shall be immediately repaired', and Napier was humbly begging for a passage to Macao.

This fanciful version, presumably thought up by the Hong, had been deeply considered by all the Imperial Officers, 'maturely consulting together'. Lord Napier had insisted that as he was 'an official Eye amongst the barbarians, there is no distinction of honourable or low rank between him and the officers of the Inner Land . . . but the dignity of the Nation sets up a wide barrier, and we, Your Majesty's Ministers, would not suffer the progress of encroachment'.

The presumptuous barbarian ships had pushed in 'ostensibly' to protect goods; but Chinese 'naval and land forces, ranged out in order, arranged as on a chess board', had compassed the warships round about so closely that their lives, the lives of all their crews, had been completely in Chinese power. Had these overwhelming forces closed in upon the ships? No, they had not.

'Our August Sovereign cherishes those from afar virtuously, and soothingly treats outside barbarians, exercising to the utmost limits both benevolence and justice'. Wrongdoers were corrected, and, if repentant were forgiven; 'never are extreme measures adopted toward them'.

'Although Lord Napier has entertained extreme visionary fantasies he yet has shown no real disregard of the laws. It would not be well precipitately to visit him with extermination measures.' No cutting off of his head; or at least, not yet. Besides which, Loo stated authoritatively, the several thousand barbarian merchants all considered that Napier's disobedience to the law was wrong, 'there is not one who unites or accords with him'. Here he spoke correctly for the firm of Dent and Co. and for the Parsee firms, who were all for letting sleeping dogs lie, as far as the China trade was concerned. And as Laboriously Vile himself had been repentant and submissive, 'there should certainly be some slight indulgence shewn, and he should be driven out of the port, (rather than exterminated) to the end that while the foreign barbarians are made to tremble with terror, they may also be rendered grateful by the favour of the Celestial Empire, shown in its benevolence, kindness, and great indulgence'.

Accordingly, on the 21st, officers 'took Lord Napier, and under their escort he was driven out of the port', and told that he was 'to wait reverently at Macao' until the Imperial Mandate has been received. The

warships too had been, next day, driven out of the Bocca Tigris . . . drag-
ging over shallows the whole way.' Capitulation complete; and Loo was
commanding 300 soldiers to reinforce the garrison at Macao, at the
same time ordering all local naval forces 'to cruise about with real activity in the anchorage near to Macao'; [in case the repentant and
submissive Barbarian Eye should have a change of heart].

The luckless naval commanders – 'careless and negligent' – who had
allowed the barbarians past the Bogue, were being brought to trial, 'that
they may suffer the punishment of their stupidity'.

'We unite in forming this reverent memorial, to be forwarded by the
post conveyance, whereon we, prostrate, beg our August Sovereign to
cast a sacred glance, and to grant instructions.'

Thus Viceroy Loo hoped to get away with it. But in spite of the Hong
merchants giving the Viceroy the version most likely to soothe him, and
he likewise giving the Emperor his, an altogether tranquil dénouement
did not ensue.

* * *

About three miles out from Canton, down the Inner Passage to the sea,
Alexander Johnstone was surprised to find their Macao-bound boat coming to anchor at the Pagoda Fort. It was well before midnight, and the
darkness was not great; what could have happened? Looking out over
the black water, he was horrified to find that though they had started out
quite alone, they were now 'in the midst of several mandarin boats, and
transports with troops'. Acting through the linguist, he and Dr Colledge
both protested against the halt, in view of the state of Lord Napier's
health – 'such unbargained for treatment'. In vain. They were powerless
to move; and the troops 'kept up during the night one continued sounding of gongs'.

'It is needless almost to say', Johnstone's report continues, 'that a
man in the state of health his lordship was then in suffered considerably
from want of sleep, and the constant annoyance of the most piercing
noise. On Monday morning, the 22nd, we left Pagoda Fort, and were
under sail the whole of that day and the next, with the exception of a few
hours when we anchored at the side of some large rafts extending from
the land to our boats, near a village.'

'His Lordship had here to undergo another species of annoyance
and insult.' Several times they protested through their linguist to the
mandarin in charge, asking them to stop this particular torment, but no
moves were made. 'I allude to the annoyance practised by the lower
orders of the Chinese', went on Johnstone, 'of coming to the window of
his Lordship's boat, pushing the curtain aside, looking in, and with

screams using the insulting epithet of '*Fan-Quie*'. [Foreign Dog]

'This, on any other occasion, might have been tolerated but on the present, with a sick man, and under an escort of armed boats, which was no longer to be concealed, was anything but an amicable mode of treatment which the Mandarin's speech would seem to imply.' All that day the nightmare screams and the furious faces dodged in and out of the dreams of high fever, as the boat lay idle on the water in the brazen heat of noon. [At the end of the journey, the mandarins in charge, with their usual bland and smiling mendacity told Dr Colledge that they hoped that Lord Napier would impute nothing that had happened to hostile feelings towards himself.]

'We proceeded slowly and tediously ', Dr Colledge reported on the Monday morning when they were at last under way, 'under a convoy of eight armed boats, two transports carrying military', plus the civil Mandarin's boat with its dragon prow and painted shields along the sides. He was in charge of the party, but to Johnstone it appeared that several mandarins had come along. At an almost imperceptible pace, the convoy crept on in the baking sunshine, between the neatly bordered green rice fields, the busy sampans and the occasional pagodas. Boxed up in the hot cabin, William John's state was perceptibly worsening and his fever now as high again as it had ever been. Colledge was seriously worried; two days had passed and already the medicine he had brought for the two day journey was dwindling. The fever was now so high that other medicines were essential, but where could he lay hands on them? His feelings as he made the report a week or two later still ran high.

'We arrived at Heang-Shang about midnight of the 23rd; and it is now that I have to describe a scene of treachery practised upon his Lordship, which was not only annoying, but so greatly injurious as to exasperate the symptoms of his complaint, and cause a relapse of such as he had nearly recovered from, previously to his leaving Canton.'

Here at Heang-Shang they were held for all but two more days 'amidst a noise and confusion that his Lordship could barely support'. At Hoan-Shang (sic) Johnstone took up the tale: 'We were detained to all intents and purposes a prisoner . . . his Lordship was subjected to every species of noise and disturbance which it was possible to have brought together – the sounding of gongs, the beating of bamboos, the saluting of mandarins on their arrival or departure, and the splashing of oars, kept up during the whole of these two nights'.

It was impossible for the sufferer to have a wink of sleep, and the noise seemed to be effectively concentrated round his boat. 'Dr Colledge repeatedly, and at one occasion four times during the night, sent the linguist to the mandarins to beseech of them to stop from making such a noise.'

Disciplined as the Chinese were, [and are] they could certainly have been quieted if anyone in authority had wanted to quiet them. But the linguist received no change; no orders were issued from the mandarin's boat, and the mandarin himself contributed nothing. His eyes considered the linguist as woodenly as the dragon eye painted upon his curved prow.

It all seemed part of an ingenious plan; no-one knowing better than the Chinese that there are more ways than one of killing a cat. Through the two stifling long nights at Heang-Shang 'they continued this mode of annoyance to the distraction of his Lordship and the increase of his illness'. Another morning dawned, breathless and baking, amidst a continued din. As early as possible on the 25th, the fourth day of their journey, Colledge had himself rowed across to the mandarin boat with the linguist, to say that Napier would almost certainly die if he were kept here motionless in this oven heat amongst the increasing din. The Mandarin, registering pained surprise, said that of course the journey could continue; he was only awaiting a 'chop' or passport, from the Heang-Shang Customs House. [The official Chinese reason for this delay was that the authorities wanted to make sure that the frigates had really left the river; but as, by the Viceroy's account as well as Brickdale's, they were out by the evening of the 22nd, and news of this kind travelled up the river like wildfire, delay until the late afternoon of the 25th does not thus seem explicable.]

Another long hot wait ensued; but at last, on the afternoon of the 25th, the convoy resumed its snail-like passage. Again the rice fields slid slowly past. A pagoda, rising ahead of their passage, became by infinitely small degrees a pagoda astern. Johnstone had now resorted to bribery to induce the boatman to go faster; the main result of this was that the linguist, once they had arrived at Macao, staged a further delay of some hours in clearing the luggage through the Customs, in hopes of a little something for himself. It might have stayed there longer, but for some timely help from Mr Pereira.

In the early hours of the 26th, the boat at length arrived in Macao Roads. William John, more dead than alive, had at last been borne up the steep hill and was at home with his much loved wife and children. He was, reported Dr Colledge 'altogether in a worse state than he had ever been since the commencement of his illness'.

* * *

Hopeful as ever, William John lay in bed making plans. They would, in any case, have to wait for six months before fresh instructions from home could arrive, which he hoped that they would, after Grey and Palmerston had received his letters asking for firm backing in his plans for reorganizing the trade on a more rational basis. He and Eliza would take a holiday, would explore, perhaps the cool greenness of New Zealand's South Island, or perhaps Australia. He felt a great longing for rationality and comprehension. Eliza abetted him. Sometimes in these first few days he would even be out of bed on a sofa in the next room for an hour or so. Sea breezes would blow gently in, cool drinks would soothe, the nightmare was over, his spirit was refreshed by affection. Together they looked forward.

'A week later', Eliza wrote home to William's parson brother Henry, who was particularly close to them both, 'his complaints took a different turn . . . His throat and chest seemed affected, and from Wednesday morning, when first a spasm came on at awakening, I had no hope in my heart though words of hope came often to my lips.' Her husband continued in fever, up and down, for a fortnight, becoming increasingly weakened. 'Throughout', wrote Eliza, 'his patience and sweet and generous placidity of temper was conspicuous. He evidently thought recovery doubtful, but was anxious for it, and spoke sometimes as if he expected it.' He was 48, a lover and enjoyer of life, and had always been strong.

Elizabeth read to him, and 'every day, by his desire, a very good man of the name of Bridgman, an American missionary, read and prayed every evening by his bedside. My beloved had known him at Canton, and appreciated his simple, pious, and judicious character'. William John had attended his services in the little church in the Factories and had learned to like and admire him. He had asked for Bridgman on the evening of his first arrival back in Macao.

'Indeed, dearest Henry, my dear, dear William's mind was in a happy Christian frame, and it is a great and unspeakable blessing to me to be assured of it.'

19

Death at Macao

It had not always been so; there was a day when William John went down into the depths, into those dark waters which at some time seem to rise up as if to swallow the dying; when the sense of failure and of bitter regret, the sense of all that he had hoped to do and all that he had failed to do lay like lead on his spirit. At no time did he rail or distribute blame. On the two or three days before delirium, 'He was low,' wrote Elizabeth, 'he spoke much more than was his wont of death.' In this extremity his faith did not desert him; he had prayed, and Elizabeth heard him repeating verses from the Bible. 'From all he said in this way', she told Henry, 'I think he viewed himself in the humblest light, and looked alone to the merits of our Saviour'.

'He was never but one night and one day uncollected and decidedly wandering; this was just before his complaint took a bad turn, and even then reading and prayer soothed him.'

From his depths he had made Eliza read to him from the Book of Job – here was one who had suffered and triumphed from worse depths than any. He dwelt on this ancient despair, and on the resilience and faith that had mastered it. The sun filtered through the shutters of the house on Macao ridge, scents from the garden blew in to the high room, and Elizabeth would begin on Chapter 19, while her husband silently cried out to God from his besetting lowness.

> He hath fenced up my way that I cannot pass, and he has set darkness in my paths.

> He hath stripped me of my glory, and taken the crown from my head.

> He hath destroyed me on every side, and I am gone; and my hope hath he removed like a tree . . .

And then would come the triumphant affirmation that the dying man had wanted to hear, with its sturdy realism and its unquenched hope, in verse 25 and its followers. To this he made the patient Elizabeth return, in what felt to her like a hundred times.

I know that my redeemer liveth, and that he shall stand at the latter day upon the earth.

And though after my skin worms destroy this body, yet in my flesh shall I see God.

Whom I shall see for myself, and mine eyes shall behold, and not another, though my reins be consumed within me.

His lips would move silently, in this unrelenting struggle through which a strong man's spirit seeks release from the flesh while the flesh battles to retain it. '*Yet in my flesh shall I see God*', he would repeat, in a voice still reassuringly strong; '*whom I shall see for myself, and mine eyes shall behold, and not another.*' Read it again, my dearest, read it through again; and the patient Eliza would comply. 'These words', she told Henry, 'seemed ever present to his mind.'

'In the last few days he was perfectly collected, though of course by the Doctor's desire I kept as silent and quiet as possible. He knew my voice to the last, and his last words were for me.'

Others reported differently, saying that his last audible enquiry had been on 8 October, when guns from the Portuguese forts had saluted an arrival from Lisbon. Some discussion went on at his bedside about the flag the vessel was wearing – 'if it is the Portuguese arms between white and blue, it is Donna Maria's flag', he said. To Mr Maurice Collis this seemed only to illustrate William John's limited understanding, 'interested only in sheep and ships'; but in fact the flag mattered to William John very much, his clan feeling enduring to the end. When he left home the previous February, the struggle in Portugal between the 13 year old Donna Maria, supported by his cousin 'Black Charlie', against her usurping uncle Dom Miguel, was still undecided. If it were Dom Miguel's flag flying from the newly arrived Portuguese ship, it would mean that 'Black Charlie' was defeated, disgraced, and either dead or languishing in a Portuguese prison; and William John, however near death, minded very much about this. Fortunately for his peace of mind, the flag at the Portuguese masthead turned out to be Donna Maria Gloria's.

'He named all our children and friends individually during his illness', Elizabeth told her brother-in-law Henry. Perhaps he felt confident that his daughters would flourish in the charge of this admirable wife. The two who were with him, Maria and Georgiana, now 17 and 16, were all but grown up and a source of help and comfort to their mother, but Elizabeth, Anne, Alice and Eleanor were all little girls, and Lucy, their afterthought, had only been a year old when they left

Scotland, though she must now be walking and talking and altogether being a joy to a parent.

The boys were another matter. 'Often, often he spoke of "the dear boys", and his anxiety about them was great.' Francis was 15 and Willy was 12; no age at which to leave boys fatherless. Francis was a clever, sophisticated boy, easy to converse with; his father thought of a civilian career for him, perhaps the Foreign Service? Willy was inclined to be wild; he had better go for a soldier; the sea was no place for such as had no special inclination for it. In any case, both William John and his wife agreed, neither was to be persuaded into jobs for which they had no wish – there must be no moral blackmail. 'I will never urge', Elizabeth promised him. [Not for one moment did it occur to William John, nor to his cousins General Sir George Napier and Admiral Gerard John Napier at Pennard in Somerset, that their sons could do other than spend their lives in service to their country; such a notion was inconceivable.]

It seemed to Elizabeth that her husband had thought of everybody, sending his love all round, and expressing his gratitude to King William and Princess Augusta, and to Sir Herbert Taylor. Perhaps the Queen might see his two dear boys, who were learning German at Meiningen? Thoughts of favour may have flitted through his mind; and he fancied that the King might be sorry to see him go. In this he turned out to be right.

Duty haunted him to the last, as it is wont to haunt the dutiful. 'Up to the very morning of his death he spoke of his anxiety to fulfil the objects he had in view for the good of his country', Elizabeth wrote. Some part of him, perhaps, still hoped for recovery, for backing from home, for power to set the China trade on a rational basis, away from trickery and greedy speculation and opium smuggling.

Brave throughout, Elizabeth allowed herself a moment of self-pity in writing to the understanding Henry of 'the sad sad and unexpected misfortune which has fallen upon us, we are now widowed and fatherless in this distant strange land. Oh my dearest Henry, I can scarcely realize to myself that it is so. So short a time, only three months to-day since he went to Canton expecting soon to return, in good health and good spirits'. In two months he had returned 'much reduced, weak and ill, and brought to that state by bad climate, harassing duties, and anxiety of mind, which was much aggravated by a severe relapse of fever, induced by the long detention and annoyance he met with from the Chinese Government or authorities on his way here'.

She braced herself for the future. 'His precious life is over, but his reputation is yet mine.' There was the consoling thought that 'his life was as much sacrificed to his duty as the Sailors' who fall in battle, for his anxiety to fulfil his instructions made him remain in Canton while a hope remained of accommodation, and some time after Dr Colledge urged his leaving it. Nor did he come away until unequal to it entirely, when Colledge took all the responsibility upon himself of his removal'.

There was the further consolation that William had been much loved; 'even in the short time he was here, people had come to estimate his upright and benevolent character'. People had been immensely kind, particularly the Thornhill family, who had welcomed Elizabeth and her daughters under their roof for the essential week of peace and quiet in which to come to terms with their loss. Next time Henry was in London, would he, she asked him, go and see Mr Thornhill at the East India Company's Offices and tell him how very greatly all this had been appreciated?

The Portuguese Governor had behaved with kind consideration too. He came to the funeral, as did many officers from Her Faithful Majesty's Navy. Better still, the bells from Macao's 12 churches had all been silenced on his orders so that William John could enjoy a little fitful slumber; and his relief at being once again in a Christian world where individuals mattered had been great. The day before he died he had sent his thanks and appreciation to the Governor. Sir George Robinson expressed his own 'admiration and regard' for Napier: 'I would have gone through fire and water for him', he wrote. The Canton business houses were closed for the day after his death, and most of the Macao community came to the funeral, which was attended by Portuguese troops as well as British. Minute guns were fired by *Andromache* in the Bay, and by British shipping at Lin Tin and Whampoa. The Canton Register went into black edges for its next two issues, and spoke of Napier's 'estimable qualities' and the very general sorrow and sense of loss, both public and private; extolling his 'pure and straightforward love of justice', his patient weighing up of the value of conflicting arguments, 'the energy and perseverance in all pursuits, with a placidity of temper and benevolence that were singularly engaging . . .'.

'His Lordship was of a vigorous constitution, and a spare frame, and his turn for pursuits in the open air, simple tastes, and abstemious habits gave his family the right to expect a good old age, and the end of a useful and honourable career in his native land.' This was not to be. Napier had died comparatively young, in this far country, dying, the Register concluded, 'of an illness (so far as limited mortal intellect can judge) brought on by his arduous duties in a burning climate, and his fate hastened by unusual delay, harsh and irritating treatment during his passage from Canton to Macao'. When subscriptions were asked for, for a memorial, the money was subscribed five times over. After a 'suitable and handsome' ornamental stone had been paid for, the remaining sum was used to endow a charitable trust in the name of Napier.

Six naval captains carried William John's flag-draped coffin – Blackwood, Chads, Elliot, Yonge, and two from the Portuguese Navy, Loureiro and Da Souza; and he was followed to the grave by the Governor, Suarez D'Andrea, most of the Portuguese civil and military establishment, all the local British merchants and many of the Macao foreigners. The Reverend Elijah Colman Bridgman took the service and preached a sermon on the melancholy theme that in the midst of life we are in death. He took his text from the Book of Numbers – 'Let me die the death of the righteous, and let my last end be like his'. He dwelt on the sudden death of Dr Morrison, and of a very young man recently drowned while bathing, passed to a description of the 16th century John Napier who had 'devoted his life to the study of the Holy Scriptures and of mathematics', and went on to enlarge upon William John's efforts to better the lot and the living conditions of his Border tenants and dependents.

'His ancestors were all pious and devoted royalists', Bridgman continued; they had been Episcopalians, 'for which church he ever had a high respect', though he had taken a line of his own and become a Presbyterian. 'He had a humble opinion of himself, and a charitable one of all mankind. The prevailing benevolence and liberality united with great decision and energy of mind.' In coming to China he had hoped, 'through the gradual extension of commerce and a free and well-regulated intercourse with China', that knowledge would be diffused and prejudice removed. This, he had felt, must surely lead to 'the overthrow of idolatry and the complete triumph of pure Christianity'.

The Reverend Elijah then enlarged upon the edifying scene of Lord Napier's deathbed. Humble but faithful, 'he knew where to look for help . . . the great truths of the Holy Scriptures, which he had so often and so fondly pondered in the season of health, yielded him rich consolation in the last days and moments of his life'. Napier's last words, insisted Bridgman, 'uttered in feeble and broken accents', had shown 'More clearly than ever before, his hope and confidence in God'. His end had been very peaceful. [William John seems to have had a number of last words, but perhaps those around him chose the ones they liked best. Georgians and Victorians were keen collectors of last words, rather as people now collect old seals or old documents.]

On this warm October morning, in the sunshine and sea breezes of Macao, the Reverend Elijah preached happily on for a full hour, emphasizing the Christian message in general, and pleased, perhaps, with an unusually large captive audience. After the funeral, the British merchants went in a body, headed by Sir George Robinson and William Jardine, to thank his Excellency, the Portuguese Governor for his kind and liberal conduct to the British subjects at Macao, and for his spirited and effective protection of the British ladies and families 'when harassed by the Chinese authorities during the discussions at Canton, and finally for the honour showed to Lord Napier's remains'. After which they all parted in a mutual glow of sympathy and compliment and the Reverend Elijah was able to go home and remove his stiff collar.

William John was buried alongside his friend and interpreter Dr Morrison; but a year or two later Elizabeth, fearing for his body's desecration if ever the Chinese repossessed Macao, took advantage of an offer from the captain of a warship to have it brought back to Ettrick, so that his bones should lie in his own green valley beside the tumbling river. This afforded great satisfaction to his workers and tenants who flocked in great numbers to the re-burial, pleased to have so helpful a laird at hand for the Resurrection and the Day of Judgment, which they feared might prove a bewildering event.

From the Viceroy at Canton, a final and most non-Confucian shaft of malice was directed. So hierarchic was Chinese society that even death, the great leveller, was not permitted to obliterate the differences of its ranks. Different ideographs stood to denote the deaths of people of different status. Writing to Howqua and Mowqua on behalf of Dr Colledge, to acquaint them of the death of Lord Napier, Mr Morrison had used the character that denotes the death of a nobleman. The Viceroy, replying through Howqua, used the character denoting the death of a beggar, a nobody, a nothing man.

* * *

In due course the memorial stone was carved and erected.

To the Memory of
the Right Honourable William John, Lord Napier
of Merchiston.
Captain in the Royal Navy
His Majesty's Chief Superintendent
of the British Trade in China
who died at Macao, October 11th 1834
Aged 48 years
As a naval officer he was able and distinguished
In Parliament his conduct was liberal and decided
Attached to the pursuit of science

and the duties of religion
He was upright, sincere, affectionate and kind
He was the First Chief Superintendent
chosen by our Sovereign
on the opening to the trade in China to British Enterprise
and his valuable life
was sacrificed to the zeal with which he endeavoured
to discharge the arduous duties of the situation.

This monument is erected by the British Community in China.

No blame or malice here. The stone eventually disappeared, and probably spent a peaceful 150 years as part of the back wall of someone's house. Recently it was discovered, propping up a shop in Wanchai, bought back by the Royal Navy, and held *pro tem* in Hong Kong.

* * *

Six years later, a dinner was given in Selkirk to the new Lord Napier on his coming of age. Long and eloquent speeches were made, in one of which Mr Hubbard, who had married Maria, introduced a note of caution to his much younger brother-in-law, for Francis had grown up into a lively spark. He warned the young laird about the treacherous temptations that would come upon him, 'from the very "joyousness" of his heart'. Francis Napier, 10th Lord, in a long, sensible and well-expressed reply, uttered his father's best memorial. He had himself been abroad, learning French and German over the last years, and the neighbourhood, gathered in large numbers, scarcely knew him. They were giving him this sumptuous dinner and warm welcome because of his father – 'so potent is the charm of his goodness, that he can even win a fair character for his children, and invest them gratuitously with that affection which his life was spent in deserving'. The cheers were deafening, and Mr Aitchison of Menzion, toasting the memory of William John, declared that 'his whole life was a history of honour, and his entire bearing the very essence of independence and noble-mindedness'.

* * *

William John had been right in thinking that King William might be sorry to hear of his death. The King was sorry for some tune. Elizabeth found there was to be no government pension for her husband's years of service, either for her or for her six daughters, but King William gave her a pleasant grace and favour house on Richmond Green, where she lived rent-free to the end of her days. Sadly, her youngest, Lucy, died at the age of 10; the other five daughters all married.

Part Four
Open Conflict

20

Aftermath: A Time of Drift

However much the whole débâcle had been due to his serious illness, the retreat of William John and his subsequent death had been a resounding smack in the face for the British community in China, and thus for their homeland; and the recriminations were correspondingly bitter. Stinging letters shot into the *Canton Register* and *Chinese Repository* like a flight of arrows, and were none the less indignant for being mainly anonymous. This last newspaper was run by missionaries and often contained articles showing a real interest and sympathy over purely Chinese affairs; but its subscribers were mainly the traders and it printed many letters from them.

Perhaps what most enraged the British community, though it found no utterance in the correspondence, was that the Chinese had proved themselves so emphatically the cleverer. Without violence, without raising a finger to strike him, they had got rid of an unwanted envoy and finished him off into the bargain. No-one at the time doubted the deliberate policy of this, neither the forgiving missionaries nor the furious traders. At the time, William John largely escaped the censure that has since been heaped upon him. Later historians, understandably ashamed for the subsequent treatment of China by Britain and other Europeans, have perhaps unconsciously turned their wrath upon William John, who is described as bad-tempered, light-headed, downright stupid, and seeming to set out deliberately to offend every Chinese susceptibility. Hardly a good word is ever said of him; although Palmerston is occasionally allotted his share of blame.

At the time William John was seen as a good man and an intelligent one; no-one considered him, as some historians have since seen him, as the tool of William Jardine who, indeed, complained that he would not take advice. He had kept calm and made no attempt to start blaming his colleagues, still less his country, when things went wrong. Even the merchants who had disagreed with his policy lamented his death, though this may have been on the time-honoured principle of *de mortuis nil nisi bonum*. There was a sensible letter in the *Register* pointing out that no-one with long experience of China would have put out a direct proclamation to the people of Canton, impugning their authorities as he did, without having a sizable force at hand to back him up when the inevitable riposte came; but on the whole it was anger with others that prevailed in the contemporary letters.

Why, the more aggressive letter-writers demanded, had not Captain Blackwood gone ashore in the Bogue, spiked the guns of the Chinese fortresses, or dumped them all in the deepest part of the river, as Weddell had done 200 years earlier? Why had the *Imogene* and *Andromache* dawdled up the Pearl River, waiting for their English pilots, waiting for Elliot and the *Louisa* cutter, waiting for the wind? The frigates should have been warped up at all speed, arriving in Whampoa before the Chinese had had time to gather troops to block the river and line the banks of the last 12 miles of waterway up which the *Louisa* and the boats' crews from the frigate had hoped to go to the rescue?

The deliberate delay in getting William John down to Macao and the long sleepless nights of unrestrained noise that he had endured from the orchestrated efforts of the troops in the accompanying boats, were described by one writer as 'torturing Lord Napier to death'. This had turned a high fever into a fatal illness. Even the level-headed Dr Colledge in his official report, and the sober-sided secretary, Alexander Johnstone, considered that this prolonged ordeal had made the difference between recovery and non-recovery. Subsequent historians have seen the whole noise as produced by the spontaneous rejoicing of dwellers along the river banks at the expulsion of the hated foreigner; but most of these would hardly have known what was happening, and would only doubtfully have spontaneously stayed up all night to express their feelings, after a hard day's work in the paddy fields. In the view of many quite rational characters at the time, the Chinese authorities had subtly but deliberately killed Lord Napier. Of course, in the bitterness of the moment, when the natural instinct is to allot blame, they added it to the Chinese and subtracted it from their climate.

In fact, there seemed to have been a kind of fatality about the whole affair, as if China herself, the whole massive, glorious, learned, crumbling edifice of Imperial China had carried out his *coup de grâce*. The message urging him to wait in Macao had just missed him, as had the second message at the Bogue. The decision of Viceroy Loo not to receive him, despite the fact that previous Viceroys had received many another man who had come up river without permit and without official backing from their home government, the stern quality of Napier's ingrained obedience to orders from the King, his liberal assumptions that made him believe that direct approach to the oppressed Chinese people was a possible option, had all combined. The sudden death of Dr Morrison had kept away his experienced advisers for the last vital weeks in Canton, since they had gone down to Macao for the funeral of this admired man.

William John's own spare and robust constitution had failed before the onset of the Chinese virus, the merchants of Canton had failed to present a united front, the steady breeze up-river had failed the two frigates at Chuenpee. One correspondent to the Canton Register blamed it all on the Pearl River itself, as if a powerful spirit dwelt within it to avenge the people of the plains that it watered. Lord Napier had gone down river in a Chinese boat, Midshipman Brickdale pointed out, 'putting himself in the hands of a treacherous set of rascals'. But whoever could be blamed or absolved, the mission from which so much had been hoped had proved a failure, and came to be known as 'Napier's Fizzle'.

The great volume of criticism was levelled at Palmerston and the home authorities. Why had they tried to deal with Canton in the first place, from whom no concessions or rational decisions could be expected; why had no attempt been made to get in touch with Peking, from whence all authority emanated? Above all, why had the Superintendent been originally forbidden to get into direct touch with Peking himself? To send an envoy discouraged from employing the only effective pressure within his range, was to send a man out with his right hand tied behind his back, it was insisted. Permission to explore the best method for getting in touch with the Emperor had eventually been granted; but this was not the same as full permission for direct access. As for Napier's determination to deal direct with the Viceroy and not through the polite but devious and unreliable Co-Hong, and his firm stand against being brow-beaten, both had been right. Such appeared to be the opinion of all but Mr Dent and the Parsee merchants, and of the shipmasters whom the Viceroy's decree had kept hanging around outside the Bocca Tigris well into the hurricane season.

There was a general sense of malaise and frustration amongst the British. The climate of China in the listless airs of September was affecting the spirits even of Midshipman Brickdale. Going ashore for the Superintendent's funeral had at least been a change from ship life. 'Lord Napier was followed to the grave by a pretty long procession and I was there', he wrote home. Already illness, a local fever, had caught up the *Imogene* at Lin-Tin, the pencil sharp smuggling island. 'We just now began to feel sickness creeping into the ship', he recorded on September 22nd. 'two or three men were taken ill every day with fever or ague which is called the Whampoa fever . . . at one time 69 on the list, and we lost three men.'

These had included his best friend, 'poor dear Daniel who departed this life on Wednesday the 8th of October, perfectly insensible poor fellow and had been so for 24 hours he had only been four days ill and during that time I think I did everything for him', Brickdale wrote, grief overwhelming punctuation. 'I do not think that you can fancy how much I loved him. I think I should have got ill had it not been for Captain Blackwood who left word that if he did not live I was to go over to Macao in the *Andromache* . . .'

At Macao friends of his family had all been very kind to him, – 'Mr Edgell, Mr Astell and Lady Robinson who knew Papa at Taunton about 11 years ago . . . her name then was Matilda Douglas'. By November, Charles Brickdale had recovered his spirits. 'We have only 40 on the sick list', he wrote; 'we sail tomorrow for Manila and then to Singapore, Penang, Madras, Trincomalee and then H.O.M.E.!' Eleven years later Charles John Brickdale was killed, as a lieutenant, aged 26, serving in HMS *Comus* in an action off Punto Obligado on the Parana River in South America, on 20 November, 1845. It was a rough life, in the British Empire. 'An officer of great promise', his captain wrote, 'and would have been an ornament to his country had he lived.'

* * *

Viceroy Loo did not entirely get away with the Superintendent affair. The Emperor wrote to him in the special scarlet characters of imperial rage; Loo had let in the Barbarian Eye and allowed tranquillity to be disturbed; he was moved down a rank in the hierarchy of mandarins, and the peacock feather was plucked from his mandarin hat. The luckless war-junk commander who had permitted *Imogene* and *Andromache* to pass the Bogue was ordered to wear the dreaded *Kang* until further notice, a yard-square collar of wood in which he could neither feed himself nor lie down to sleep. The whole trade system was now in a disarray worse than the previous state had been, and the Viceroy sent a swift command through the Hong. A new chief must be sent from England, but he must be a taipan, a super-merchant, and *not* a Barbarian Eye. Someone, in other words, who could be bullied or cajoled because his own financial interests were involved. The whole business of trade along the Canton river was an affair for merchants, not to be involved with royal officials on one side or the other; and the sooner the nation of shopkeepers [whom Napoleon had condemned as such] realized this the better.

* * *

Through November, the local British wrath swelled and, in early December nearly 100 China merchants petitioned King William directly, in a long, closely-reasoned letter demanding support. Sir George Robinson was more passionate. 'Can England submit to such an insult?', he demanded. 'Will she pass it over in silence? I am unwilling to believe it.' He classed the Chinese authorities' treatment of Lord Napier as murder. He could not accept that no satisfaction should be demanded. There was so much to gain in preventing 'the recurrence of such degradation', both for England and for China, and in putting trade on 'that advantageous, true, and *safe* footing on which it ought to and might be'. He begged for 'responsible political relations with China', instead of 'a miserable infatuated timidity, and the evil counsels of a few interested, party-spirited, discontented individuals'. If these were to guide policy, 'I have done'; and he would hope to get away soon from 'so detestable a place as I should feel this to be'.

Under the guise of A British Merchant, either William Jardine or his partner and colleague, James Matheson, launched into a furious attack in which William John did *not* wholly escape censure. 'Lord Palmerston may be a very clever negociator in Europe, but in China *he is nought!* . . . HM Representative must not be joined in the Commission with notorious tea-dealers . . . must not be carried to knock heads with a set of merchants in Leadenhall Street, which act was known to every shopkeeper in Canton long previous to Lord Napier's arrival here . . . must not be sent here with a numerous suite to partake [as if by favour] of the run of the Company's Servants' kitchen. A powerful interest in the shape of a finance committee must not be established in hands animated with the keenest desire to ruin his plans, whose access to the ears of the Chinese is better than his own, and whose baneful influence on Chinese and British subjects has on this occasion been an important cause of failure.

'It appears that Lord Napier very early perceived that there were enemies in his own camp, but not knowing whom to trust, he gave his confidence to none and was deprived of good advice', Jardine [or Matheson] went on. 'And it is with boldness asserted, no faithful adherent acquainted with the Chinese would have advised his Lordship's Chinese proclamation. Such a proceeding *anywhere* implies complete powers of self-protection, which his Lordship had at no period.'

No more had his letters to Howqua written in his illness been advisable, as in addressing him, Napier gave up the principle of direct communication with the Government of Canton, for which indeed 'his whole cause of struggle was'. As for the Home Government, this had been 'equally ignorant and presumptuous in withholding Napier's power of appeal to Peking . . . that which a corrupt secondary government most fears . . . To deprive HM Representative here of such a hold on their fears and wishes was to deprive him of his right arm.'

'Do we owe this scene of disgrace and loss to some petty official struggle for patronage?', a British Merchant demanded. 'This we suspect it was.'

In criticising Lord Napier for mistakes on the spot, it was 'with feelings of high respect . . . But his Lordship should have arrived here in the face of day, and in his own war-boats'. He should have made no declarations as to intended acts: 'these convey to the Chinese recollections of the wild threats of the Honourable Company, *abandoned* before the echo was done repeating them'.

'Having once fired at the Bogue Forts every gun should have been sunk in 15 fathoms water'; and with a little more briskness in the frigates' arrival, their boats, 'gunned and manned' could easily have reached Canton. Having got this one off his chest, Jardine [or Matheson] gathered strength for a further broadside in a fortnight.

One correspondent, a student of the Kin-ting-e-le, tried hard to argue the case in Chinese terms. He claimed that this honoured manual contained instructions (Book 5, page 43) on how to treat an envoy coming from another royal household as an honoured guest. It was a work with which he assumed the Viceroy was familiar. 'We find no passage in this ample treatise of ceremonials consisting of 36 volumes which ever introduces the designation of Emuh, Barbarian Eye, and rather fear that this is an innovation, neither sanctioned by antiquity nor laws of rites. Could it have been overlooked by His Excellency?'

'A Commonplace Writer', admitted to tears at the death of William John, but pointed out crisply that 'if there is no sufficient power to resist Chinese insolence, it should never be attempted. Canton ought *never* again, and we repeat it, *never* again, to be made the scene of negociation, but strictly be considered a place of trade, where nothing of the slightest importance can be settled . . .'

'We view the whole as a *national* quarrel and expect that this time, the soi-disant celestials may experience that they have wounded the honor of a powerful nation; if not matters will grow worse', Commonplace Writer concluded. He was right about the growing worse.

Contemplation of the Viceroy's edict deepened the gloom. He wanted the immediate appointment of 'a Commercial man acquainted with affairs, to come to Canton and sustain the duties of a Taipan – to direct buying and selling and to restrain and control the merchants.

'Specially do not again cause a Barbarian Eye to come hither to control affairs, thereby occasioning, as Lord Napier did, the creation of disturbances in vain.' Let there be obedience to the old rules, 'then may there be mutual tranquillity'. On this point at least, *trade only* to be under discussion at Canton, the Viceroy and A Commonplace Writer were as one.

Still indignant as the year wore on, the correspondents of the *Canton Register* continued to comment upon 'the Napier fizzle'. If the newly appointed Superintendent, Mr Davis, were to negotiate on any other terms than Lord Napier's, declared the Editor, 'he will in our opinion betray the commercial interests of Britain in China'. If he could sum up local opinion, 'we should address our August Sovereign in the following words – "We entreat your Majesty either to leave us to our own resources in resisting Chinese oppression, or, if Britain resolve on interfering, let it be done effectually, not by half measures, producing all the evils of contest without any chance of the benefit of success" '.

Launching a second broadside, Matheson (or Jardine) fulminated against 'the *trick* of inducing the British Ministry to accept from the East India Company one third of the annual amount of the expenses of HM Commission in this country; a measure which to anyone acquainted with the Chinese character must appear certainly effectually to damn the cause'. The Chinese had simply 'looked upon the new state of things as the old one in disguise'. Why should they therefore treat the new Superintendent as something new, or different, or in any way grander or carrying more authority?

'They are led to indulge the hope that the reign of the Company', a British merchant went on, with the deep dislike felt by the Free Traders for John Company in all its monopolistic works and ways, 'the golden age of the Hong merchants, and the triumph of monopoly and folly may yet again return. Add to this the contrast between the easy pliability, and "laudable docility" of the Company's servants, intent only on the obtaining of tea even though at the sacrifice of National Honour, and the independence and opposition which the knowledge of the British character would lead them to expect at the hands of HM Representative, we need not wonder at the hostility displayed towards him'. This was all very fine, but there was almost no knowledge of the British character in China, except such as could be gleaned from parties of drunken sailors creating mayhem ashore, or resolute adventurers driving a hard bargain over tea and silk or smuggling opium along the coast.

'The British Government', went on Jardine/Matheson, 'be it spoken in plain terms, has by truckling to the East India Company for the sake of a few thousands annually, framed such difficulties in the way of any man anxious to assert his country's independence that Lord Napier's failure was more to be expected than wondered at . . . Whatever might have been wanting in measures framed at home to render success impossible, has been afforded here: personal and private feelings have been opposed to public good . . . "A house divided against itself cannot stand";' and of course the Chinese had very well known this. 'They have calculated upon it as an engine against his Lordship, and one which they have used to good effect . . .'

'We have seen the futility of all attempts to reason with the corrupt and ignorant officers of local government into an amelioration of the present system; it now remains to try the result of a sensible and well-directed appeal to headquarters, of the success of which few men acquainted with this country could be found to doubt.'

By 7 October 1834, the Emperor had decided that Viceroy Loo had done well enough, on balance. Not all his honours were to be restored, but he was kept on in his job and the peacock's feather flew back again into his hat. The luckless Captain Kao had the Kang removed from round his neck. Loo and colleagues were pronounced to have 'acted in this affair with skill and correctness. Though at the beginning they failed to take adequate preventive measures, for which failure they have been duly punished, yet they were able in the end to settle the thing well and securely, without loss of national dignity and without shedding blood. We hereby declare that We are highly pleased'.

At Canton and Macao, the British community continued to feel highly displeased. Although almost nobody in England was aware of the opium smuggling or of its terrible effect on the Chinese people, even the Free Traders were becoming conscious of the shame of the thing, and feared that unless something drastic were done, their honest branches of trade would be swamped. The opium trade was infinitely the most profitable, but, centred upon Lin Tin, it bade fair to turn into one huge smuggling racket. Even the dirtiest conscience among the China traders was aware that this would not do; violence would increase, sound trade would be lost in the struggle to unload this noxious drug.

They accordingly addressed a petition to King William, signed by nearly 100 of the merchants, beseeching him to set the China trade on a rational basis of fair trade and non-noxious goods. If Napier had been supported by a proper armed force, there need have been no bowing to insult, no disgraceful exit; and the merchants themselves would be no longer at the mercy of the Chinese authorities or exposed to their corruption and petty caprice. They begged for a Plenipotentiary backed by a ship of the line, two frigates and some sloops, demanding an open trade and backed by a threat to the capital, to Peking itself, in which, if necessary, troops should be landed at the mouth of the Pei-Ho river. It would work, they assured King William – 'We are confident that resort even to such strong measures as these, so far from being likely to lead to

more serious warfare . . . would be the surest course of avoiding the danger of such a collision'. Whether this plea ever reached the eyes of King
William is not to be known; in government circles it fell upon stony
ground.

Napier had reported home that it was 'an idle waste of time to negotiate with the Chinese without adequate means of compulsion'. The
next Superintendent adopted a policy of 'absolute silence and acquiescence', pending fresh instructions from home. But none came.

In their dealings with China to date, the British Government had
tried a variety of approaches – grandeur, threat, a Marine band, thunders
from her native oak on the Bogue forts, a fortunesworth of presents,
ineffective menace, good manners, a letter from George III, a letter
from the future George IV, promising trade offers, a squadron of British
cavalry in full fig, Lord Macartney in his cocked hat and feathers, Lord
Amherst without his, a succession of fighting-drunk seamen, and regular
pained reproaches from the East India Company. Every wave had
expended itself in vain upon the great wall of China's indifference; sighing away before what a hostile witness saw as 'a nation nursing itself in
solitary, sulky grandeur, and treating as inferior all other nations, most
far superior in civilization, resources, courage, arts and arms'.

'It seems strange indeed', wrote this contributor to the Repository,
'that the whole fabric of the Chinese Empire does not fall apart of itself.'
One good push by a foreign power, 'and it would totter to its base'. How
could it last? With its laughable army and its ludicrous navy the wonder
was that it had lasted so long.

Upon this mingling of the frantic boast and foolish word with loud
complaints about Chinese behaviour, 1834 in Canton drew to a dour
close.

* * *

After this, there was a five-year lull in British proceedings during which
things went from bad to worse and the opium smuggling increased by
leaps and bounds; nearly one third more was landed in 1839 than in
1834. By the irony of fate, it was the admirable activities of the able and
forceful Commissioner Lin that really sparked off the Opium Wars,
which settled absolutely nothing except continued bad feeling between
East and West. Opium went on being landed in China until 1908.

John Francis Davis, who had not signed the petition to King William,
(neither had several of the leading merchants) succeeded as Chief
Superintendent and made no attempt to press home any of Napier's
points; or indeed to do anything at all. He remained 'in a state of
absolute silence and acquiescence', he told Palmerston, while trade went

merrily on at Canton and Whampoa, and opium smuggling boomed at Lin-Tin. It was as well that William John was no longer there to receive the answer to his letter to Lord Grey, whose place as Foreign Secretary had been taken by Wellington in the short-lived ministry of Lord Grey, November 1834 – April 1835. The old Duke told Napier roundly that he had not followed his instructions as to maintaining friendly relations with the Chinese authorities, and informed the Canton merchants that he did not consider Napier's treatment a national insult. What mattered was the tea trade – 'that which we require now is, not to lose the enjoyment of what we have got', Wellington wrote firmly.

Perhaps the old Duke, as he grew older, no longer cared to take or send his indefatigable redcoats to the ends of the earth on errands not seen as vital, to die a dusty death on some far strand. No forces would be sent. Be that as it may, when the crunch became crunchier in 1839, his tune changed. 'It is not by force and violence that His Majesty intends to establish a commercial intercourse between his subjects and China', Wellington had written crisply to William John in early 1835: by 1839, he announced in a debate in the Lords that he would not take upon himself the responsibility of advising Her Majesty 'to submit to an insult and injuries such as he believed had never been before inflicted on this country'. But by now the naval officer involved was still alive and vocal, and a very great deal of money was involved.

James Matheson had travelled home with Lady Napier and Maria and Georgiana, in hopes of stirring the home government into action; but found no takers, not even Palmerston, returned to power in April. 'The fact is', he wrote back to Jardine, 'the people appear to be so comfortable in this magnificent country, so entirely satisfied in all their desires, that so long as domestic affairs, including the market, go right, they cannot really be brought to think of us outlanders . . . Lord Palmerston means to do nothing'. He had found even the Iron Duke 'a strenuous advocate for submissiveness and servility', when it came to China.

Matheson had managed clearly to describe English attitudes – to the opium trade, to the transportation of convicts for minor offences to Botany Bay, to the Slave trade in its day and to the Irish famine in its. Most people did not *know*, and what the eye does not see or the mind know, the heart does not grieve over. [This is not an excuse or a reason that will be possible for us, continually informed as we are by television and wireless.] It must be said that any Foreign Secretary of that day had a very great many outlanders to think about – could the Canadian frontier be held in the event of another stab at it from America as in 1812? Could Boers in South Africa be reconciled with Kaffirs? In 1833, nearly 7,000 convict prisoners had been shipped to Australia – how to feed,

guard, employ and generally sort all of them out? [A great pity that
William John's obvious talents and humanity were not employed in New
South Wales rather than China: General Charles Napier in 1835 was
offered and accepted the job of Governor of the newly founded province
of South Australia, but unluckily never went there, as the home government would not agree to his insistence on funds to enable settlers and
ex-convicts to set themselves up in a new land. Aborigines should be protected, he had written, no governor should countenance 'the usual
Anglo-Saxon process of planting civilization by robbery, oppression, and
murder . . . That the population would be immoral and bad I know, but
the greatest rascals would have been satisfied to see Kennedy, Light, and
myself, and other good fellows working hard to forward those very rascals' own wishes and success as colonists'.]

Quite apart from the kith and kin, other outlanders absorbed a great
deal of Palmerston's time and attention. France was not wholly settled
after her latest revolution; where next might she not break out? The situation in the Eastern Mediterranean was, as ever, menacing and
obscure; and what was the Icy Muscovite, The Emperor Alexander I,
about on Russia's eastern borders, pushing ever south-eastward towards
India? And how to raise the money with which to govern that immense
country without selling opium to China?

It seemed safer to do nothing to protect the traders, and Palmerston,
if he had been able to manage it himself, could not have been cleverer
in contriving that dispatches should always arrive in mid-August, just
after the government had departed *en masse* to shoot grouse or flog the
rivers for salmon, so that any decision on China could be postponed; for
the British, in addition to their addiction to tea and trade, were hopelessly addicted to country pursuits. Opium continued to pour into
China, and the Emperors, very naturally, redoubled their efforts to stop
it.

Over the next few years, the home government made no decision of
any kind. Davis retired and went home and Robinson succeeded him as
Chief Superintendent of Trade; he gave up living at Canton and settled
himself at Lin-Tin, from whence he wrote home to the British
Government telling them that if they really wanted to stop opium smuggling he was well placed to take action against it. The instructions
remained the same as they had been for Napier – no authority to interfere. Superintendents were ordered to go on pressing for direct access to
the Viceroy, without being given any help in obtaining it, either by force
or direct reference to Peking. After four years on the pencil-sharp island,
watching the opium clippers reef their sails on arrival and spread them
on departure across the beautiful and dangerous Bay of Canton,

Robinson retired, to be succeeded by Captain Charles Elliot, RN, who was to bear the brunt of the inevitable crunch.

* * *

After Viceroy Loo had been given back his peacock's feather, and the luckless war-junk captain had been relieved of his kang, Loo continued steadily to feather his nest, landing the opium in broad daylight in his own mandarin boats, while from time to time ordaining the strangling of unfortunate coolies who had actually done the work of unloading the stuff. But pressure from Peking was mounting. Although the Ch'ing Dynasty was increasingly corrupt, memorials submitted by high officials were still seriously considered at Peking; and many of these between 1836 and 1838 dwelt strongly on the need to stop the use of opium. So much now came into China that it exceeded the value of the tea and silk that were being sold, and constituted a grave drain on China's silver. Two per cent of her population were now addicted: if nothing were done to stop it 'it will mean the end of the life of the people and the destruction of the soul of the nation', the Censor Yuan-Loo-Lin wrote to the Emperor in November of 1836. But how to stop it without 'irritating' the Barbarian traders whom previous Governors had sought to 'soothe'?

The obvious answer was to free trade, open the ports, and import foreign goods, on condition that no more opium should ever be either imported or smuggled. But suspicions of the British still understandably haunted the Imperial heart; had they not recently moved into Burma and Malaya? Where would they stop? The authorities seriously hoped to end the opium trade without a single concession to legitimate trade. Under pressure to be more severe, Viceroy Loo ordered that a coolie who had been caught smuggling opium should be publicly strangled in the very forecourt of the foreign Factories; [Loo had already confiscated a token load of opium from a boat at Whampoa.]

The British and American contingency at Canton would not stand for this operation; seeing the gallows erected virtually outside the windows of what they had come to look upon as their private property, the shouting crowd, the desperate victim who had never even been tried, the magistrate sweetening his labours by incessant cups of tea, they rushed forth and put a stop to the proceedings. Pulling down the gallows, they argued hotly with the magistrate who pointed out that had they not smuggled opium they would not have been subjected to the insult and affront to their feelings of which they now complained. But William Hunter, the American trader, and the whole body, declared their refusal to allow the execution to happen, and a party of British sailors from HMS *Larne*, landing at this moment, entered heartily into the protest, broke up the gallows, and belaboured the executioners with the bits and pieces. Chairs and tables and tea-cups all fell in the mêlée; but the main object of the exercise was frustrated; the Chinese guards were able to whisk away the victim and he was duly strangled just outside the Factory walls.

A large crowd from Canton's least reputable quarters now gathered and swarmed into the Factory square, and the younger and more dashing among the traders set forth with sticks to drive them out. They were answered with stones and bricks, and soon a crowd of 8,000 Chinese had gathered and were hurling stones through the Factory windows and bringing battering rams to the doors. William Hunter and a colleague bravely crept from roof to roof and out of the Factory area to seek the intervention of the ever-ready Howqua; who saw himself being obliged to pay for the damage, and quickly got in touch with the City Magistrate who duly arrived in his sedan chair and directed his police force to lay about the rioters, dispersed them, and posted the guard. It was described by the *Chinese Repository* as a moderate riot. From Whampoa, Charles Elliot despatched 100 armed sailors, but the trouble was all over by the time they arrived. Some traders had been hurt but no Chinese killed except some unlucky members of the crowd who were driven into the river by the police and drowned, no-one present taking the least notice of their cries for help.

Elliot was deeply concerned, foreseeing a crisis whose imminence he had no power to avert. Hoping to ease the situation he forbad the carrying of opium into the Pearl River by British cutters, a practice that had recently grown up. But he had no authority to enforce this; the traders knew it, and continued to ply up and down. Elliot had irritated them without appeasing the Chinese, who meant to halt the entire trade in opium and under Viceroy Teng, who succeeded Loo, they all but succeeded. Howqua warned Elliot of the wrath to come, and the Superintendent wrote gloomily to Palmerston of the 'sinister aspect of present circumstances'.

On the last day of 1838, Commissioner Lin was appointed to Canton to sort out matters. On hearing of his appointment Viceroy Loo, deeply implicated in opium smuggling and corruption, fell into a dead swoon. Shortly afterwards, with his usual savoir-faire when it came to avoiding trouble, he breathed his last.

Lin Tse-Hsu, a mandarin of the first class, was a clever and powerful man who had been Governor of Hu-Kwang, in which province he had stamped out opium smoking by confiscating all pipes and all stocks of the drug, and by frightening all officials who had shielded either the addicts or the traffickers, and punishing by death all who persisted. He planned to do the same in Canton, and made this clear at once upon his arrival in Canton in March 1839 – 'I, Lin, Imperial High Commissioner of the Court of Heaven, President of the Board of War and Viceroy of Hu-Kwang, issue these my commands to the Barbarians of every nation.' The Son of Heaven had most graciously allowed them to trade with his realm, and they had responded by selling opium, 'seducing and deluding the sons of the Middle Kingdom'.

He issued his ultimatum. 'Let the Barbarians deliver to me every particle of opium on board their store ships. There must not be the smallest atom concealed or withheld. And at the same time let the said Barbarians enter into a bond never hereafter to bring opium in their ships and to submit, should any be brought, to the extreme penalty of the law against the parties involved.'

Nothing could have been clearer; but the traders, as so often, underestimated the strong will behind it. They were given three days to obey; if they did, Lin would ask the Emperor to forgive them for former misdeeds. If they did not, the army and the navy would be called into action against them, and all trade would be at an end. 'Do not indulge in idle expectations', Lin warned, 'or seek to postpone matters, deferring to repent.' The Hong merchants were also summoned, and on their knees, told to show an earnest severity with the merchants – no trifling over the opium surrender, or some of them would be for strangling. 'Never say that you did not receive early notice.'

Next day, all foreigners were forbidden to leave Macao, and the river between Canton and Whampoa was closed. The merchants shilly-shallied, offering to surrender some opium; there was much to-ing and fro-ing, and Howqua and Mowqua presented themselves in the Factories with heavy chains around their necks and pleaded their imminent destruction. News was sent through to Elliot, at Macao, who ordered Captain Blake of the 18-gun sloop *Larne*, to gather all the British merchant ships outside the Canton river and take them to Hong Kong where they could be defended in case of need. With some difficulty he made his way to Canton, a favourable breeze and 'the admirable steadiness of the four people of the *Larne* enabling him 'to baffle the attempts to obstruct me'. He ran up the Union Jack on the British Factory, but still felt that they were all in 'a dismal strait'. Far from home and without authority, Elliot was unnerved by the situation and made no serious attempt to bargain with Lin, by asking for free trade in return for the surrender of the opium. As in Napier's time, the Factories were surrounded by armed men, supplies were cut off, and all Chinese employees disappeared. Elliot became convinced that British lives were in danger and that it was, therefore, wiser to sacrifice British property. On 27 March, he called upon all merchants to surrender their opium. Lin took over, and 20,000 chests of opium were landed from the ships at Whampoa and Lin Tin, destroyed by salt and lime and flushed away into the Bay of Canton, the Reverend Elijah Bridgman being one of those called on to bear witness to its total destruction.

The British taxpayer, Elliot assured the merchants, would repay them the £6,000,000 of the opium's value; and they, feeling that this destruction could only raise the price of the next crop due from Calcutta, were far from unhappy. Matheson had already begun to organize opium distribution through Manila, and the merchants took the oath against further importation of the drug with silent reservations – an oath taken under duress is no oath. Lin wrote delightedly to the Emperor, and congratulated Elliot on his 'real sincerity and faithfulness'. When the last trace of the odious drug had melted into the sea, the ban on movement was removed and most of the merchants, (only Dent and Matheson were permanently exiled) departed for Macao, never to return. They had had enough of siege and armed surroundings in Canton, though the hardship of the siege had not been great, and Howqua had sent in fresh vegetables and fruit throughout. He and Mowqua were amazed at the easy surrender of *all* the opium – 'six, seven thousand so would be enough'.

Lin was well aware that opium would continue to be grown in India, and he addressed a letter to Queen Victoria, now 20 years old, which, sadly, was never delivered. Had it been published, or sent to *The Times*, it might have considerably influenced public opinion in Britain.

Politely, Lin congratulated the Queen on her respectful and obedient predecessors; this demeanour had aroused the kindness of the Emperor whose gracious condescension had enabled Britain to become a flourishing kingdom, sustained as it was on Chinese tea, rhubarb, and silk. But this incomparable benevolence had not been met becomingly; barbarous pirates had brought and sold a deadly drug, though 'doubtless you, the honourable chieftainess, have not ordered its growth and sale . . . In your honourable barbarian country the people are not allowed to inhale this drug; if it is so harmful how can it be reconciled with the decree of Heaven that the evil power of the malign stuff be imposed on others for profit?'

How indeed? 'You should immediately', Lin went on, 'have the plant plucked up by the very root, and the land hoed up anew . . . Let your reply be speedy . . . Do not by false embellishments evade or delay. Earnestly reflect hereon. Earnestly obey'. Though not exactly accustomed to be addressed in this tone of voice, Victoria might well have seen the force of all this. Heaven, Lin had assured her, would ward off

misfortune, if she thus displayed a clear apprehension of celestial principles.

So far, so splendid; but in a memorial to the Emperor, Lin was to display a far from clear apprehension of the range and reach, let alone the
pride and determination, of this Queen's far distant island. At this critical moment he advised the Emperor not to take the British threat
seriously: had they not been stopped dead at Whampoa in 1834? The
way to deal with them was the old way – alternate indulgence and rigour.
It was needful first of all to soothe them, and then to impress them with
awe. 'Here is the reason why men are dazzled by the name of England.
They call her powerful because she has strong ships and angry guns.
Because she spends so extravagantly she is called rich.' But, 'these warships of these same Barbarians are low in the water, needing the depth
of tens of feet. They can succeed only on the Outer Seas, where they
break the waves and can sail even beneath great winds.'

Why fight them on the sea? 'In harbour, their ships become unwieldy.
One Barbarian, called Laboriously Vile, was bold enough to enter the
Bogue: he was soon struck with fear and driven to Macao where he
died . . . Their soldiers do not know how to use their fists or their swords,
their legs are tightly bound with cloth and they move with difficulty. It is
clear that on land the English can do little harm. Their so-called power
can easily be dealt with.'

Thus wrote Lin, in the fateful autumn of 1839. Away from Canton, the
smuggling along the coast continued as briskly as ever, and Elliot
decided to evacuate the British Factories at Canton until he had instructions from London, which would take about a year to reach him. All
British ships were to stay out of the Pearl River meanwhile, lying at
anchor at Macao or in the anchorage between Hong Kong and the
mainland. He had written to Palmerston urging 'a powerful intervention' not on account of the opium trade, 'so discreditable to the
character of a Christian nation'; but because of the threat to British
lives, and the arbitrary seizure of British property '.The merchants also
wrote home emphasizing their case for protection.

This departure rattled Commissioner Lin: the last thing he wanted
was the cessation of trade at Canton. He shortly appeared near Macao
and encamped with a large body of troops just across the isthmus. All was
complicated by an inopportune visit ashore in Kowloon by British sailors,
provoking a drunken affray, after which the body of a Chinaman was
found. Lin demanded that the culprit be handed over to the Chinese
courts – this since the treatment of the *Lady Hughes* seaman, the British
had always refused to do. It was quite impossible to discover who had
actually done the deed, but Elliot court-martialled six men and subjected

five of them to imprisonment and fines, while handsomely compensating the family of the murdered man. Lin continued to demand that someone be delivered over to him, and the Portuguese made plain their inability to defend the many British subjects in Macao.

Alarm was widespread. 'Living in the greatest misery, I assure you', lamented the artist Chinnery to Matheson. 'To be away is everything to me. I should like to paint a few good pictures (at least try at it) before I am put to the sword. Rely on it, something serious if not dreadful is coming.' Parties of Lin's soldiers roamed Macao at nights, and at least the British women and children now 'trembled exceedingly'. To avoid peril, Elliot ordered them all to leave their houses and goods and take refuge on board the British merchant ships anchored off Hong Kong, hot and crowded as they would prove at this season. The *Larne* had now departed, and the British community, huddled nervously into small boats, crossed the open Bay of Canton on 26 August 1839. 'All alike were hurried from their residences; what will now happen?' asked the *Chinese Repository*. 'Would that timely and friendly interposition of Western governments had prevented such an issue.'

Lin made no attempt to attack the embarkation: he was not that kind of man, and contented himself with a triumphal march at the head of his troops through Macao, where the delighted Chinese community hung garlands on beribboned arches and set tables covered in flowers at their front doors. The red-haired barbarians had been sent packing.

Lin now ordered the people of Kowloon to refuse supplies to all British ships – no food, no water; they would thus be forced to send their women home and themselves return to trade at Canton. 'If any of the said foreigners be found going on shore, all and every of the people are permitted to fire upon them . . . or make prisoners of them.' Not a drop of water was to be allowed them. But on this very day, a second class frigate, HMS *Volage*, Captain Smith, hove over the horizon, shortly followed by another, a third class frigate, HMS *Hyacinth*. Earlier that day Captain Elliot, in the *Louisa* cutter, accompanied by Gutzlaff as interpreter, had held long parleys with the captains of three war junks, anchored under the protection of Kowloon's shore batteries, asking to be permitted to buy food and water. After six hours of Gutzlaff's best eloquence, no progress was made; the last junk captain sent orders to load to the battery commander on shore, and Elliot moved away, sending a boat further along the coast for supplies. These had just been successfully loaded, when the Chinese police arrived and forcibly removed their stores. Elliot was by now very hungry, thirsty, hot and cross; he lost his temper and fired the first shot of the war, on 5 September, 1839, almost single-handedly in the cutter battering three large war junks into silence and finally driving them into flight. There were now, by chance, two frigates to back him, and the war had begun. Never before had the British fired upon the Chinese without being first fired upon; and Elliot, an essentially pacific character, apologized in his report to Palmerston for the irritated feelings that such trying circumstances had aroused and betrayed him into firing.

Lin, retaliating, sank a merchantman off Macao, which turned out to be Spanish; and by proclamation, threatened to destroy Elliot's merchant ships unless they at once returned to Whampoa and continued to trade. Failing compliance, fleet and army would be launched against him.

Peace, of a sort, might still have been kept. Seeing the rout of Lin's junks, local officials were conciliatory; supplies for the ships poured in. Lin felt that if he could get those 60 British merchantmen, complete with all the women and children from Macao, up to Whampoa, they would be within his power; he would have won and could then make his own terms.

Threatened by fire-ships at Hong Kong, Elliot stationed his merchant ships at some distance off Chuenpee, and *Volage* and *Hyacinth* confronted 18 heavy Chinese war junks and 14 more fire-boats emerging from the Bogue. With these Lin now planned to destroy the merchant fleet or compel it up the river. Captain Smith of the *Volage* sent the Chinese admiral a polite letter, which the latter returned unopened. The day wore on in abortive discussion. Elliot was trying to continue the trade as usual, with the same dues paid to the same customs officials, but conducted from Chuenpee rather than Whampoa and Canton, and Chinese officials had agreed that British merchant captains need no longer fear decapitation if any opium were found in their vessels.

But Lin's fierce proclamation carried more weight; it was now November, and Smith reasonably feared that, in the darkness, this huge assemblage of Chinese ships and fire-boats could slip past him and his two frigates and destroy the merchantmen. After a second day of negotiation, in which the Chinese admiral demanded a victim in exchange for the Chinaman killed six months earlier, Smith had had enough; the Chinese fleet were advancing towards him, he raised anchor and sailed towards them. Upon this they anchored in a long row parallel with the shore, which enabled *Volage* and *Hyacinth* to sail past them at a distance of 50 feet, raking them first with their starboard guns and then with their larboard. The Chinese fired back fiercely but ineffectively, the British frigates came so close that Chinese shot passed over them. Four junks were sunk, many disabled, the rest fled or were deserted by their crews, rowing desperately for the shore. Undiscouraged, Lin reported this as a victory, the Chinese admiral was decorated, and this and two skirmishes off Kowloon were recorded in the official history as The Six Smashing Blows. Since the Son of Heaven ruled the world, this was not technically war and the affray could be looked on as only a little civil disturbance.

War was, therefore, not an obligation; and a lull followed. Although 1,500 chests of opium had been taken by Lin from their holds, American ships were not banned and continued to ferry tea to the waiting British ships, and made almost as much money so doing as if they had ferried it across the Pacific; but their co-operation was much appreciated. Lin continued to report hopefully to the Emperor, having no idea of the hornet's nest he had stirred up in the country that had been so pityingly described by the sympathetic Chien Lung – 'I do not forget the lonely remoteness of your island, cut off from the world by intervening wastes of sea'.

21
War

Things had now reached a pass when all would have to come out into the open and be debated at home, where ignorance of the whole opium business still reigned. As it also did in India. 'I was glad to see that the people were at work in their poppy grounds, and that the frost had not extended far', Bishop Heber of Calcutta had happily recorded in his journal in the 1820s, blithely unaware of the end product of all those nodding white heads of *papaver somnifera*. Later on, Archdeacon Dealtry of Calcutta was taken wholly by surprise when he learned of the existence of the opium traffic, its enslavement of addicts, and the terrible agonies of mind it created; and protested strongly. Those who knew kept quiet, except when giving evidence to a Commons Committee of Enquiry into the East India Company in 1832 – 'the strangest of all governments . . . designed for the strangest of all Empires', as Macaulay was soon to describe it. Holt Mackenzie had bluntly told the Committee that without selling opium the Indian Government could hardly continue; 'the revenue cannot otherwise be got'. To these the maintenance of government in India seemed more important than the lives of a few lucklessly addicted Chinese.

The chorus of those who *did* know, and were horrified, began slowly to swell in Britain and they tried hard to rise above the theme of those pointing out that without the opium trade the whole expense of running India would fall upon the British taxpayer, in a country still struggling to recover its economy after the 20-year drain of the Napoleonic wars. 'It is a curious circumstance', John Barrow remarked mildly in the *Quarterly Review* in 1836, 'that we grow poppy in our Indian Territories to poison the people of China in return for a wholesome beverage which they prepare almost exclusively for us'. A London clergyman called Thelwell brought out a pamphlet on the wickedness of the opium trade. It was murder; 'and he who stands by unconcerned . . . is justly deemed an accomplice in the crime'. He was echoed by C A Bruce, who had seen the effects of opium on the coolies of his tea plantation in Assam; to keep up his supply 'the coolie will steal, sell his property, his children, the mother of his children, will finally murder'. On 1 August 1839, Lord Ellenborough demanded further information on the trade; it would be 'very difficult for any man to say one word against the grounds on which the Chinese Government insists on its discontinuance'.

Feeling against the whole opium transaction continued to swell. 'Everything in India is disgraceful; we are reduced to the level of the French', declared Lord Ashley; but then, with him, indignation was a kind of hobby and produced diminishing returns. Admirably exercised on behalf of little chimney-sweeps and against mill-owners and their employment of small children in factories, it came to seem slightly ridiculous – 'the dishonesty of the Americans individually and as a nation is perfectly shocking', he was to declare *à propos* of the Oregon boundary. More influential possibly was Thomas Arnold, famous head-master of Rugby and father of the poet Matthew, who declared in 1840 that war in China would be the most impossibly wrong-headed action that ever disgraced a great nation – 'So wicked as to be a national sin of the greatest possible magnitude'. But louder voices were to prevail.

Maclay was to pronounce that the Chinese mind had 'an intuitive logic of rare vigour and certainty, praiseworthy for its quickness, shrewdness and pragmatism'. De Quincey thought the Chinese 'imbecile' and 'obstinate', hampered by their 'feeble brain'. What was the non-expert to think?

The average knight of the shire or burgess of the city in the Commons knew not *what* to think. Conflicting voices assailed their ears. Matheson, after 17 years' experience around the Bay of Canton and in Canton City, thought the Chinese were 'characterized by a marvellous degree of imbecility, avarice, conceit and obstinacy'. 'Why are not thousands of our bayonets bristling at this moment on the shores of China?' demanded Samuel Warren (The Opium Question) early in 1840. Hobhouse in the Commons described the Chinese as 'a barbarous and uncivilized people'. On the other hand there was Sir George Staunton, who had lived for years amongst them, extolling and admiring them; but then Staunton was a dead bore and induced an irresistible temptation in his listeners to fall into a deep sleep five minutes after he opened his mouth. There were all those marvellous things the Chinese had made – the bronze vessels cast when Achilles and Hector were still battling it out before the walls of Troy, the exquisite carved jade, the lacquered furniture, the porcelain, the brushwork calligraphy. How possibly condemn such a race as barbaric? But were they not, in this instance, behaving barbarically?

When in doubt, it is easier to feel than to think – a glow of moral indignation suffused Britain for all those women and children driven forth from Macao, for all those Britons starving in the besieged Canton Factory with the Union Jack flying bravely overhead (though these had, in fact, been handsomely fed throughout by the Hong merchants, and Lin himself was far too much against a 'disturbance of tranquillity' to have ordered an actual attack and destruction). Alas, there was no Chinese Ambassador to plead his country's case. Such a proceeding was inconceivable to the Son of Heaven. Imperial officials never argued or pleaded with the barbarians, they just pronounced.

Peel, now in opposition, saw the dangers and the wrong-headedness of fighting the Chinese Empire for such a cause; he feared 'a terrible retribution for the most absurd and insane project that was ever undertaken in the wantonness of power;' and Wellington, the trusted elder statesman, spoke extremely highly of Peel – 'I never knew a man in whose truth and justice I had a more lively confidence'. But Peel was in an awkward position; he would have liked the Government to have dealt with the opium problem themselves. He did not relish the prospect of their fall, and of having to cope himself with the enormous difficulty of running India without the opium revenues.

* * *

In September of 1839, ominous date, Melbourne and Palmerston, having stalled as long as possible, were obliged to make up their minds. Should they abandon Elliot and reject the responsibility of paying for the destroyed opium, and leave the traders to their fate? Or should they compel the Chinese Government to pay compensation and at the same time 'accompany that demand by a further demand for a treaty placing the intercourse of British subjects with China on a footing of security for the future, and also by a demand for an apology and reparation of some kind for the great indignity put upon an officer of the British Crown by the whole character of Chinese proceedings'? Even if this meant war? The destruction of Lord Napier had rightly not been seen as an occasion for war; but it would have been a very much better one than a struggle that could be, and was to be, forever associated with the opium trade.

Considerably egged on by William Jardine, and ably advised with his maps and charts, the government plumped for war. Lin had used force and had put British lives in peril; the flag could be waved, and British anger could be roused.

Debate in Parliament in April 1840 provoked a great deal of eloquence and deeply divided views; except that almost all deplored the way in which Palmerston had allowed matters to drift until war was inevitable. William Fry and John Crawfurd, in vigorous pamphlets, had supplied the Opposition with a wealth of damning facts and figures about the opium trade, but Sir James Graham opening for them, based his attack on Palmerston's inability to make up his mind. Both Napier and Elliot, he said, had been given contradictory instructions, told to respect protocol, but equally urged to defy it; so that whatever they did must land them in trouble. Both had been left virtually helpless; and now the British merchants were compelled to withdraw from Canton. He spoke for two hours; with a sigh of relief the House saw Macaulay take his place. This was no time, Macaulay suggested, to deplore the lack of instructions in the previous year as, from enquiry to answer, they took a year to arrive anyway, so nothing would have been altered. With immense eloquence and a certain amount of inaccuracy Macaulay swept into a diatribe against the behaviour of Lin – women and children bundled out of their homes, women with babes at the breast launched onto perilous seas . . . there was a limit to our famous forbearance . . . the name of Englishman respected as ever the name of Roman citizen had been . . . my earnest desire that this most rightful quarrel may be prosecuted to a triumphal close . . . this was a country unaccustomed to defeat, to submission or to shame. And anyway, who was going to police the whole coast of China to prevent the landing of contraband? Sir George Staunton launched into a fence-sitting waffle; of course the war was just, but would be no walk-over; a fast frigate could still countermand the orders. [He had gone as a page on the Macartney embassy to Peking, where Chien-Lung had congratulated him on his decorous behaviour, and he had gone on being decorous ever since, but carried little weight.] Sidney Herbert concluded the day's debate by saying that only those blinded by faction could fail to see that we were off 'in a war without just cause . . . a disgrace to the British flag'.

The second day of the debate passed in two very long and immensely boring speeches saying nothing much, before the young Gladstone rose to his feet and let them have it, with real passion and considerable authority. Sensibly, he pointed out that there was no need to police the Chinese coasts for opium smugglers; we needed simply to stop its growth in India, and its export therefrom. 'The great principles of justice are involved in this matter; . . . a war more unjust in its origin, a war more calculated in its progress to cover this country with disgrace I do not know.' The Chinese 'had the right to drive us from their shores on account of our obstinacy in persisting in this infamous and atrocious traffic'. As for the flag, 'under the auspices of the noble Lord [Palmerston] that flag is become a pirate flag to protect an infamous traffic . . . indolence and apathy have brought about this pass'. But Gladstone was still, in Parliamentary terms, a very young man: frock-coated members on either side looked on all this vibrant youthful passion with a certain cool detachment. Poor young fellow, he would soon learn some worldly wisdom.

Peel, as leader of the Opposition, would have liked to oppose; but he thought that as we *must* now take action in defence of our people, he could not sweepingly condemn the man about to conduct it, and contented himself with blaming the long inaction that had brought us to such a pass. It was the third day of the debate; those not hopelessly confused over the issue were becoming hopelessly bored. Palmerston, concluding it, reckoned he would have an easy ride, and he was right.

Ever since he was a curly-headed young man, Palmerston had been noted for having a way with him; the years had not robbed him of this quality. Handsome, clever, and amusing, he had evaded the matrimonial designs of a thousand women without causing real offence, before settling with a perfectly charming widow who was also exceedingly rich. He did not now practise rhetoric, or invoke passion. He carried a restless House by being shrewd, funny, and down to earth. He spent five minutes being amusing at the expense of Graham, before coming to the point. Where was the use of our stopping growing opium in British India, when it would simply be grown in India's Princely States and in Persia and Turkey? No English law existed that would have entitled him to tell Captain Elliot to expel every smuggler and drive away every opium clipper. The morals of the Chinese people were not our concern – they were disposed to buy what other people were disposed to sell them. The objects of the expedition would probably be achieved without resort to war – the Emperor of China was very different from Commissioner Lin; he was said to have a strong sense of justice and would prefer an amicable settlement to end the dispute.

Redress must be secured for the many humiliations inflicted on British subjects from Lord Napier onwards, and even before him. Unless Britain now acted with energy and firmness, 'the trade with China can no longer be conducted with security to life and property or with credit or advantage to the British nation'. He anticipated no international repercussions, and quoted from a memorial to Congress sent in January by the American merchants of Canton, denouncing Lin as a robber and giving it as their belief that if a naval force from England, France and America were to appear on the coast, it would place foreign trade on a safe footing, and that without bloodshed. When the long-winded Sir James Graham attempted to launch into further speech, he was shouted down by cries of Divide! Divide! For all Palmerston's charm and wit, the Motion of Censure was defeated by only nine votes. The expedition was already under way: as Florence Nightingale was soon to pronounce in her cool incisive tones, 'Palmerston was a humbug, and he knew it'.

* * *

When, in June 1840, the 16 British warships plus four paddle-steamers and troopships bearing 4,000 British troops anchored off Hong Kong,

Lin continued to square up to them, verbally at least; instructing the unarmed fishermen of Kowloon to attack any who landed and to burn the ships. 'Valiant heroes, let not the heads of the base foreign devils long be wanting! Act like men!', and he offered rewards, ranging from 20,000 dollars for a 74-gun ship, down to 20 for a sepoy. And when, acting on their instructions, the body of warships and armed and shallow draught paddle-steamers moved north to the mouth of the Pei-Ho river, there to try dealing directly with the Emperor at Peking, Lin sent a triumphant message to that potentate telling him how he had driven the barbarians away.

Commissioner Lin was forceful and effective, though little inclined to respond to Elliot's genuinely pacific words and intentions, but he had many other matters beside British traders to attend to. He suffered from asthma and rheumatism, and was responsible for the civil service examination results, for the choice of a name for his new grand-daughter, and for making offerings to the spirit of his late grandmother, for the elimination of opium in remote country places as well as at Canton. He was also preoccupied in writing poetical couplets for the decoration of pillars. His job was no sinecure.

Alas – the bluff of the only Canton Viceroy who had made a serious and effective attempt to rid his country of the opium imports was about to be called. The Emperor declined to be treated with in person, but finding the red-haired barbarians on his doorstep in the flesh, and in formidable numbers, he was furious at having been so deceived by Lin. 'You have caused the waves of confusion to arise', the Son of Heaven thundered at poor Lin. 'A thousand interminable disorders are sprouting', he prophesied, more truly than he knew. Lin was summarily dismissed, and sent to end his days by the chill waters of that far northern river, the Amur, the Emperor thus foregoing the services of probably the most vigorous and least corrupt of his servants.

Chi-Shan, known to the Europeans as Kishen, who replaced Lin, was a subtle operator. He took a clever line with Elliot, now in joint command with his cousin, Admiral George Elliot, in the fleet off the Pei-Ho mouth, 100 miles from Peking. The two Elliots were persuaded by Kishen that the whole matter had much better be discussed at Canton, which was where the original dispute had originated, and where the facts could be found. He represented Lin as a rude fellow, and insisted that the Chinese Emperor's well-known love of the stranger from afar would soon see that things were put right. Elliot, who had not wanted to use force anyway, was delighted to comply. Kishen told the Emperor that however bold and defiant the red-haired barbarians affected to be, they were easily managed by a little judicious flattery. His Majesty had so many real problems with which to contend that such trifles (as the appearance of a considerable British fleet at his gateway) 'are not worth a turn of the Holy Glance'.

The ships accordingly trekked the 1,100 miles south again. On their way north, they had left three warships to guard the mouth of the Yangtse, and had occupied (without more than token opposition) Ting-hai, the port of the island of Chusan; but so many British troops had died there of fever that it was thought wiser to transfer the base to healthier Hong-Kong. To the Chinese, this pacific move to the south did but evidence British weakness: Kishen was told to play for time at Canton while the Imperial forces were gathered. 'After long negotiation has exhausted and wearied the Barbarians, we can attack them suddenly and subdue them', the Emperor told Kishen.

In the preliminary letter that Palmerston had sent to be delivered to the Emperor's Minister of State, he had asked that the century old trade between Britain and China be peaceably continued, that the unprovoked outrages against British merchants by Chinese officials be apologized for and damages paid. The law against the importation of opium which of course, he conceded, the Chinese government had a perfect right to make, had become a dead letter, with many of the Emperor's subjects taking part openly in the trade; and then suddenly Commissioner Lin had acted with violence, imprisoning the British merchants and threatening them with starvation unless the opium were delivered up. For this Elliot was instructed to require the Emperor 'to cede one or more sufficiently large and properly situated islands' where British merchants could live and trade. This condition could be waived if the Chinese would guarantee security and freedom to trade in several other ports along their coast. An indemnity was demanded, as well as the costs of the expedition. Palmerston was careful to avoid demands as to the opium trade, but suggested that as it was beyond British power to prevent the introduction of opium from all alternative sources, the Chinese should regularize the trade and stop the vast smuggling enterprise by allowing in a legal and strictly controlled amount which would bring them in large sums of customs dues.

At Canton, the negotiations with Kishen dragged on interminably. Meanwhile hearts were hardened by the atrocities inseparable from war or threat; British men and women, landing peaceably along the coast, were seized, put in tiny wicker cages ($3\frac{1}{2} \times 3 \times 2\frac{1}{2}$ feet) and exposed in the market place. By January 1841, Elliot realized that he was getting nowhere with Kishen, and decided to move on Canton with his available force. He attacked and silenced the Bogue forts, capturing Chuenpee, and though he halted before Tiger Island, it was plain that the way to

Canton now lay open, and Kishen capitulated. Both Lord Auckland (as Governor General of India, nominally in command of the expedition) and Elliot himself were anxious not to alienate Chinese opinion more than was necessary. In the Convention of Chuenpee, Elliot settled for Hong Kong, indemnity for the seized opium, and – the point for which Lord Napier had held out – direct access to the Viceroy, and no more petitions. To these terms Kishen agreed: Elliot had long thought the Chinese 'the most moderate and reasonable people on the face of the earth'; he hoped to save them from further humiliation. Five thousand Chinese had died in the Bogue forts; scores of British soldiers had died of dysentery and fever at Chusan: surely enough was enough? And freedom to trade at Hong Kong, accessible from the sea, was all that the British needed?

* * *

Unhappily, their respective bosses felt differently. Palmerston wrote to Elliot in real fury – 'You have disobeyed and neglected our instructions'. He had failed to make use of the forces at his disposal. Hong-Kong was 'a barren island with hardly a House on it'. Feelings, stirred by Palmerston, ran high. Even the Duke of Wellington was heard to say that the settlement made his blood boil; fire-eaters in the Commons wanted to know why 'the attack had not been pressed home?' Melbourne, the reasonable, was not happy; concerned that his government should be connected with the growth and export of opium and wishing to abide by Elliot's Convention of Chuenpee, he feared that any extra compensation to be gained would not offset the loss of Chinese goodwill. Queen Victoria, briefed by Palmerston, expressed vexation to her Uncle Leopold of the Belgians – '*All* we wanted might have been got if it had not been for the unaccountably strange conduct of Charles Elliot . . . who completely disobeyed his instructions and *tried* to get the *lowest* terms he could'. Elliot was recalled, Sir Henry Pottinger sent out in his stead, a fresh expeditionary force prepared. The war became steadily nastier.

Kishen fared even worse. The Emperor was furious. By attacking the Bogue forts the Barbarians had displayed their wonted fickleness of temperament. Troops had been ordered to Canton to 'extirpate them'. The rebel leader (Elliot) must be taken and sent to Peking for punishment. Poor Kishen replied in a panic: he could neither eat nor sleep, he told the Emperor, he was so terribly worried. He had no thought for himself, and was only concerned for the whole nation. 'I beseech the Heavenly Face to take the lives of the masses into consideration . . . the work of extirpation can be carried out later . . . There is not a shred of timidity in me.' This plea did him no good. Kishen was taken to Peking in chains, and condemned to death. His house was razed to the ground, his immense fortune of £10,000,000 was confiscated, his wives sold by public auction. But his death sentence was commuted to exile.

It is difficult to keep a good mandarin down. According to Evariste Huc, who with his fellow French priest, M. Gabet, went on a brave expedition in the early 1840s to convert the Tibetans to Christianity, by 1845 Kishen had become governor of Tibet, from which province he briskly evicted the two Frenchmen. Asked by a bold colleague to say why, if he was such a brilliant general, he had not defeated the Ing-Kie-Li, the English, the Sea Devils, Kishen replied superbly that he was far too compassionate to do any such thing.

* * *

Long before Palmerston's bombshell of disapproval could explode upon Elliot, he was aware of Kishen's disgrace and knew that the Emperor, his coffers replenished by the huge sum extracted from Kishen, was gathering further armies in Canton province. These Elliot forestalled by again forcing the Bogue, bringing some of his warships up to Whampoa on 2 March, and even making another truce, during which trade was re-opened and the season's tea shipped – rather more briskly than usual, since Imperial forces were moving upon Canton. On 10 May, the Chinese Tartar general sent fire-ships against the vessels moored at Whampoa; and the British Factories, evacuated in the nick of time, were plundered and burned down. By the end of May, the desperate vulnerability of China had again been amply demonstrated, when Elliot, with fewer than 2,500 British troops caused the capitulation of Canton, defended by 30,000 Chinese soldiers. The only real fight was put up by some local peasants, passionately angry at the outrages committed upon Chinese women and children by some Indian sepoys who had become separated from their British officers. Canton was redeemed for $6,000,000, Elliot fearing to occupy it lest his troops should get drunk and disappear and be murdered among its myriad alleys.

In June, Hong Kong was settled by the British and its new town laid out. Elliot, not knowing quite what to do next, did nothing. Pottinger, arriving to relieve him in August, set out for the north again to re-take Chusan and demand the original settlement from the Emperor. Elliot, like Kishen, was deservedly a survivor; he went on to become an admiral, and governor of a succession of islands – Bermuda, Trinidad, St. Helena. William Jardine and James Matheson too survived; colossally rich, they went home to become landowners and members of Parliament, and though satirized by Disraeli's Lord Egremont – 'a dreadful man . . .

McDrug, fresh from Canton with a million of opium in each pocket' –
their skins were sufficiently thick to obliterate the smart. It is easy to hate
Jardine and Matheson for their wickedly irresponsible drug-running,
but difficult not to admire the courage, skill and tenacity which founded
a great merchant empire. Elliot, when recommending Jardine to the
notice of Palmerston, spoke of his charitable generosity, which it is to be
hoped found its way to the poorest Chinese.

Howqua too survived; though rudely squeezed by his superiors in fulfilment of the terms of the peace treaty, he still had plenty of money, a
magnificent house, rich silks, gilded boats. He was painted by Chinnery.
Long-faced, intelligent and graceful, the epitome of civilized culture,
Howqua's portrait is now in the Tate Gallery.

* * *

No looting was the order of the day to the new expeditionary force, but
as Lord Jocelyn, who went north with Elliot pointed out, though this was
an excellent idea, anybody who knew about armies on active employment must be aware of the difficulty of carrying it out'. (*Six Months with
the Chinese Expedition.*) Seeing that the Chinese looted every city the
enemy took, the British troops not unnaturally decided to get in first.
The plan was to destroy the defences of the hoped for treaty ports, and
thereafter to dazzle the inhabitants with the justice and mercy of our
administration. Not surprisingly it failed to work out like that. Stragglers
from the British forces were cut off and butchered, and when a Captain
Stead brought his merchant ship into a Chinese harbour without knowing that the British had gone, the local Viceroy had him tied to a post in
the market place, and publicly flayed alive. Good resolutions broke down
before the cruelties of war.

Misunderstandings naturally increased. Chinese sources admit that
the Chinese wounded, left on the field, were succoured by the British
exactly as were their own wounded, but this was not put down to kindness but to a plan to suborn them and destroy their fighting spirit.
Chu-Shin-Yun, a poet living just outside the walls of Chinkiang, recorded
that 'when the foreign ships anchored off Kiangyin they did not do any
harm to the people, and even insisted on their keeping out of the line of
fire in case they should be hit by accident . . . When they entered the City
in strength, they did not wantonly kill a single person, and let everyone
who wanted to, man or woman, leave the city'. According to his report,
and that of Ts'ao Sheng, of Shanghai, almost more Chinese must have
been killed by their own authorities, under suspicion of treachery or spy-
ing, than were killed by British fire-power.

Starting north on 21 August 1841, the British forces took Amoy,

Chusan, and Ning-Po. The seizure of Chusan particularly alarmed and enraged the Emperor; it could be used as a launching pad for an assault on Peking or for blockade of the mouth of the Yangtse. In the winter, the British force returned south, and Elliot organized the seasonal tea shipments from Hong Kong, since the home government had decided that the Emperor could best be compelled to treat by an assault on Nanking, where the great canal from Peking joined the Yangtse river; this would be best attempted in summer. The campaign to the north was duly made, the British troops having been reinforced from home so as to make up an army of 10,000. Chinese capitulation was arrived at in August 1842, when everything for which Macartney, Amherst, Napier, and Elliot had sought, and much more beside, was conceded in the Treaty of Nanking. Hong Kong was ceded 'in perpetuity', (lease of more land in Kowloon was later purchased) besides which the ports of Canton, Amoy, Foochow, Ning-Po and Shanghai, afterwards known as the Treaty Ports, were made open to British trade and British residents (complete, this time, with wives and families). Here they could import under a fixed customs tariff, and trade without the Hong intermediaries. The £6,000,000 of opium compensation exacted was described in the treaty as 'ransom'. Nothing whatever was said about opium, though a vague phrase announced that 'it was hoped that smuggling would cease'. Pottinger, who had been delighted by the charm and civilized manners of the Chinese Minister of State, Ki-Ying, who came to treat at Nanking, declared on going home that 'every hour I have passed in this superb country has convinced me of the necessity and desirability of our possessing such a settlement' [as Hong Kong] 'as an emporium for our trade, and a place from which Her Majesty's subjects may be alike protected and controlled'.

The opium trade increased by leaps and bounds: by 1850 no less than 50,000 chests were being imported annually. It went on until 1908, by which time the Chinese were growing enough themselves to supply their wants.

* * *

Views on the war held by Tom Bourchier, captain of the Frigate *Blonde*, were probably held by many of the British combatants. In August 1841, he wrote home from Hong Kong to his great friend and old shipmate, Captain Henry Napier, RN, in some disgust at 'the miserable career of this ill-fated and ill-conducted expedition. When we arrived last year we had 4,000 troops, ill-commanded it is true but in themselves equal to anything before them, ships in abundance, an enemy totally unprepared and very, very ignorant as to the proper mode of applying the resources for defence in their power, so that with common vigour we might in one season have at least humbled China to such a degree as to have made her concede any reasonable damages and conclude a peace at once honourable to our country and beneficial to our trade . . .'

'Nankin should have been the point of attack. I have little doubt that *Blonde* could get near the mouth of the Canal in the Yang-tse; once there we should cut the main artery of the Empire and . . . have set our terms and awaited reply, if we had put through our force sufficiently to advance on Peking'.

As to the Chinese – 'they perform prodigies of labour in a space of time incredibly short. They are a race but little known, those who have mixed with them have done so with views purely commercial, and gave them no further consideration than as they could turn them to profit. The Chinese have great aptitude for learning anything, and are by no means deficient in personal courage, as you will readily conceive, that on a wet day when our muskets would not go off, they advanced and speared our men in their ranks, and those fellows were not soldiers but peasants. In fact, they only need teaching, arms and leaders to become excellent soldiers and sailors'.

'We might have astonished them with the superiority of our warlike knowledge, and the vigour of our measures, but alas we have done nothing of the sort; the strength of the Chinese has been passive resistance, the weakness of the British, the credulity of her Plenipotentiary [Elliot] and I blush to add the incapacity or imbecility (whichever you like) of our naval chief . . .' [Admiral Sir James Bremer].

'Nor is it possible for any man honourable in Downing Street to carry on a war in China. We have given up Chusan, a very nice island with an excellent port where I have no doubt we should have opened up a trade to beat the Emperor with dollars instead of shot . . . We hear Charlie Napier gets South America. That is the sort of fellow they ought to have sent here.'

Eighteen months later, Tom Bourchier was still more impressed by the Chinese and disgusted with the war. 'They are a highly civilized people, of great intelligence and ingenuity, possessing most of the arts we have, especially the mechanical ones. In science they are deficient, but when once the system of exclusion which has hitherto been the principle of their government is broken down, I have little doubt they will keep pace with the world for they appear to have both industry and aptitude.'

'At present they are decidedly not a warlike nation. It is not that they want, as a people or individually, personal bravery; we have had many and striking proofs to the contrary; but they have not that courage which arises from discipline and organization. The progress we have made must convince you of that. We are now with a force not exceeding three thousand men holding positions in the three largest and richest provinces of the Empire – to wit, Canton, Fokien, and Che-Kiang . . . We have held Ning-Po, a city of some 300,000 inhabitants for four months with 800 bayonets . . .'

'I hope to get *Blonde* up to the mouth of the Canal . . . we shall then I suppose take Nan-King, and if the Emperor ever means to treat he will do so at this point . . .' [Treating was still far from the mind of General Nin-Chen of Nanking. 'A brilliant plan has been made which assures us of complete victory', he proclaimed as the British ships neared Chin-Kiang.]

'We have just advanced from Ning-Po where we remained all the winter', Bourchier went on in May 1842. 'During our stay, the Chinese attacked the town once and made repeated attempts to burn the ships, but their efforts failed in both cases and we pursued their forces on one or two occasions in the neighbourhood and of course thrashed them. But I think I perceive an increased firmness in their stand; on one occasion on the heights of Sigram about 20 miles from Ning-Po we got hold of about 8,000 of them, some of the Emperor's Body Guard, and they absolutely wrenched the bayonets from our people's muskets while in the act of charging. Give them arms and discipline and they will make first rate soldiers . . .'

'My next letter will, I hope, tell you that *Blonde* is in sight of the Porcelain Tower of Nan-King. I have some hope of their offering to treat at that point . . .'

Bourchier's disgust at the whole business continued. 'We have neither been at peace nor at war. A mawkish sensibility has pervaded all our acts, and in this way, with the cry of moderation on our tongues we have done more mischief to China than war would. Every place we have taken has been by us plundered, pretty well, and by the Chinese after us, the greatest thieves and the most expert in the world, and we get the credit of all. We shoot these poor devils by the hundred on the day of fight, and are then told – Oh, do not hurt the poor people, we are not at war. I am sick of such stuff . . .'

By July 1842, they had seized the Canal, 'which we did without opposition save from a tide of six knots . . . Once through the channel the celebrated Garden Island bursts upon you; it has a Pagoda on it, and is wooded, and studded with buildings in the oriental style. It is here what Isola Bella is in the Lago Maggiore, but there is more poetry in the latter'.

'We seized 700 junks, chiefly empty I am sorry to say, but some had salt and some coal, precious to us for our steam arm. This is a noble river, we are 190 miles from the sea and have lost the tide of flood and have from 10 to 20 fathoms; it is much free-er from danger than the Thames . . . The Chinese have sent to propose to treat, but no-one clothed with sufficient power to do so has appeared. Yet at Nan-King I think we shall make a peace or the Emperor will lose the Southern and richest half of his Empire which is already in a state of anarchy.'

'I hope all your dear children are well?'

So it was over at last, and Tom Bourchier was free to sail *Blonde* home, to rejoice the heart of his Napier god-daughter with presents from the East, and to marry Jane Codrington, daughter of Admiral Sir Edward of Navarino fame; and China was left to recover; or never quite to recover. 'My dear friend', he had told Henry Napier in an earlier letter, describing the attack on Amoy, 'I did as little injury as I possibly could; but the individual humanity was of little account; the great injury was all the while being done, the desultory progress far more cruel than the short sharp *coup de grâce*'. The merciful Bourchier did not long survive; China had given him another of her slow but lethal germs and he died four years later, though not without leaving another little Tom to mitigate the desolation of Jane.

Epilogue

Could Palmerston in fact have been biding his time all along, using first Napier and then Elliot as the 'fall guy'? Waiting until things slowly hotted up into explosion, and the Chinese made a false move which would enable him to stir the Commons into a sufficient state of indignation to sanction action against them? In other respects he has a good track record and does not seem a Machiavellian type. He had denounced Slavery, forwarded Catholic Emancipation, blamed the British Government for countenancing Dom Miguel in Portugal, [known as this usurper was to employ torture and to imprison without trial]. In 1831, Palmerston had been instrumental, and most diplomatic, in persuading the great powers in Europe to alter the terms of the Congress of Vienna to allow Belgium to be independent of Holland. He had taken a hand in the establishment of Greece's frontier in 1832, and in coaxing all Europe's great powers into guaranteeing constitutional government in Spain and Portugal whilst these two countries were under two very young Queens, and threatened with absolutism under their respective and would-be usurping uncles.

He had spoken with real passion over the Abolition of slavery in the British Empire in 1833, voted at a cost of £20,000,000 – calling it 'a splendid instance of generosity and justice unexampled in the history of the world': [it took the Americans another 30 years and a bloody civil war to arrive at the same action] and he had spoken long and eloquently on the subject; in 1841 his efforts were rewarded by the Slave Trade Convention of the European powers. On the Continent by now he was a very influential figure, if less so at home. Though extremely tenacious of the rights of Britons abroad, he behaved admirably to refugees.

Could someone so confident and mocking, so forceful and resourceful, such a good fellow and such an amusing one, be so culpable? In a four hour *civis Romanus* speech, largely in defiance of France, in 1851 he made what Peel, his opponent (who was to die in a riding accident next day) called 'a most temperate and able speech, a speech which made us all proud of the man who delivered it'. Palmerston defeated the whole range of the considerable opposition and his speech was greeted by volleys of cheers from both sides of the house. Could this prince of good fellows really be a demon in disguise? And have engaged in such dirty work over China? Who knows what goes on inside the heart of man?

* * *

The war was over, but misapprehension was not. When the two French Fathers, Huc and Gabet, were on their way to the hoped-for conversion of Tibet in 1844, they were accused by officials in Szechuan of being 'some of the Englishmen who were fighting at Canton', a charge which they indignantly denied. They were still in some danger, when their lives were saved by another official. Of course they are not, he said; all the Ing-Kie-Li, the English, the Sea-Devils, have blue eyes and red hair, which the two priests had not. And furthermore, being Sea-Devils, the English were unable to exist on land; like fish, 'they trembled and died almost at once'. Huc and Gabet, relieved, were enabled to go on their way. [*Travels in Tartary Thibet and China by E Huc, translated W Hazlitt.*]

The struggle was far from over. War was renewed in 1856 with a joint Anglo-French expedition against the Imperial régime. Again it was in connection with opium; a Chinese *lorcha* called the *Arrow*, carrying opium but flying the red ensign was arrested; again Palmerston was to move the Commons with tales of insult to the flag. Again British prestige dropped to zero; in 1843, Balzac (*An Inventor's Tale*) wrote that before all this the world had thought of the British as 'noble-hearted'; after this and the humbug over the opium trade, we were *perfide Albion* all over again. The Chinese empire had already been badly weakened by the Taiping Rebellion, 1851–64, led by a communist rebel from the south, preaching Marxism before Marx was, laced by draconian notions of equality picked up from American missionaries, and causing more deaths than those suffered by everybody on both sides in the First World War. He all but reached Peking, burning beautiful Hangkow and Nanking, moving steadily on through scenes of great bloodshed and destruction, complicated by Japanese incursion. In 1860, in revenge for murder of their nationals, the British and French marched on Peking, where they looted and destroyed the Summer Palace (fortunately looting more than they destroyed).

And so it went on. The French made war on China in 1884, the Japanese again in 1894. The Empire was far too weak to resist; and the jealousy of the greedy powers among themselves was probably all that saved China from total dismemberment. '*Thou shalt not covet*', was a precept which Europe appeared to have forgotten. The Russians seized an immense stretch of Chinese territory beyond the Amur, moved on later beyond the Usuri river, and established Vladivostok. Steadily, China chafed against the foreign demands; steadily, the European nations

closed in on her, demanding ever more concessions – the Russians, the
Germans, the Dutch, and the Portuguese, as well as the English and the
French.

After what seemed to them a treacherous attack, the European powers converged upon Peking to save their embassies, at the time of the
Boxer Rebellion. The British had meanwhile advanced into Burma, the
French took Indo-China, the Germans demanded, and got, concessions
in Shantung, the holy land where Confucius had been born and buried.
At Tientsin 13 French missionaries and their 300 Chinese converts had
been murdered in 1870: enmity between East and West thickened and
occasionally boiled over in increasing mistrust. The Americans, on the
whole, kept out, enjoying the trade advantages won by these successive
aggressions and being a great deal holier-than-thou: all the same, they
were known along the China coast and in the Treaty Ports as second-
quality Englishmen; a series of honest and admirable men having
restored the British good name.

As early as 1843, American warships had appeared off Japan, declaring 'Open up to trade, or we fire': the Japanese had complied, opening
up to some tune. Forty years later, having entirely retooled, the Japanese
defeated the Chinese with their modern weapons and acquired further
slices of Chinese territory; in 1931 they took Manchuria, original home
of the Manchu Emperors. Short of actual partition, China's disintegration seemed complete.

Still to be suffered by China were ravaging war-lords, full-scale Japanese
invasion, Communist massacre and confiscation, the fanatical destruc-
tions of the Red Guard, secret police, forced confessions, all the dreary
paraphernalia of a police state; and the disappearance of the compassion
and toleration of the old Confucian values. For those broadsides on the
Bogue Forts from *Andromache* and *Imogene*, so cheerfully applauded by
Midshipman Charles Brickdale and his seamen, had blown the gaff. They
had exposed the extreme vulnerability of Imperial China, that magnificent old three-decker commanded by the insufficient man, and laid her
open to her period of hopeless drift, and to untold misery for all those
innocent and industrious millions that made up her ship's complement.
The last Emperor but one was not in himself an insufficient man; he proposed wide-scale reforms, but he was insufficiently suspicious to
counteract the wiles of the Dowager Empress who dethroned him and
seized his power, completing by her wickedness the Ching downfall.

* * *

Some good came of it all, after 1842. Like one of her exquisite Ming
vases in the hands of the Red Guard, the mould of the old China had

been cracked; but she was now in touch with the rest of the world, and much enriched thereby. Soon intelligent Chinese would be travelling to London, to Paris, to Washington, to Rome. As early as 1844, Wei-Yuan was pointing out to his countrymen that among the foreigners there were 'people who understand propriety and practise virtue, who possess knowledge of astronomy and geography, who are well-versed in things material and events of past and present. They are extraordinarily talented and should be treated as our good friends. How can they be called barbarians?' In 1860, the help of the foreigners 'in quelling the bandits near Shanghai was unquestionably a demonstration of their peaceable intentions and friendship', the co-Regents of the Empire declared.

By 1884, Hung-Hsun was pointing out to those still at home that in European countries the interests of government and people dovetailed and were jointly considered, to the benefit of both. Other Chinese sojourners in England were impressed by the 'greatness' of Oxford, or felt that Cambridge had 'opened my eyes, given me my craving for knowledge.' A debate in the Commons in 1919 gave rise in Lian-Ch'i-Ch'ao to 'an admiration beyond description'. 'Having been in Paris, one loses one's wish to go to Heaven', Hsu-Chi-Mo wrote in 1925. Many Chinese students enjoyed the benefits of education in the United States. This access of riches to the Chinese imagination did not quite equal the artistic stimulus that had come to Europe from China in the 18th century, but it was something, to set against the grievous losses.

Hung Hsun was full of admiration for the West's roads, waterways and harbours, their hospitals, their clean prisons, their public libraries and their theatres; but it was not long before the critical minds of Chinese travellers were to sort the various Westerners out – the Americans were sentimental, the French profligate, the Spaniards and Italians lazy, the English cold, the Germans brutal.

Somehow, and in some places, through the high intelligence of their intellectual travellers, the hopeful possibilities of democratic government trickled through to the Chinese authorities. But these, though determined to learn the skills of science, could not bring themselves to alter the time-honoured structures of their administration, nor the tight family rule by the aged, so discouraging to progress. So that it was all no good – the mixture somehow failed to gel into a modern state capable of holding its own against the West or against the predatory modernism of Japan.

All these bright observers from China did not fail to connect the greatness and success of the European nations with their Christian religion; but this faith, in their estimation, was only partially responsible. The strength of the West and of Christianity lay in the fact that, like tea, it was unquestionably a Chinese import. Jesus Christ had gained his following, and civilization had prevailed in Europe, simply because Christ had translated the Confucian classics into Latin, Wei-Yuan announced with great firmness, untrammelled by the tedious need for supportive facts. Others besides Hsueh-Fu-Cheng, Chinese Minister in London in the 1890s, thought that the actual story of Christianity was laughable, more to be despised than a low Chinese novel. Anything of worth in its doctrine had been derived from the Chinese philosopher Mo-Tzu, who died in 392 BC. All civilization, it was felt, derived from Chinese civilization, including Greek philosophy: if there had been a Jewish myth of Moses and his laws it was probably derived from the similarly named Mo-Tzu. This romantic concept died hard, whatever the contradictions of dull fact and duller date might provide, and still perhaps lives deep within the Chinese psyche.

But if the precepts of Confucius on the cherishing of strangers from afar had indeed been followed by Viceroy Loo, even to the extent of receiving and reading Lord Napier's friendly letter, a sensible agreement to open trade could have been, however slowly, arrived at; and the misery and disintegration that China endured through the next 100 years avoided.

Or might not: perhaps William John had been right in his opinion, that the mighty brass-bound doors of Imperial China would swing open only to the sound of gunfire. By this means only could the Chinese be persuaded to descend from their ivory tower and join the non-Chinese inhabitants of the planet, to the great enlightenment of either body of men.

Collingbourne Ducis
1986–1994

Select Bibliography

The Canton Register (Private, 1833–34)

The Chinese Repository (First XII volumes)

Maurice Collis, *Foreign Mud.* (1946)

Vincent Cronin, *The Wise Man from the West.* (Collins, (1961))

Dr C.T. Downing, *The Fan-Qui in China 1838–37*

John King Fairbank, *The United States and China*, 4th Edition. (Harvard University Press, (1979))

Pao-Chang Hsin and I.C.Y. Hsu, *The Rise of Modern China.* (Oxford University Press (1970))

Evariste Huc, *Travels in Tartary, Thibet and China*

W.C. Hunter, *The Far-Kwae in Canton before Treaty Days*

Brian Inglis, *The Opium Wars.* (1976)

Jardine Matheson Archives, Cambridge University Library

P.C. Kuo, *A Critical Study of the First Anglo-Chinese War*

K.S. Latourette, *The Chinese, their History and Culture.* (Macmillan (1946))

H.B. Morse, *International Relations of the Chinese Empire*

David Owen, *British Opium Policy in China and India.* (1934)

Aldo Ricci, *The Travels of Marco Polo*

Elizabeth Seeger, *The Pageant of Chinese History*

Arthur Waley, *The Opium War through Chinese Eyes.* (Allen and Unwin (1958))

Index